Kelli,

Thanks for being you and for remembering ✓

#YouAreEnough

#Rockstar!

x oxo

Evict the Bully in Your Head

Mentions:

pg 221

pg 222 Stevie

Vicki ♡

#YouAreEnough

Evict the Bully in Your Head is a cohesive and cogent book that will help everyone change the way they think and act. Vicki examines the numerous Bullies we all deal with and gives step-by-step directions to the Eviction Process. She's taken years of experience of coaching and working with people in business, as well as having a special needs child, and made a fun, informative and life changing book. This book should be required reading for counselors. It uses cognitive behavioral principles but adds a little spice to make it fun for everyone. Highly recommended.

—**Stacy Lynn Harp**, M.S

Being someone who has been plagued with a Bully in my head since as early as I can remember, I found *Evict the Bully in Your Head* fascinating, delightful and easy to read. Vicki has masterfully taken complex subjects and broken them down in language that even a 5-year-old can understand. This book is so powerful, it is a must read for everyone and should be required reading in schools, anger management curriculum and anywhere that people are struggling with self-esteem or a history of abuse.

—**Rocky Jacobson**, Stage Manager for Tony Robbins

If you have ever lacked confidence, doubted yourself or questioned your worth, *Evict the Bully in Your Head* was written for you. ETB is refreshingly unique. The writing style is engaging and entertaining, infused with stories that will make you laugh and cry. Vicki has the ability to have you reach into your heart and pull out courage for real life change. *Evict the Bully in Your Head* provides a strong framework of practical information in a compassionate and challenging way. If you are looking for hands-on solutions to replace negative self-talk, this is the book for you.

—**Jody Summers**, Certified Nutritional Therapy Practitioner, HealthKindness.com

After reading ***Evict the Bully in Your Head,*** I realized I didn't have just one... I had an entire Bully Brigade running around up there! I found Hope in Vicki's vulnerable stories of her personal Bully Births and challenges. Although some of this can be very sensitive, she made it fun and easy to read and blended in simple ways to start the Eviction Process. I discovered where my Bullies came from and am now aware that my negative thinking and self-defeating behavior was keeping them around. But no more! I am excited to recognize my value and to be part of the **#YouAreEnough** campaign. This book provides amazing value, and I highly recommend it to everyone. We all have a Bully in our head and Vicki shows you how to make sure they board the Eviction Express and get dropped off at Eviction Isle. I feel better already and can't wait for the next book in the series!

—**Dorothy Boyd**, Chapel Hill, North Carolina

From Vicki's ***Evict the Bully in Your Head***, revealing and heart-wrenching podcast series to this amazing compilation and "guidebook" to truly EVICT said bullies, you are in for a brilliant and beautiful ride. Having been blessed enough to choose to be **#Fitchslapped** by Vicki as a client of hers, I can attest that this book reveals in print what Vicki delivers in her coaching sessions. What you will read in these books is not only the writing of an amazing, ambitious, yet down to earth human being, but one who has the gift from Creator to gently guide others toward their Dreams and help them slay bullies to get there. She not only teaches the talk in this book, but I can firmly attest to her walking the walk in all you read here. As a Clinical Social Worker for over 20 years, I can easily say Vicki and her lessons match, if not exceed, many seasoned therapists I know. I hope you are as blessed as I am and have been by the lessons and wisdom Vicki brings to this and all of her work.

—**Stacy Braiuca**, MSW, MPH, LCSW, LSCSW, Entrepreneur/
Owner of Braiuca Enterprises, LLC

Evict
the
Bully
In Your
Head

How the Negative Self-Talk
Got There and How to
Evict it Forever

Vicki Fitch

Evict the Bully in Your Head

How the Negative Self-Talk Got There
and How to Evict it Forever

Published in Chino, CA by Headspace Publishing House

ISBN: 978-1-950622-00-9 (Paperback)
ISBN: 978-1-950622-01-6 (Ebook)

Library of Congress Control Number: 2019903637

Cover and Map Design by
Jay McKey
www.JayMcKey.com

Interior Illustrations by
Ceecee Acot

Interior Design by
Marlo Borda

HOPE ISLAND

OUTSIDE THE 5000 FOREST

QUIRKY COAST

CHRISTIANPRENUER COVE

LIGHT THE WAY LIGHTHOUSE

PROFIT IN THE PAIN PENINSULA

AUDIENCE OF ONE ARENA

N
W   E
S

EVICTION EXPRESS

REASSURANCE REEF

Sea of TRANQUILITY

ROCK THAT DREAM

ROCK THAT ST

PAIN PERF

SUCCESS ISLAND

Fitchipelago

MONEY ⊙   ⊙ MINDSET

⊙ MOTIVATION

the M³ Philosophy

FOLLOW UP FERRY

STAND OUT DECK

STEP UP STEAMSHIP

Sea of SAMENESS

OWN IT OCEAN

OCEAN of OVERWHELM
HOPE HELO
Sea of
EDIOCRITY
EVICTION ISLE
BULLY BAY
CONVICTION COAST
QUIT YOUR FITCHIN' CAVE
HATERS GONNA HATE HABITAT
FITCH ISLAND
SLAP
RED IS ALWAYS
RIGHT REEF
STABILITY SHORE
DREAM IT BELIEVE IT ACHIEVE IT BRIDGE
ONSISTENCY
TIDE OF TEMPTATION
DIRECT SALES SAILBOATS
Sea of STATUS QUO
DEPTHS OF DISCOURAGEMENT
HIGH GROUND
NOT VALLEY
GH
EY
OUGH
NATION

Dedication

This book is dedicated to every person who has ever thought they were **Not Enough**. To those who have ever felt discouraged, disheartened or even depressed. I know what it feels like to have **NES, (Not Enough Syndrome)** and I know how damaging the **Bully in Your Head** can be.

I wrote this book as part of the **#12Books12Months** series to give a voice to your pain and to acknowledge you, but also to give you **Hope** and a plan to eliminate it from your life so you could become the version of yourself you always knew you could be.

Stand tall, stand strong and get ready for a bumpy ride because **Bully Eviction** takes strength. You must remember, **#YANA (You Are Not Alone)** and the challenging emotional journey is worth every minute of it.

To those of you who have already tamed the **Bully**, kudos to you, use this book as a way to encourage others by using the simple analogies to inspire those that are drowning in the **Depths of Discouragement** or floundering in the **Ocean of Overwhelm**.

I **Believe** in YOU and we can do this together!

Table of Contents

Foreword

I met Vicki in Fiji at the end of 2017. She had just come from being the keynote speaker at the Social Media Conference in New Zealand and had hopped the plane over to Fiji for ten days to experience the ***Tony Robbins Life Mastery and Wealth Mastery*** events before heading home. As Tony Robbins stage manager, the intimate setting of Fiji allows us to get to know the participants, and Vicki and I had an immediate connection. I loved her warmth and grace and ability to connect with other people in a way that was authentic and kind.

Being as busy as it is to keep an entire 10-day event going for 16 hours plus a day, didn't give us a lot of time to actually get to know each other, but we became Facebook friends and could see a glimpse into each other's lives. On one particularly rough day I posted,

> *"Sometimes you just have to let [certain] people go, even if they are family… GOODBYE!"*

Vicki replied with a note about this new book she had written and replied, "Sounds like you need to do a Bubble Bump!" I was immediately intrigued about what that was, and she sent me a pre-release copy of this book. I was blown away!

I felt like I was reading my life as it unfolded on the pages of her book. She was telling my story in a way I hadn't been able to articulate before. The **Bubble Bump**, although a serious and challenging thing, was written in a way that made it humorous and OK to remove the people creating negative influences in my life. The quote about the *Intimacy Bubbles don't represent Love, just how much vulnerability you are willing to allow access; to* felt like freedom! I didn't have to feel Guilt or Shame about my decision to take care of myself. She gave me, as a reader, the permission to recognize my value and to enforce the reminder she writes about in this book:

Don't Accept Unacceptable Behavior.

It was like a declaration that I was worth something.

I am a confident, powerful woman who knows who I am, but I still have Bullies running around in my head that make me Doubt myself and my abilities. But I now understand the Bully Eviction process and can start with the "Not today, Bully! Not today!" philosophy as I work on sending these negative influences (Bullies) to Eviction Isle where they belong.

What many people don't know about me, is that I was adopted when I was very young. When I was five years old, I overheard my grandmother and my mom talking. You see, my mom adopted me when she was unable to conceive, but when I was five she had a miracle baby that she was very happy about. I understand the Joy in being able to conceive but I was devastated when I heard my grandmother say this about me:

"Can't we give her back? We have our little girl now. Tell them they can keep the adoption money."

At that moment I believed it was better to be a miracle then it was to be chosen. I was no longer necessary.

I know now, after reading Vicki's book, that was my first Bully Birth. I Believed they didn't want me anymore and I Received it as my truth and it has affected my life ever since. I was infected with NES (**Not Enough Syndrome**) and I accepted the lie that I was Not Enough. The only way to be enough for them was to be a blood relative and that was not something I could change.

There is so much more to my family story including bullying at home and school, mental, physical and sexual abuse, running away, foster homes and more. I will have to share all of that in my own book someday, but the exciting part is that because of those people and the trials I went through, I was open to understanding myself and those around me better.

My life turned around in an amazing way when I met my wonderful husband Greg, who introduced me to Tony Robbins at a UPW event. That event lead to my understanding myself and recognizing my value. I went on to crew for him and moved up through the organization and am now honored to be his stage manager. That in itself is special, and I feel blessed, but the real power is that because of my difficult childhood, and the Bully Brigade hanging out in my head, I learned the power of a PMA – Positive Mental Attitude and was able to raise my children around the positive, self-affirming qualities of the great Mr. Tony Robbins. He and Mrs. Robbins have had a tremendous impact on my life that has abundantly flowed over to my family.

My hardships lead me to seek out better relationships and to avoid Bully Births in my own children by reminding them they could do and be anything they desired. At eight years old my youngest son started Firewalking. He learned, just as all four of my children did, to Believe in himself and the possibilities that were in front of him. No limiting beliefs stopped him. He was raised believing **#IAmEnough**.

Granted we all have Bullies, but Vicki uses the amazing Headspace Heroes to Evict those Bullies, so you can step forward into becoming the best version of yourself. Her **#YouAreEnough** campaign should be embraced by schools, hospitals, organizations, businesses and corporate America. We all need to remember that We Are Enough, just the way we are!

In my opinion, this is a must read for everyone. I am proud to know Vicki and honored to have written this foreword. I am excited about this book and I believe it will change people's lives. I can't wait to read the other books in this series. If they are anywhere near as interesting, entertaining and insightful as this one, they will be on the best seller list for sure.

I am going to take her advice and share it with those that I know.

Dream it, Believe it, Achieve it!

And while we are at it, let's **#RockThatDream!**

—**Rocky Jacobson**, Stage Manager for Tony Robbins

Acknowledgments

Where do you begin when trying to acknowledge all the people that participate in a project of this magnitude? There are so many, and I am afraid I will forget someone. If I have, I ask for forgiveness because when you are writing **#12Books12Months**, it is easy to forget who you have already thanked and those you may have missed. It is truly a fast-paced project so let me try and highlight a few.

First and foremost, as always, my family. My husband **Terry** and my sons **Zach** and **Elijah** have brought me meals to my room, understood why I couldn't take on some additional activities, and took several trips out of the house so I could finish my manuscripts. Thank you for your patience and understanding. I also owe you gratitude for allowing me to add your stories into these books. Stories are what connects people together and although I make up a lot of scenarios in each book, there are some that are right out of our family's experiences. I appreciate your willingness to be vulnerable throughout the series to allow other people the opportunity to grow from our experiences.

Terry, you are still my greatest supporter, my speaking agent and my most cherished accomplishment. Being your wife has been quite a ride and our two boys are truly amazing. Thank you for being my love.

Zach, you are a family connector. You have a heart as big as they come and have continued to extend all that you are to our family for whatever is needed. You are a blessing to everyone who meets you and I am forever grateful that you are my son. I couldn't ask for anything more than who you are. Thank you from the bottom of my heart.

Elijah, you have the heart of a lion. No matter how hard things get, you continue to show up and try. You work every day on becoming the best version of yourself. Thank you for allowing me to share your journey in the pages of my books. Your stories will bless others and help them recognize their value! That is a gift of incredible value.

Next, I must thank **Érick Ramirez**. You are not only Elijah's teacher, but have become a valued member of our family as well as my book editor. Your commitment to getting so much done, in so little time is truly inspiring. I appreciate your support, participation and assistance in our lives. You have been a true gift from God. Thank you for going through this journey with us.

Next in line, is my wonderful team. **Iris** for doing editing and research, **Yanna** for creating entertaining graphic content for our social media posts and **CeeCee** for being my assistant but then stepping up to do the illustrations when **Jay McKey** had personal family health issues that prevented him from doing the inside illustrations. CeeCee, when I asked you if you knew anyone who could do illustrations and you said, "No, but I can try.", I was grateful for your commitment and willingness to help. When I saw what you meant by "try" I was amazed. You are such a talented lady and I am blessed to have you on my team! You are a **#RockStar**!

Since we are talking about illustrations, I must thank the great **Jay McKey** who designed the cover and the map of **Fitchipelago**. When we had our first call, I remember trying to explain the Bully to you and what I meant by it. You instinctively picked up on what I saw in my mind and delivered it on paper. I fell in love with it immediately. It resembles my son Elijah and since the **Pseudo-Sequel** to this book was inspired by Elijah, it was perfect! I am sorry that you were unable to finish the illustrations inside, but your contribution was critical and the launchpad for so much in the series. Thank you for all you do!

A late arrival to our **#12Books12Months** team is **Abby Wiegers**, who tackled her FEAR and helped with the interior design and layout of this book. She also started creating some covers for us, so I think you will see more of her amazing talent in the future!

There are those people in life whose small contributions make a big impact. That describes my friend **Kevin Madison** who is a self-proclaimed contrarian. He challenges himself and others to think differently, which is what my entire **#12Books12Months** series is about. Thank you for your wisdom my friend. I look forward to hearing more from you… and perhaps even a debate or two. I cherish you!

To my dear friends **Jim** and **Misty Means** whom I met in Fiji after speaking at the Social Media Conference New Zealand. They graciously allowed me to stay at their home to have solace during the final edits of this book and to continue on with the **#12Books12Months** series. I enjoyed my time there with your precious pugs and hope to be invited back again someday. You are kind and lovely people and I am blessed to know you!

I am forever grateful to another person I met on my trip to Fiji. **Rocky Jacobson**, I am amazed at all you have been through and all you continue to do to bless others and help them recognize their personal value. Your positive outlook and never give up attitude are exactly what this book embodies. **Tony Robbins** is lucky to have scooped up a warrior with a heart for people like you. You make running those events seem almost effortless even though you put so many hours into making sure everything runs like clockwork. Thank you Rocky for delivering such value to everyone and being willing to share your stories to inspire the world. What a beautiful bit of God's grace to connect the two of us there in Fiji, to keep us connected via social media, (**#DoTheBubbleBump**), and to have you at that party I attended where you agreed to write the foreword for this book. I know it was a scary thought, but you changed your state and committed. I am so grateful for you and love the woman you are. You are a hero Rocky and I may have to create a new character after you in a future book!

I would be remiss if I didn't mention my dear friend **Jody Summers** who encouraged me as she started reading the pre-release copy. I was blessed when this popped up in Messenger.

This one quote is worth the book alone:
"Friendship is caring enough to listen until you
understand, not until you agree."

It was statements like that which inspired me to keep moving forward even when I had bad days. It reminded me that the message was important and was delivered in a way that was not only palatable but filled with Hope. Thank you, Jody, for your insight and input. I appreciate you and your kind heart!

Then there is the unbelievable **Brandon Love** who poured out his heart and shared his story on my *Evict the Bully in Your Head* podcast when he was only 19 years old. He was bullied and tormented and let an entire Bully

Brigade attack him to the point of no longer wanting to live. Brandon rose above those Bullies and has been flourishing with his business Wax Crumbles. He is a trailblazer in the area of bullying and I asked him for a testimonial, but he was so busy fighting the good fight and building his wax empire he couldn't fit it in LOL. Love you Brandon and am proud of the man you are as well as the man you desire to grow into. **#YouAreEnough**, I adore you and know you are an Overcomer. I look forward to watching you continue to **#RockThatDream**.

No acknowledgment would be complete without the outstanding assistance of the **Fitch 5000**. You are supportive, helpful and fast with your praise and your suggestions whenever I ask. I can't imagine doing this without you all. I feel invincible with this project because of all of you. I know if I stumble or things don't go right, you all Believe in me. Your Faith in my ability, my mission and who I am, are humbling! You are the most supportive people I've ever met, virtually or in person. Thank you from the bottom of my heart for joining my journey. You make a difference in my life!

Rounding off the additional inspiration and sanity stabilizers would be my best friend **Kathy Thorsell** (Parsons & Hainault Forever!) We have gone through the most difficult times together and even in the sadness, it has made us stronger. We are proof that Friendship is strong and can carry you through the situations that seem unbearable. More about our journey is coming up in future volumes. I am grateful to have had you in my life for almost forty years. (I mean, that would be true if I wasn't only 22!)

If you have that connector in the family, you know the character of my sister **Susan Shannon**. She is always there for me and my family and she is the person you can count on to come through and stand by your side. (Even in 3rd Grade when I had to fight the boys in Elementary School. That is a story for another book! You will have to keep reading the series to find out about that!) I am truly blessed to call you my sister. You have been there to support my Dreams and goals, to teach me to drive and lend me your license (and your bicycle!). I don't think I tell you enough how very much you mean to me and how your heart has influenced me. Thank you for being my sister and choosing to be my friend.

Although there are so many other that have inspired me on this journey, including those that bullied me, it is my parents, **Joan** and **Henry (Hank) Hainault** that deserve the lion's share of my thanks. Although you will find out throughout the pages of my books that we didn't always have the best of relationships, I came to know, beyond a shadow of a doubt, that they loved me and did the best they could. That is all we can really ask of anyone, including ourselves, that we do the best we can. I was not the easiest child to raise. Intelligence and **Confidence** can get you into trouble without someone guiding you. I recognize the trials I went through probably didn't even compare to their own. I am forever grateful for my experiences because they are what made me the woman I am today and inspired me to share what I know with others. I miss you both so much and am sorry that you never got to see me achieve this amazing goal. I pray you both greet me in Heaven when it is my time to come.

Which leads me to the last and always most important acknowledgment to my Lord and Savior, **Jesus Christ**. Thank you for being with me through all those years of bullying, pain and anguish. Thank you for holding my heart and influencing my mind, even when I wasn't sure you were there. I am nothing without you Father and I pray this **#12Books12Months** series will be the change our world needs to start recognizing the value of others. It is only because of you Lord that I know **#IAmEnough**.

Introduction
READ ME FIRST!

If you read *Direct Selling 101*, book #1 of the **#12Books12Months** series, you already know why I started this project, but as it comes to fruition and each one rolls out, I am proud that they have created an additional layer of support for each of the foundational principles captured here. It is my sincere desire that you will gain even more clarity about yourself as a person, a parent or an entrepreneur as you read more of the series.

For those of you who haven't read *Direct Selling 101*, I will be honest, I highly recommend you add it to your reading. Not because I want you to buy my book, which of course I do, but because each book represents different parts of your life and your perspective and the information found in each one, will help build a stronger, healthier, more equipped version of yourself. I've outlined why I wrote them and how they will bring you value so as you dive in, you can ponder how much more the rest of the series will add dimension and support to what is taught here.

I know some of you are thinking, I'm a...

- Stay at home mom
- Retiree
- Student
- Child
- Corporate executive
- Business owner

... but I am not in the Direct Sales industry, so that book isn't for me.

I understand your hesitation, but I promise, even if you don't think it is applicable to you and your life, the lessons here apply to everyone.

DS 101 describes that we are on our way to the ultimate destination of **#RockThatDream Ridge**, which is located on **Success Island**. It also lays out the principles of how to create a life that is full of connection and meaning, while assisting you with your communication skills and understanding your own perspective.

The journey we are about to take together is one that can change your life forever. This may be your first experience with my writing, or you may have read my other books first. Either way, it is my sincere desire that when you read this series, it will inspire you to become all that you can be.

Each of the twelve books can stand alone and deliver value on their particular topic. But as a whole, all twelve books build on each other, inviting and encouraging you to grow in amazing ways. The **#12Books12Months** series will seamlessly provide a place for you to develop your **Confidence**, character, and community, while turning your passion into your profits. I **Hope** you will **Trust** me when I tell you that this will be a life-changing experience. There is no need to do it alone! Invite your friends to **#JoinTheJourney**. It's time to live the life of your **Dreams.**

The inside cover of this book is a map to help you navigate your way around **Fitchipelago**. In case you weren't familiar, an **archipelago** is a sea or stretch of water containing many islands. **Fitchipelago** encompasses the numerous islands and bodies of water that are depicted in my books. I want to help you successfully navigate the rough waters of life and business, so you can end up at the ultimate destination of **Success Island**.

If I am new to you, you may not know about my **#BHAG (Big Hairy Audacious Goal)** of publishing **#12Books12Months**. Many think I am crazy, but that is what a **#BHAG** is—a goal that is so big, it seems out of reach.

If you KNOW you can achieve it, it isn't a #BHAG.

The map will help you understand how each of the books are connected. I have put the titles of future books in ***Bold & Italics*** to give you a precursor of what is coming ahead. All of them are part of the **M3 Philosophy (Money, Mindset & Motivation)** and will provide you with clearly defined, actionable steps to guide you on your journey.

You will learn to overcome the **Ocean of Overwhelm**, defy the **Depths of Discouragement**, and sail through the **Sea of Status Quo** on your way to **Success Island**. It will be my privilege to lead you to the **Pinnacle of**

Peace on **#RockThatDream Ridge** where you will have a 360-degree view of your future.

I promise to make you laugh, and maybe cry, because my journey has not always been fun. It's also been painful and frightening at times, but I made it through, and you will, too.

I have always found humor to be a great way to communicate, and I use a lot of my own lingo I call **Fitchisms**. I'm confident that my unique vocabulary will **Edutain (Edu**cate and Enter**tain)** you. This creative dictionary provides easy access to the terms I use and the often-humorous meanings behind them. I Trust you will come to Love and embrace them, like my existing **Friends, Followers**, and **Fans** already have.

For easy reference, I have included them in the **Fitchtionary** in the back of this book and added map locations, industry terms, specialty hashtags, and words or phrases that might not be widely-recognized by different cultures. I have tried to **bold** them throughout the text to make them easier to identify.

Many people wonder why I am taking on such a huge project in such a short period of time, so I wanted to clarify a couple of things. I did not decide to do this because I had something to prove, nor am I sacrificing quality for quantity.

I took on this #BHAG because the world needs Hope.

I started **Livestreaming** several years ago and I quickly attracted an audience of people who resonated with my unique, heartfelt, but "tell it like it is" style. During those daily broadcasts, I recognized the same struggles and questions over and over and made it a point to create fun analogies to help educate and empower the audience.

My consultations became very popular and as the questionnaires poured in, I noticed another pattern emerging: people across the globe were struggling to **Believe** in themselves, their talents, and their businesses. No matter what state, country, or province, the recurring theme was the same. There was a "**Bully**" in their heads who was repeatedly lying to them by telling them they were "**Not Enough.**"

Some were discouraged, and some felt defeated. Helping them recognize their personal value became my mission. My success in business was the catalyst for some; recognizing the extensive trials I had overcome provided **Hope** for others. The same foundational principles are needed in life and business, so these books are a compilation of those principles.

- We all need to "sell" ourselves to others to be respected in our communities.
- We all need to "recruit" others to complete projects or tasks.
- We all need to "lead" people who are watching and learning from us.
- We all need to "connect" with others to find those who appreciate who we are.
- We all need to "market" our skills to the world in public and private.
- We all need to "brand" ourselves personally and in business.
- We all need to accept that technology can be used to help or to hinder.
- We all need to **Believe** in ourselves, so we can withstand life's challenges.
- We all need to appreciate others for who they are and not who we want them to be.
- We all need to seek to grow and become the best version of ourselves.
- We all need to recognize that **Social Media** is a method of communicating and that leveraging the power of **Livestreaming** is powerful.
- We all need to understand that we will have difficult times and it is not what happens to us, but the way we handle them, that defines who we are.
- Even if you think one title may not apply to you because you aren't in "sales" or you don't use **Social Media**, I promise you will learn something valuable in every book. The principles, analogies, and stories in each one will inspire you to understand others and increase your desire to be the best **YOU**, you can be.

Every title in this **#12Books12Months** series will add an additional layer of support to help you grow and learn, because we know there is always room for improvement. That is incredibly different from wanting to change because you don't **Believe** you are worthy or that you are under the false assumption that you are **Not Good Enough**. Remember, **#YouAreEnough** just the way you are.

Having a **Tribe** of people who **Believe** in you and your journey makes it easier and improves your chances for success. For that reason, I am inviting you to be part of our **Tribe**, the **#Fitch5000**. You will see a section in the back of each book listing these steadfast supporters who have helped me take this from a **#BHAG** in my head, to a reality. They are also helping me expand the **#YouAreEnough** global campaign into schools, corporations, and homes across the world.

If you would like to **#JoinTheJourney** and be part of the **#Fitch5000,** go to **www.VickiFitch.com/5K**. We will add your name to the list and who knows? If you participate in the group, you may get an acknowledgement, a thank you, or even a character named after you!

In closing, I want you to know that I am honored that you are reading this book. In an effort to make our journey even easier, I have provided you with a lot of additional resources at **www.VickiFitch.com/ETB** to help you on your way.

I **Hope** you will join me on my daily broadcasts, so I can answer your questions and help you arrive safely at your ultimate destination. When you do, you will recognize the way I close every broadcast to keep you focused on the possibilities.

I want to remind you, like I always do, to…

Dream it,

Believe it,

Achieve it!

Vicki Fitch

Follow Us on Social Media!

Facebook @VickiFitch1
LinkedIn @VickiFitch
Pinterest @VickiFitch

Twitter @Vicki_Fitch
Periscope @Vicki_Fitch
Instagram @Vicki_Fitch

Preface
On A Mission

In a world where suicide has become an epidemic, and where feeling like you don't "measure up" is as common as drinking a cup of coffee, I was inspired to write something that would encourage, motivate, and inspire the world by casting away the outdated, inaccurate opinion that you are **Not Enough** and replacing it with not only the idea, but the confirmation, that **#YouAreEnough** just the way you are.

My MISSION:

To Edutain in schools, churches, hospitals, organizations, and companies worldwide; to help people recognize and Evict the culprits that have taken over the Headspace between their ears and replace them with an army of positive reinforcement.

The process is fun and simple, but not always easy. Understanding ourselves in a way that allows us to start using the underutilized **Empathy** over the unfortunate pandemic of **Apathy** takes some time and creative thought. I believe this book is the perfect mix of **Edutaining** (both **Edu**cating and Enter**taining**) you. It initiates a new way of thinking about yourself and your circumstances, while helping you to see others through a different **Filter**. One that engages **Compassion** instead of **Control**, **Anger**, or **Apathy**.

Throughout the pages of this book, I will introduce you to a variety of **Bullies** that have been plaguing you, and to the **Headspace Heroes** who are ready, willing, and able to handle these inconvenient intruders.

- If you have ever fallen prey to the idea that you are **Not Good Enough**, **Not Strong Enough**, **Not Smart Enough**, **Not Pretty Enough**, **Not Thin Enough**, or just **Not Enough**, you have been infected with **NES** (**Not Enough Syndrome**), and this book is the cure.
- If you have ever been angry, annoyed, or aggravated with people at work, home, or out and about in public, this book will provide you alternative ways to handle the situation that are easy and effective.
- If you have ever felt disconnected, disheartened or depressed, this book will guide you out of the **Depths of Discouragement** and back onto **Stability Shore**.
- If life, or your circumstances have had you feeling overworked, overtired, and underappreciated, this book will guide you from the **Ocean of Overwhelm** to the **Sea of Tranquility**.
- If you have been feeling empty, lost, and alone, this book will bring you **Hope** and a **Tribe** of people who will care about you and connect with you.
- If you know someone else who has been feeling like this: a child, an adult, a parent, a team member, a co-worker, a boss, a patient or a friend, you have the answer in your hands to help them heal. Be the hero that provides **Hope**.

As we travel together through **Fitchipelago**, this book will move you forward on your journey to becoming the best version of yourself. Opportunity, community, and connection are the answers most people are looking for, so read this book and share it with others. Become **Part of the Solution**, by helping to inoculate future generations, while curing those who have already contracted this often-debilitating disease.

If you implement these simple strategies, your life will change because your perspective and your attitude will change. What's more, your ability to see the best in yourself and others will improve, and you will become a catalyst for positive change. That ripple effect will transcend the local boundaries of your family, organization, or community and can impact the world.

I'm on a mission to help every individual recognize:

#YouAreEnough… Just the way you are!

It is time for you to make a difference. Let's get started and find out why we ask ourselves, "What's wrong with you?"

Part I
Recognizing Your Bully

Chapter 1
What's Wrong with You?

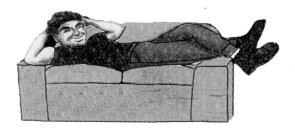

"Heavy hearts, like heavy clouds in the sky, are best relieved by the letting of a little water."
—Christopher Morley

"**W**hat the hell is wrong with you, you little floozy?" My father yelled at me after he dragged me in the house by my hair from my front yard, humiliating me in front of all my friends and neighbors.

My mind was a blur, and my head was spinning…

- What is a floozy?
- What did I do?
- Why am I in trouble… again?

It seemed like this would never end. I was never going to get it right. I was never going to please him, I was never going to be good enough… so why bother?

The pain and agony of being a misunderstood child can compound itself into a myriad of things.

- Some children become bullies themselves, taking their anger out on other younger, weaker, or quieter individuals.
- Some will stuff it down and develop anxiety disorders or become a volcano of anguish and resentfulness that results in an angry, unfulfilled adult.

- Some will become violent and become full-on abusers who hurt others because it is the only way to temporarily distract themselves from the devastation that has occurred in their own lives.
- Some will put up a façade that they don't care and try to parade around letting others believe they are confident when inside they just want someone to appreciate who they really are, so they can let down their guard and receive… acceptance.
- Some will jump from relationship to relationship trying to please a partner to find the ever elusive… love.
- Some will throw themselves into work or service or relationships, as a way to "prove" their worth, only to feel abandoned when their efforts aren't appreciated the way they expected.
- Some will develop OCD in the pursuit of being perfect or getting things "right."

And yet…

- Some will figure out who they are and learn to understand why others do what they do, so they can go on a mission to change the world.

Chapter 2
Bully vs. "bully"

"I don't know that there's any rhyme or reason to bullying...
it's not even the bully's fault,
which is why it's such a difficult thing to combat."
—*Dove Cameron*

As you will soon come to understand, we encounter both **Bullies** and **bullies** in our lives and I am going to break down these definitions for you. The **bully** with a lowercase "b" is the one you can see hear and touch. They are in the physical realm:

> **bully** - /ˈbo͞olē/
> **A person who uses strength or power to harm or intimidate those who are weaker.**

The **Bully** with the capital "B' is the one that resides in your head and there is an entire **Bully Brigade** that wants to visit and take up residence in your **Headspace**.

> **Bully** - /ˈbo͞olē/
> **The tormentor that lives rent free in your head, that holds you hostage with insults and constant reminders of your past.**
>
> **The Typhoid Mary of NES (Not Enough Syndrome)**

This book will focus on the **Bully in Your Head** as they are often more dangerous, more difficult, and trickier to manage than any **bully** you can see.

Bullying is not specific to gender, race, age, or geography. It occurs in schools, at work, in public, in private, and in politics. It is everywhere, and the only universal thing it seems to look for is "different."

"Different" can exist in any of the places mentioned above, but, it also can include people that look, speak, act, or believe differently than someone else. That is why it is imperative that we start recognizing that *anyone* can be a **bully**, and *anyone* may be subjected to bullying; it does not matter how big, strong, or effective they think they are.

In addition, each of us has a **Bully** in our head that has an **All-Access Pass** to our vulnerability. No matter how much we try to protect ourselves, we cannot get away from … ourselves. Since the **Bully in Your Head** has one goal, and that is to stay securely planted in your **Headspace**, he will do whatever it takes to stay right where he is. He is a carrier of the dreaded **NES** (**Not Enough Syndrome**) and he infects you the moment he is born and will continue sharing his disease until we **Evict** him and his **Bully Buddies**. They all must be **Quarantined** on **Eviction Isle,** so they can't infect anyone else.

If you are like me, there have been days when you felt like you were **Not Good Enough, Not Smart Enough, Not Strong Enough, Not Pretty Enough**… or just **Not Enough.** Those are the symptoms of **NES** that we need to cure you of. The longer you are infected, the lower your resistance is to the friends your **Bully** will bring over. You may have encountered **Despair** when you started feeling that no matter how hard you tried, things just weren't going right. When **Doubt** dropped by, your ability to accomplish things was hindered and you may have falsely believed that things were never going to get better. The longer these losers stuck around in your **Headspace**, the further you fell into the **Depths of Discouragement**. You may have even started to believe that the scraps left at the bottom of the barrel were the best life had to offer you.

I want you to know that is just a big fat lie the **Bully in your Head** has tried to convince you is fact. Through the pages of this book, I have tried to transparently share my personal situations, so you know I understand where you are coming from and why you are fearful of making changes. Remember this, the journey is easier when you realize that **You Are Not Alone #YANA**. I am here with you, and we can do this together.

One of my objectives with this book is to help you see that most **bully** attacks aren't personal. They are the result of a **Bully** residing in the **Headspace** of the **bully** who is bothering you. This may sound tricky, but I will explain it in greater detail soon. After we recognize how those two tormentors interact with each other, it becomes clear how to correct the situation and start implementing the **12-Step Bully Eviction Process**.

Let's start with understanding the different types of bullies we encounter in the real world by doing a **bully** breakdown:

"bully" Breakdown

The three main types of **bullies** you will encounter and their identifying characteristics:

- **Physical bullies**
- **Mental/Emotional bullies**
- **Cyberbullies**

Physical bullies are tangible and capable of being in proximity to you. They can touch you and torment you by being close or can make you uncomfortable when you know they are around.

Mental/Emotional bullies may or may not be within your proximity. They could call you to tell you how you aren't meeting a set of undefined expectations, make fun of you, or harass you. They might even get others to remind you about any of your perceived inadequacies. (For example: teasing you about the size of your nose, insulting you over the color of your skin, or judging you based on your socioeconomic background.)

Cyberbullies don't have to be in proximity to you. They can torment you through email, texts, **Social Media**, etc. They can be complete strangers and even someone you know: a neighbor, relative, coworker, or someone you grew up with. Unfortunately, they may even be someone you considered a friend.

Anyone feeling insecure that has access to the internet can be a **Cyberbully.**

Many of the **bullies** we encounter are a combination of two or more types of **bullies**, which makes us feel even more vulnerable. They have access to us on multiple fronts, which limits where we ultimately feel safe. In addition, they sometimes show up in places we weren't expecting…

Authority Figures

Some people in authority or leadership positions, like doctors or teachers, have bullied us into doing things their way, because they have a degree or because they have more information than we do. In some ways, society has encouraged us to submit to this less recognized form of bullying. Keep in mind:

Secure, confident people don't engage in bullying behavior.

It is the **Bully in Your Head** that stops you from asking great questions and weighing the expert's information with your own intuition. The **Bully** stops you from finding the **Confidence** and **Courage** to ask questions until you are completely satisfied with the answers given.

I will be sharing stories with you from both sides of the **Bully** versus **bully** spectrum. This is to assure you that I understand you and acknowledge that I've likely been where you are. I will help you see the differences, identify how they are directly related to each other, and how easy it is to **#EvictTheBully**. So, **Pull up Your Bootstraps #PUYB** (That is a **Fitchism** to say, "Prepare yourself! It may get rough."). It's time to dig in!

Chapter 3
The Bully in Your Head

---

*"I woke up one day and thought,
'Enough is enough with bullying myself.'
The war is within you, and that's also where it's won.
You just have to tackle your insecurities
and then let them go."*
—*Keala Settle*

For the ease of writing, I am going to address the **Bully** as a "He" for the most part. Feel free to substitute "She" if you find that it serves you better. I am fully aware that the **Bully** can come in both the male and female roles. In some cases, your **Bully** may be a bit more gender neutral, look more like a **Troll,** or lack definability. Keep in mind that the noun or pronoun used is not important; it is understanding what is happening and how to change the situation that really matters in the long run.

Before I explain how the **Bully** got so firmly planted in your mind and in your life, I am going to share an analogy with you that may make some of you uncomfortable. You may have experienced this situation in real life or know someone who has. Therefore, the reality of what I am about to share could make you feel uneasy.

As you read, please remember there is no **Judgment** here. Any **Judgment** you feel is the **Bully in Your Head** trying to dissuade you from continuing this journey. I promise to help you **Evict** him, so be prepared for some intense feelings and emotions to be present. Continue to the end, because that is where the magic happens.

The **Bully** doesn't want you to change or to become the best version of yourself. He likes things the way they are. You are an amazing human being that God planned to not only grow, but flourish.

Lisa's Love Story

Lisa was a lonely sixteen-year old girl who had never had a boyfriend. She was of average height and build. She listened with envy as all her friends talked about boys, because so far, she had not had anyone interested in her. She dreamed of "the one" and sang every romantic song on the radio as if there were someone special in her life.

One day, a boy named Trevor smiled at Lisa. She felt herself blush a little and glanced back, noticing that he was still looking at her. He came over to where she was standing, and they started chatting.

"You are so beautiful!" said Trevor with a charismatic smile.

With a slight blush, Lisa smiled and drank in the attention as she glanced up at him. Everyone likes to feel pretty; he was so handsome, and he was talking to ***her****!*

They continued to chat, and he asked if he could see her again. With her heart pounding, she gave him her number. She was not sure if he would ever really call, but she secretly hoped he would.

The next day, to her surprise and delight, he did call. They chatted on the phone and he asked to take her out. She coyly said, "Yes." and they made arrangements for the next day.

Upon arrival, he complimented her hair and her clothes. It made her feel lovely and special. Already, she was starting to fall for his kind words and his longing gazes.

She told her friends about how wonderful Trevor was, and even though it was early, she thought to herself, "He might be the one!"

Lisa and Trevor started spending a lot of time together, taking walks and talking. Lisa realized she was definitely falling in love, although she would never say it out loud, at least not until he did.

On one of their dates, he picked her up and, as usual, he complimented her and said, "You look so beautiful tonight... but what did you do to your hair?"

Lisa reached up to touch it and smooth it into place, not sure what he meant. When she asked, he said, "Oh never mind, it's fine."

Lisa reluctantly let it go, but not without thinking to herself, "It must have been out of place, or maybe a leaf from my walk earlier had gotten tangled in it." Still, she went on to have a nice evening, realizing that she was really crazy about him.

"He gets me." she thought. "He is always telling me how much he loves being with me, he just hasn't said he loves me yet." Silently, she wondered if he was falling in love with her, too.

The two talked every night and grew closer. Trevor started to share more personal things including details of his life that made Lisa feel teary. "He is confiding in me! I will never let him down! He can trust me!" Her commitment to Trevor was becoming stronger every day.

Their next time together, Trevor greeted Lisa with a smile. He looked into her eyes with a stare that seemed to say how he couldn't live without her. Lisa's heart melted. "He is so wonderful. I've never felt so close to someone before," she continued to think to herself.

His gaze drifted down to her clothing and instead of a compliment, this time he said,

"Where did you get that dress?" The expression on his face fell short of admiration.

"Why do you ask? Is there something wrong with it?" she replied quickly.

"No, it just makes you look fat." he casually tossed back.

Lisa drew back feeling hurt at this quick retort. She offered to go in and change while at the same time trying to process that the man she had been falling madly in love with now thought that she was fat.

He declined her offer and said, "No, it's OK. We will be late for our reservation. It isn't your fault; it's the dress that makes you look that way."

Still trying to figure out how she felt, she shuffled into the car to not keep him waiting. The conversation became fun, and soon Lisa forgot all about the misfired comment.

Dinner finally arrived as the two were chatting and having a great time. Things were going along splendidly, and the waitress offered them the dessert menu. Trevor ordered the usual dessert to share. All the while, they were still talking and smiling.

As their dessert arrived at the table with two spoons, Lisa picked one up and started to take a bite. Trevor gazed at her with a wistful look that said, "You don't want to eat that, do you?"

Lisa smiled and put down her spoon. She watched as Trevor devoured the entire thing. The conversation from earlier in the evening came rushing back. She started thinking to herself, "He really does think I'm fat." After a while, she became withdrawn.

On their car ride back home, things were a little strained as she quietly sat in the passenger seat. Trevor asked her what was wrong. She hesitated, then told him how he had hurt her feelings.

He immediately pulled the car over to apologize for how insensitive he had been. He begged for her forgiveness and offered to get her some ice cream. He then showered her with kisses and told her that she was perfect just the way she is.

All was well again. Lisa gazed longingly at him, all the while thinking, "He made a mistake and he is so sorry for it. He really is wonderful!"

Their phone conversations got more intense after that night, and Lisa shared her heart with him. He was such a good listener!

The next time she saw him, she wore a pair of jeans that she knew fit her well. She wanted to make a good impression and she wanted to make sure that he noticed she had been paying attention to what she looked like. She wanted him to be proud of her.

"What do you think?" Lisa asked playfully as she spun around. His eyes dodged about a bit as he said, "You look fine."

Lisa could tell by his expression that something was wrong. She pursued the true answer until she finally got him to ask, "Have you gained some weight?"

Devastated, she ran into the house; her confidence eroded as she burst into tears.

He ran to her side, hugging, caressing, and showering her again with kisses. Telling her how sorry he was for being such an idiot. "How could I be so insensitive to the girl I love?"

Her heart skipped a beat as she quickly drew in a breath. She forgot all about the anger and the hurt... "He LOVES me! He must have been having a hard time dealing with his emotions. He told me he had never said that to anyone before."

Their embrace lasted a long time and Lisa felt closer to Trevor than ever before. She whispered, "I love you, too." In Lisa's world, this was the perfect moment!

The conversations on the phone got longer and more intimate. They couldn't wait to see each other. Trevor wanted to come over the following night, but Lisa already had plans with her friends. Trevor was very disappointed. He reminded her that he just couldn't wait to see her, and he begged Lisa to cancel because he was going to miss her so much.

Lisa's heart fluttered. It felt so intoxicating to be wanted! She agreed to cancel with her friends. They were disappointed, but they understood.

*Her friends started calling them **Treva (Trev**or & Lis**a)** and the couple started spending more and more time together, and Lisa spent less and less time with her friends.*

"This must be love." Lisa thought to herself as she drifted off and started thinking about the romantic songs she always listened to.

*The more time they spent together, the more Lisa started to notice that Trevor's compliments were now being replaced by bits of **Sarcasm**. Sometimes, he would tell waiters, "She'll have the salad because she is watching her weight."*

Lisa tried to hide the sting because she never said anything about watching her weight. She just smiled at the wait staff and nodded in agreement. She convinced herself that Trevor was just trying to help her.

Then, one day, Trevor told Lisa that she might want to start working out because her arms were getting a little flabby. She glanced down at her arms and started thinking that he must be right.

Soon after, he said, "That chub around your middle is cute." She looked down at her nearly flat stomach and started thinking that maybe her body was not OK. When she protested, Trevor apologized and reminded her that she was "too sensitive" about things. He essentially dismissed her concerns.

*Time passed, and Lisa had not seen her friends in months, which frustrated them. When she told Trevor she wanted to go out with them, he flared up in **Anger** and forcefully grabbed her arm.*

Lisa pulled away shocked that he would touch her like that. Trevor immediately apologized. He then held her and showered her with kisses like he used to.

"I'm so sorry. I am so in love with you! I have never felt this way before and I miss you so much when I'm not with you. I just felt crazy for a second. It will never happen again."

His gaze was directed downward as he began to share, "When my Mom left my Dad, it started by her going out with her friends. I just don't want that to happen to us. You are happy with our love, aren't you?"

Shattered that she could have hurt him so much, the tables turned, and Lisa started apologizing. She explained that she had no idea about what happened with his mother. No wonder he was so sensitive. Lisa recognized that love is emotional and of course, she understood and agreed to stay away from her friends.

This appeased Trevor but the tension with Lisa's friends was still mounting. She knew they were getting bitter. They started making comments about how she was ignoring them, and about how she wasn't being herself anymore.

Guilt *over letting them down versus hurting Trevor again became difficult to deal with, so she thought of a solution.*

She lied.

She told her friends they were right and committed to going out with them that night. Then she told Trevor that she had something to do with her parents. Lisa felt content that this would make everyone happy. Trevor wouldn't feel abandoned and she could connect with her friends again. It was the perfect plan!

The evening was a lot of fun! Lisa had forgotten how much fun she had with these girls! Trevor continued to text her all night, and she replied each time to make sure he felt safe.

Without Lisa realizing it, one of her friends posted a picture of the four of them on social media. This was where things went off the rails.

When Lisa got home, Trevor was outside of her house waiting to talk and he didn't look happy.

Lisa apologized repeatedly as she tried to explain why she did it, but Trevor didn't want to hear any of it. He called her names and the two of them argued. Lisa, feeling frustrated, then said, "Trevor, you are being ridiculous. It was only a few..." but before she could finish her sentence, she felt a sting across her cheek.

Stunned, Lisa looked at him and for the first time, saw the **Anger** in his eyes. She didn't move. "Did he just slap me?" she thought to herself in disbelief. It couldn't be. "He loves me. He would never do that!" But, the sting on her cheek and the welt from his ring told a different story. It...was true.

As the tears started rolling down Lisa's cheeks, she tried to catch her breath to figure out what to do. She noticed Trevor started crying, too.

He begged Lisa to forgive him and explained how the lying and sneaking around is what his Mom had done, and it left him feeling devastated, just the way his father had felt. To Trevor, it was like Lisa was cheating on him, and that wasn't supposed to happen when you loved someone.

He looked sincere as he slumped on the ground. Lisa found herself instinctively putting her arms around him to comfort him. Still not exactly sure how she felt about what just happened, Lisa felt a combination of **Sadness**, **Guilt**, **Anger**, and **Confusion**... There were too many emotions to keep track of, so she just stayed and listened to his words. She felt his apology kisses, which were starting to seem all too familiar after each uncomfortable incident.

The welt on her face put her in a predicament. She had to dodge her parents when she went in the house. When they saw it the next day, Lisa laughed and made up an excuse about how she and the girls had been goofing around and how she got in the way of some play acting.

She retreated from her friends. Lisa couldn't allow them to see the mark on her face. They would ask questions and she wouldn't know what to say. She didn't want them to judge Trevor. They didn't understand him, although she was starting to wonder if she understood him either.

The up-and-down cycle of emotions between Trevor and Lisa continued. Lisa tried to not make any waves or do anything that would upset him. After all, love is a choice and it goes through ups and downs. If it is true love, it will weather the storm.

Lisa put effort into keeping him happy but one day she challenged him by asking a difficult question. Trevor lost his temper and knocked her down.

Lisa looked up from the cold, hard ground and thought to herself, "How did I get here?"

As you can see from this story, these kinds of relationships don't typically start out with **Abuse**.

Imagine if the end of the story was the beginning.

One day, a boy named Trevor smiled at Lisa. She felt herself blush a little and glanced back, noticing that he was still looking at her. He came over to where she was standing, and they started chatting....

... Trevor lost his temper and knocked Lisa down.

The End.

There is no second date. There is no relationship building, no deep connections forming, and thus, no **Manipulation** occurs. As a matter of fact, the police would likely have been involved. **Abuse** is a sly **Bully**. He starts out subtle. It is what I call the **Nudge**, which pushes you off course.

Another example, without using relationships as the premise, is simple geometry. If you are thinking, "Vicki, I flunked geometry," or "I'm not a math person," that is OK. This is simple, and you will get it. If you are starting out at point A and want to get to point B, you just need to go straight ahead.

On the other hand, if you start out at point A and want to get to point B but someone gives you a **Nudge**, that changes your trajectory. You never hit point B. Instead, you end up somewhere completely different and wonder, "How did I get here?"

It is the same way with relationships. Perpetrators don't start out with obvious **Abuse**; they groom you. They have you start doubting yourself, toy with your emotions, and manipulate you to get what they want.

The **Bully in Your Head** is an abuser and operates from the same playbook. This is why I need you to understand the **Bully**, so we can start the **Eviction Process**.

There are some simple techniques to help you start preparing yourself for the changes that are coming during this book. You need to get ready. Remember, the **Bully in Your Head** is very comfortable where he is. He wants to stay and will do anything to keep you stuck in the **Sea of Status Quo**, where nothing ever changes. He wants to **Overwhelm** you to the point of **Frustration** regularly each day.

This is especially true when you start identifying with parts of this book and we talk about "**Eviction**." He will tell you that you're crazy, will call you names that **Trigger** your insecurities, and will hurl insults at you just to keep you under his **Control** so you will keep giving him everything he needs to survive.

By now, the **Bully** has grown quite scary, and he can easily dominate us which is why we are not going to fight him head on. We are simply going to start by changing the way we deal with his everyday assaults. Arguing with your **Bully in Your Head** will not do you any good at this point. You have argued with him and lost so many times that you no longer believe you have the stamina to fight, let alone fight and win. You have probably chosen to give up altogether. This book is the first line of defense in your learning to **Stand Up** for yourself in a way that will not cause you to buckle under the pressure again. The days of your current, manipulated belief that you just can't win are about to be over.

Here is the first lesson in executing the **Eviction Process**. You need to practice if you are serious about changing your life.

Step Up for YOU

When the **Bully in Your Head** starts to attack you, argue with you, or consistently pummel you with lies about your being **Not Good Enough**, **Not Smart Enough**, **Not Pretty Enough**, **Not Tall Enough**, or **Not Whatever Enough**, you won't argue with him anymore. We now have a different approach.

When the **Bully** tells you,

> "It's your fault."
> "You're stupid."
> "No one likes you."
> "He doesn't love you."
> "This book is a waste of time."

You only need three little words to protect yourself.

"Not today, Bully."

For emphasis, and to remind ourselves that we can handle this for a short period of time, we often repeat the first two.

"Not today, Bully. *Not today.*"

These three words, used in repetition, can and will change your life. They are the first step in the **Eviction Process**.

Psychologically, I want you to understand the significance of standing up for yourself with a real or "imagined" foe. I intend to teach you how to take your life back by engaging your senses to strengthen your resolve the force him and his **Bully Buddies** out of your **Headspace**.

Practicing prepares you for the **Super Stance** and the hand motion we will be adding in shortly. I want you to be fully equipped to handle your **Bully** and to train others to do the same. So, let's dive into why we are doing this and what it means.

Have you ever been in a battle with a coworker or loved one and just run out of steam? You no longer had the strength or energy to continue and said, whether to yourself or out loud… "Not today…" While possibly shaking your head side to side in exasperation?

This was a decision to stop engaging with someone, or to stop discussing something that did not warrant the time it was taking, at least not at that particular moment.

It was not a declaration of you giving up. It was a decision to preserve yourself, and your mental or physical energy. The insecure, overzealous minds of people without perspective might have seen it as your throwing in the white flag of surrender. They may even have relished in what they considered the victory of wearing you down, or worse, are under the illusion that you changed your mind and are now in agreement with them.

You really didn't change your mind or your position. You just knew that wasn't the time, or perhaps the place, to do battle. You may have also realized it wasn't a battle worth fighting.

The **Bully in Your Head** works on the same premise. He is an insolent child that wants to stay in **Control** of your feelings by manipulating you and feeding you lies to keep you in "check." He will continue to make you second guess all your decisions in order to create **Doubt**, pushing your **Confidence** further away.

Every choice that doesn't go as you expected becomes a weapon in his arsenal he uses to keep you discouraged. It is time for you to #**EvictTheBully** that is taking up your precious **Headspace** and I want to explain how.

The **Bully** thought your exasperation was retreat. I will teach you how to use it to pull back and regroup to form a stronger position.

"Not today, Bully. Not today."

First, these words aren't a "dig your heels in," all-out attack; they are a small stand that the **Bully** falsely sees as submission. Internally, you say to yourself,

---

"You may have your grip on me, but today, just for today,
even just for this moment, I am taking a stand and
I am not going to allow you to destroy
my ability to see the best in myself."

It doesn't matter if you wholeheartedly **Believe** this in the beginning. It is a proven scientific fact that the brain reacts to situations that are both real or imagined. You are just trying to build up a lethargic muscle that has atrophied from lack of use.

As large and aggressive as the **Bully** has become, just like all **Bullies**, he is actually a bit of a coward. He is easily persuaded that he has won if he interprets your actions as **Defeat**. By repeating that phrase, he will likely leave you alone for the moment while he relishes in his assumption that you are under his full **Control**. That moment is all you really need. That is the moment that you start flexing the muscles you had forgotten existed.

When you recognize that three small words can calm or dismiss his attacks, you will feel encouraged to exercise that weak and flabby muscle to increase your strength and stability.

You will start to see how your **Confidence** has been buried underneath a truckload of insults, and disparaging remarks. That is all about to change.

Now that you know the words, say them out loud. I want you to repeat the first two as an extra layer of support. Ready?

"Not today, Bully. Not today."

That wasn't so hard, was it?

OK, I understand that you might feel a little uncomfortable. The **Bully** is jeering at you right now telling you how ridiculous it is for you think that three words can change the way you think and feel about yourself. I am here to help you **#EvictTheBully**, so, if you are tired of having him beat you up, keep reading and practicing the quick exercise I just gave you.

You don't want the **Abuse** to keep going. You will not resign yourself to accepting the scraps the **Bully** has been offering you. Therefore, you need to continue building your strength and a solid **Eviction** strategy.

If you have visions of making it to **Success Island** and getting to **#RockThatDream Ridge**, I recommend you take my advice and **Step Up**, practice, and support yourself.

Think about it… what is the harm in trying?

If I am wrong, you silently repeated a phrase for a while that in no way harmed you, and no one but you is any the wiser.

If I am right, on the other hand, you will change your entire life and the lives of those around you forever because they will see and emulate your ability to appreciate yourself.

There is no downside and yet the upside is so amazing that the only reason you wouldn't give it a try is if the **Bully** has that strong of a hold on you that he is holding your **Belief** hostage.

In case you are still contemplating whether the **Bully in Your Head** has power, read *Lisa's Love Story* again. Substitute yourself in for Lisa, and Trevor's "not so subtle" insults for your negative self-talk. You and your **Bully** are a lot like Trevor and Lisa. (That is a **#TruthBomb** that might take you some time to process.) The **Bully** is fully prepared to destroy your **Confidence** to get you to stay submissive to his will.

Back to those of you who are ready for change and want to implement Step One which is to **Believe** in yourself and recognize that **#YouAreEnough**. Then it's time to practice the second step in the **Eviction Process**, which is to **Stand Up** for yourself.

"Not today, Bully. Not today."

If someone is around, say it in your head. If no one is around, then who are you worried about?

It's just you, me, and the **Bully** hanging out right now. I suggest you listen to me. I am a much more positive influence, and I actually **Believe** in you. I don't have to know you personally to recognize that you have the potential to be even more amazing!

You picked up this book, whether by accident or on purpose, so I have to **Believe** something in you wants to change. Something inside wants you to stop beating yourself up every time things don't turn out as expected. Something within you wants you to stop fueling your **Doubt** and **FEAR**. You are MORE than the sum of your challenges and it is about time you started living the life of your **Dreams,** instead of the life the **Bully** has convinced you is all you deserve.

So, did you do it? Did you say it out loud?

There is POWER in saying things out loud. If you have the **Courage**, even if other people are around, say it out loud.

"Not today, Bully. Not today."

Flabby Muscle Cure

Trust me when I say you are going to need the practice to tone up that flabby muscle and that you are worth it!

OK, so now that you have the words, it's time to engage multiple senses. Let's add a little hand motion with it.

Yes, I am fully aware that the **Bully** is reminding you how RIDICULOUS this is. Why wouldn't he? Again, he likes this **Comfy, Cozy Comfort Zone** you've been providing for him where you provide for all his needs and he has free reign to do whatever he pleases. Who would ever want to give up that easy life?

So, what hand motion am I talking about? You can make up your own if you like, but you know the old "Talk to the hand" motion? You can watch me doing this move on a quick video clip here **www.VickiFitch.com/ETB**. My hope is this will both encourage and motivate you with a quick laugh.

When you get your body, voice, and mind all focused on one thing, you are using multiple senses, which makes the psychological impact of what you are doing much stronger.

Next, do it while you watch yourself in the mirror. By adding the extra sense of sight to engage the muscle, you will multiply your efforts.

Will you laugh at yourself at first? Maybe.

Will you feel awkward or ridiculous? Probably.

Want to know why?

Because the **Bully** has conditioned you to **Believe** that this is foolish and that training to **Believe** in yourself is crazy. Remember, his intention is to keep you right where you are stuck—in the **Sea of Status Quo**.

Here is your chance to show the **Bully** that you have a backbone. You may not feel strong yet, but practicing will strengthen and tone the muscles. It takes time to find the perfect **Super Stance**, so try it again with all the attitude you can muster. Your ability to do it without laughing at yourself or feeling ridiculous will probably go something like this:

Steps to finding your Super Stance	
Not today, Bully.	No power, eyes rolling or looking down. No **Confidence.**
Not today, Bully. Not today.	Quiet, trying to take it seriously but feeling silly.
Not today, Bully. Not today.	Committed, but subtle.
Not today, Bully. Not today.	Resolute in doing it, but still weak delivery.
Not today, Bully. Not today.	Recognizing your value and ready to actually try.
Not today, Bully. Not today.	**Confidence** building including a head shake or hand.
Not today, Bully. Not today.	**Confidence with full head swirl, hand twist, or attitude.**

OK, so now it is time to practice. Did you know that a hands-on-your-hips superhero pose produces a chemical reaction in the body to help with your **Confidence**? So, start out with that "open posture" stance and develop your own **Super Stance** from there.

Ready? Go!

- Drop into your **Super Stance**.
- Look in the mirror
- Get your wrist, neck or whatever other attitude you got prepared for the **Bully**, and do it while saying:

"Not today, Bully. Not today."

Which place are you on the chart? Practice a few more times to get yourself more comfortable with the process. Try not to laugh at yourself. Right now, you need to take yourself seriously. There will be plenty of time to laugh "with" yourself later.

Keep practicing and figure out what makes you feel the most confident. It is time to take a little bit of your power back. Just like the **Nudge**, in *Lisa's Love Story*, the **Bully** won't see it coming!

Now that you have taken your first steps toward **Eviction**, let me help you understand how that big bad **Bully** got there in the first place. You actually invited him in…

Chapter 4
The Birth of the Bully

---

*"People talk about bullying,
but you can be your own bully in some ways.
You can be the person who is
standing in the way of your own success,
and that was the case for me."*
—*Katy Perry*

I f you watch my daily **Livestreams** or have heard me speak about the "**Bully in Your Head**," you will recognize the reference that the **Bully** didn't just show up. He didn't come into your life as a 350-pound linebacker staring you down ready to tear you to shreds for every original thought or idea that was outside the norm. As we look back to *Lisa's Love Story* from the previous chapter, we can see that things are a bit more subtle than that. You are smart, you would have avoided that type of scenario. Now, are you wondering how the **Bully** made his entrance?

The **Truth** is, the **Bully** came into your life as a baby. The **Bully** was conceived the first time someone said you were stupid, ugly, worthless, ridiculous, insane, annoying, fat, or **Not Enough**.

It was a tiny little thing at first— not much to be concerned with, just a blip on the radar; a tiny little embryo that was easy to ignore. But over time, as these insults continued to come, and your assuredness started to shrink, it became harder to ignore. Subconsciously, you weren't aware that each of these criticisms became food to nourish the growing fetus.

Something the size of a pimento isn't strong enough to harm you; at least that is what you thought. As time continued and other comments and concerns piled on, you started to feel a discomfort in your gut which eventually felt more like getting kicked in the stomach. It was uncomfortable, but tolerable, and you just ignored it. You continued accepting the negativity that was feeding the mass of **Doubt** breeding inside. Until one day, it happened…

You **BELIEVED** the negative insults being thrown at you were true and the **Bully** was born.

He was dropped off at your proverbial doorstep. You could have called the authorities to come take him away, but you thought you could handle him. After all, he was a just a baby. A cute, tiny little baby. He was good company. He needed you and you so desperately wanted to be needed. So, you invited him in.

You fed him, nurtured him, clothed him, and cared for him. You not only accepted his presence, you sought a connection with this baby letting him become part of who you were and got used to him being around during that gestation period. You embraced his presence since he was familiar.

You held him, rocked him, and comforted him. One day, something unusual happened. The baby reached up and touched your face making you think about how sweet this precious baby was.

As the baby grew a little more, you continued with the holding and nurturing. Again, the baby gently reached up to touch your face with his soft little caress and grabbed your cheek with his chubby hands. They don't have much control, so you gently squeezed his hand and softly cooed, "No, no, baby. Be gentle." You said this just as you would to any innocent child trying to learn spatial awareness.

Time continued, and the baby got bigger and stronger. He reached up again to touch your cheek while you smiled and gazed at this familiar part of your life. Then…

SMACK! He slapped you!

Shocked, from the sting, you looked at the baby and said,

"No, no, baby. Be gentle."

You were surprised that his playful taps were getting harder and harder.

You continued to gently hold his hand and tried to lovingly show him how to treat others. But, as he grew, the frequency and the impact of the slaps got more forceful. The baby got bigger and before you knew it, you were confronted with a teenager that espoused comments like:

"You are

- **...stupid!"**
- **...a loser!"**
- **...a Failure!"**
- **...a waste of space!"**

You have lived with this baby that turned **Bully** for so long, that you have no idea what life would be like without it. You therefore keep accepting this **Unacceptable Behavior** and, in the process, you become disgruntled, discouraged, and depressed.

You have basically become a slave to him. He has set up residence in your head, like a college dorm room allowing his **Bully Buddies** to frequent the place and come and go as they please treating you the same way. They continue to leave residual trash in your **Headspace**, which only amplifies the **Lonely** feelings of unworthiness.

To the **Bully**, life is good here. You provide for all his needs, while he continues to mentally assault you with insults and disparaging remarks. You have unwittingly accepted them as **Truth**. Thus, fighting seems futile. He is a freeloader and a fraud. He is taking up valuable space in your sanctuary.

You know he needs to be served an **Eviction Notice,** but you don't know how to do it. He is bigger, stronger, and has a whole host of friends backing him up. You feel helpless as he insists on staying in this "Home Sweet Home."

Those rare occasions when you do feel encouraged and protest his insults, you realize that he has gotten so big and strong that you have no idea how to handle him, let alone **Evict** him. Somewhere along the line, you just gave up. You began to accept the daily assaults as what you deserve. You became accustomed to his version of the **Truth**. You were no longer surprised by the daily reminders that you are **Not Enough**. You resigned yourself to the idea that this nightmare was going to be your future and you settled in for the long haul feeling this was the best your life had to offer.

I am here to remind you that you may have taken in this **Bully** at birth as a surrogate parent, but this is NOT your child. You have no responsibility to continue allowing him to **Abuse** you.

The negativity others hurled at you because they were hurt or angry or discouraged in their own lives does **not** make this *your* child, nor *your* responsibility.

It is time to #**EvictTheBully,** but first we need to peek **Behind the Curtain** to where it all started…

Chapter 5
The Art of Empathy

"Empathy is a ladder out of the Shame hole."
—Brené Brown; Daring Greatly

I t's time to talk about the "Elephant in the room." We need to address the **Pain** that the **bullies** in your life are experiencing.

Empathy is not the go-to emotion for most people when dealing with **bullies**. Many people on the surface might even say it is the weak approach, but I disagree. It takes much more strength to try to look beyond our own circumstances and seek an alternative reason for why people choose to use cruelty and **Humiliation** as a way of life.

If you think about it, you probably agree with this statement:

Happy people are unlikely to try to hurt others.

It doesn't mean it never happens; it means it is unlikely. Most truly happy people look for the good in both the people they come into contact with, and the situations they experience.

Let us separate those that outwardly *pretend* they are happy, those that mask their **Pain** with a smile and a laugh, from the people that are genuinely happy. People that are truly happy feel **Joy** and contentment in their lives. They don't look to hurt or destroy others. It doesn't mean they don't sometimes get angry or upset; it means they don't choose to hold onto it and find someone else to take it out on.

When you feel frustrated or overwhelmed, is your inclination to go hurt someone, make fun of them, or make them feel bad about themselves?

If it is, I have news for you… you are not actually happy.

Happy people tend to know who they are and want to be part of something greater than themselves. They typically gravitate toward other happy people. If you are wondering if you are genuinely a happy person, look at the people you hang out with. If you are spending time with a pessimistic bunch, you may have fun despite their negativity, but you are probably not living up to your true potential.

Just for the record, we can still love those friends, but we need to recognize:

Those that always expect the worst to happen
often get what they expect.

I would try to encourage them to see things in a more positive light, while making sure to spend time with them in small doses, to maintain my energy level. While I empathize with their situation, the best thing I could do is give them a copy of this book and hope it would have a positive influence on their behavior.

Hurt People Don't Hurt People.

Some of you read that title and are saying,

"You are wrong! Hurt people DO hurt people."

I know why you are saying that. I had the same reaction the first time I heard my friend, Kevin Madison, say it. I remember the day well. It was a Saturday, and I was at the high school where we played all our CYAA games. I was listening to Kevin's **Scope** (what we call broadcasts on the **Periscope** app). I was walking near the gym where the next game would be starting soon, with my headphones in my ear. That was when I heard him say, *"Hurt people don't hurt people."* I stopped in my tracks for a minute, thinking, "Am I going to vehemently disagree with the amazing KGM?" I had enough **Respect** for him to listen to what came after that. I had been caught off guard by things he said in the past and they had always turned out to be incredibly insightful, so I listened intently. What came out of his mouth next were "3 Magic Words" that literally changed my life, the content I share, and even part of this book.

> *"Hurt people don't hurt people.*
> *Hurt people, <u>that aren't heard</u>, hurt people."*
> —*Kevin Madison*

#Boom! There it was. The magic formula. No wonder there were so many people full of **Anger** and **Frustration** who spent time hurting others. Perhaps there was an inability to express the **Pain** they were feeling or maybe the people they were sharing it with didn't really "hear." The point is that people **can** get through their **Pain** if they feel *heard* and cared about.

Think about that. People can work through the hurt they feel, if they feel they are *heard*. It is also important to recognize that to truly be *heard,* someone must **care**. I like to say it this way:

> *"The Healing begins when the Hearing begins."*

Being Heard

What does it mean to be *heard*?

Although each person may have a different interpretation of what that means, I can tell you what it means to me. My definition:

> *To be heard, means someone is*
> *Actively Listening to me,*
> *with a desire to understand WHAT I am really saying,*
> *and WHY it is important to me.*

It is not a warm body in the room who occasionally looks up from a phone or project to nod or concur. It doesn't matter to me that when asked, you can "rewind" the conversation in your mind to repeat what I have said. That is "*Listening without Hearing*" and, in my opinion, makes the person sharing, feel about as valuable as a box of rocks.

Active Listening requires the listener to fully concentrate without distraction on what is being said.

That means to listen without **Judgment** in a wholehearted effort to understand the other person's perspective. It isn't about agreeing, it is about adding the ever-important element of **Empathy** to the equation, which increases your desire to understand, more that your need to be understood.

If you want to make me feel valued, you don't have to agree with me, but you do have to care enough about how I feel to listen to what I say AND be committed and patient enough to ask questions that will help you understand.

Friendship is caring enough to listen until you understand, not until you agree.

Sometimes, we will even have to agree to disagree. But, if I know I have been *heard* and understood, I feel successful regardless of the outcome. I feel valued as a person.

When you are hurt and don't feel *heard*, you are prone to becoming a **bully**, so let's look at how that occurs.

"bullies" Beget "bullies"

How did the **bullies** in your life get the way they are? Most of them have been infected with **Not Enough Syndrome (NES)** and it shows up in various ways.

<u>Physical bullies</u> – the easiest reference we have for these is the schoolyard **bully**. This person is the one who finds the kids who are smaller, less vocal, shy, or different. We see these **bullies** depicted in movies as stealing food, stealing lunch money, and throwing other children into trash cans. These **bullies** grow up to be adults who either continue using physical **Abuse**, or sometimes move exclusively into the **Mental** or **Emotional** bullying arena. It is very sad and disturbing to realize that some of them knowingly do this to prevent detection of their abusive behavior because there are no visual signs of the damage. This is why **Mental/Emotional bullies** often go undetected for so long.

<u>Mental/Emotional bullies</u> – we often see these culprits in everyday locations—at work, at school, at home. These **bullies** use their words like weapons. Often, their words are more devastating than a bloody nose or lip. These psychological beatings are a breeding ground for **Bully Births**.

> <u>Kids</u> - When we look at a schoolyard scenario, we recognize the uncertainty of some children. Even at a very young age, their internal **Pain** will provoke them to start picking on others. The critiquing of their looks, style, or perceived inadequacies by a popular student can create an overwhelming sense of **Shame** and **Humiliation**. It isn't just kids that can cause this, adults can be just as, or even more **Guilty** of these **Bully Births**.

<u>**Adults**</u> - Adults that don't feel validated in life are often not prepared for the power that comes when they are in a position of authority. Their lack of validation tends to cause them to overcompensate to prove their worth. This often results in them treating subordinates poorly. Some of these insecure **bullies** can be seen **Peacocking** to pretend they are **Confident**, which reflects the desperation that they feel that they are **Not Good Enough**. They will continue putting others down to elevate themselves. It is just a façade, but we will address this in more detail later.

<u>**Authority Figures/Influencers**</u> - The continual berating of someone by an authority figure can cause more lasting damage to their future than any physical beating. These people in authority can be in the form of relatives, or can be work-related bosses, teachers, doctors, police, politicians, or any other person society has deemed an authority in a specific area or industry. Even celebrities, successful executives, and notable entrepreneurs can fall into this category.

<u>**Cyberbullies**</u> – these are usually the most woeful of all the **bullies.** They typically have very poorly-developed communication skills and a lack of **Courage** to say what they are thinking directly to people they are having challenges with. Instead, they hide behind a screen and use all their tactics to annihilate the **Confidence** and perceived worthiness of other people. Sometimes, they are so desperate to get reactions, or are so fearful of potential confrontation from someone they know, that they do this to complete strangers. They have no reason or grudge specifically against the "targets," they are just desperate to hurt another human, so they can somehow alleviate their own **Pain**. I discuss a lot more about this in *DS 301* in a chapter called **Troll Patrol**.

Reading that might have made you angry or upset. Maybe you have been the victim of one or more of those **bullies**, and it hurts. Maybe it is making you want to lash out at someone else, too. I understand why you feel that way, but I'd like to help you see a different point of view.

Behind the Curtain

In the movies, we tend to side against the **bullies**. We despise what they represent, which are things like **FEAR, Anxiety, Pain, Insecurity,** etc. We *"love to hate"* them. We cheer when they finally "get" what's coming to them! It is our classic "good always wins" mentality.

Don't get me wrong. I'm a hopeless romantic, a "**Rooter of the Underdog**," if you will. I am the person who always defends those who are smaller, weaker, less fortunate, or less **Courageous** than I am. That is part of my nature. It is just who I am.

I'm right there in the movie with you saying, "Get him!" So much so, that my husband laughs at me. I have an eagerness for justice to be served, and I ALWAYS want good to win. To be honest, I don't enjoy movies without a happy ending. I want to feel good and believe that everything is going to be alright. The problem is when we look **Behind the Curtain**, we see things from **A Fresh Perspective**…

"Behind the Curtain,"
we often find that the "bad guy" is just a "good guy"
in a lot of Pain, that doesn't know how to handle it.

I choose to assume that people who are rude, disrespectful, overly sarcastic, or bullying, are hurting inside. My instincts tell me to gently ask if they are having a bad day, or if they are hurting in some way. I remember the emptiness I felt during my greatest losses, and I habitually ask myself to ponder the possibility that something difficult has happened in the past, or may be happening in their lives now, that might explain their behavior. I choose to imagine it has, just to allow me to stay in a place of **Kindness**, **Forgiveness** and **Grace**.

When I ask if they are hurting or having a bad day, I am often greeted by a sorrowful face, realizing that the emotions they have been trying to hide are surfacing. Their guard tends to be lowered when they feel that people care, and often become willing to share what's causing them **Despair**.

It is CRITICAL that if you ask, it is based on genuine concern, not **Sarcasm**. To ask if they are having a bad day with a sarcastic tone would be hurtful. That would be you spreading **NES (Not Enough Syndrome)** to others. Asking without **Judgment** provides a release valve for people in **Pain** to share instead of "stuff" their emotions. This is a great reminder to always

---

"Seek to Understand more than to be Understood."
—Stephen Covey

Understanding why people act the way they do is essential information if we want to grow as individuals. When we put ourselves in a place of **Empathy** regarding those who are experiencing **Pain**, we can see our way around the angry exterior. We can look at the hurting child inside, who is being held hostage by the **Bully,** who is hanging out in their **Headspace.**

Think of a movie where you felt angry at the **bully**. You wanted him to get caught and you wanted him to pay! Then, as the backstory unfolds, you find out that his mother was dying of cancer, his father refuses to pay for her medication and the kid works every night until dawn to make enough money to help her. You also find out his dad beats him for not excelling on the football field and when the coach sees the beating, he just turns and looks the other way because he doesn't want to get involved in family situations. When we can see beyond the situation and look in to the circumstances, we are able to engage **Empathy**.

Please, don't misunderstand me and hold on to this phrase, you will need to remind yourself often. **Don't Accept Unacceptable Behavior.** I am simply reminding everyone that we have all made bad decisions, been grouchy, or disrespectful to others, and done things we aren't proud of. When we are faced with their circumstances and can identify with the physical and/or emotional challenges that have occurred, it could change our **Perspective** about the perpetrator. It doesn't change what they have done, but we can see who they are as people and use **Empathy** to let go of the negative feelings.

Granted, it is much harder if we were personally subjected to the bullying. But, if we are able to look at the situation with emotional distance, it is easier to find and engage **Empathy** towards the person as a whole.

It may surprise you to know I have been bullied for standing up for others. I've had my heart broken, I've been hurt, and I have cried because of what others have said or done to me. I've also wanted those that hurt me, to hurt, too. That is why I know how it feels and recognize the cancerous effects of holding onto **Anger** or **Resentment**.

I never became a **bully** myself, but I could have. I chose to use my energy to become the protector of those who were being bullied. I recognized it was easier to stand up for someone else than it was for myself. When you choose to do that for someone else, you know there will be at least one other person standing with you. When you stand up for yourself, you can often find yourself completely alone. Bravely facing trials when you are alone is one of the hardest things to conquer. **Believing** in yourself, when it seems the entire world has left you to fend for yourself, creates a **Lonely** space. A place many people would do almost anything to avoid... even if that means bullying someone else.

I put my energies into helping instead of hurting, but it could have easily gone the other way. That is why I understand and believe that if we view things through the eyes of **Empathy**, it may provide what we need to allow **Grace** and **Mercy** to prevent us from being part of the **Bully Birthing** process in others.

If we concentrate on seeking to understand, we will find **Compassion** to be a much better companion. We can help others heal by teaching them to **#EvictTheBully** as well. Seemingly happy individuals, that become **bullies** are often a case of **Multi-Generational Bully Births**.

Multi-Generational Bully Birth

That is a mouthful! What does it even mean?

In this day and age of fast paced, do more, and pay attention less, "microwave generation" of relationships, people and their feelings are getting lost in the shuffle.

In an earlier chapter, we talked about a **#BullyBirth** and how it happens. It does not happen at the moment someone hears the negative words or actions thrown at them, but at the moment they *Believe* that it is true, or mistakenly think that they deserve it. (We will discuss the "When you *Believe*, you will *Receive*" concept in a later chapter.) Recognizing this fact, it stands to reason that the **Bully in Your Head** would, at some point, in a less mature state, encourage you to say something mean or unkind to someone else. This starts the conception of someone else's **Bully**, and so on and so on.

Here's an example:

Let's say you have an Uncle named Bob who says unkind things to you.
Uncle Bob has a **Bully** in his head, we are going to call this **Bully**, *Bubba*. Through Uncle Bob, *Bubba* continues to infect you with **NES** by falsely reminding you that you are **Not Enough.** One day, you are feeling very vulnerable and this is the day you finally *Believe* that you are **Not Enough**. This is the unfortunate day when you give birth to your **Bully,** *Bertha*. You are young and not strong enough to stand up to *Bertha*. Thus, she pushes you to the edge all the time. You are frustrated and overwhelmed while your little sister hounds you to play with her. At the same time, *Bertha* keeps pushing you until you yell at your sister. You tell her she is "too annoying to play with" and "no one likes her because she is such a whiner!" This is not the first time she has heard these things, but today is the day she actually *Believes* it is true and accepts that she is **Not Enough**. That's how *Boonette* the **Bully** is born in your little sister.

Now you know how the **Multi-Generational Bully Birthing** process works and can see that it is often unintentional. No matter how old someone is, if they don't have the emotional maturity to withstand the **Bully** residing in their coveted **Headspace,** they will be a likely **NES Carrier**. That is why it is imperative for you to learn the **Eviction Process** to protect yourself and help inoculate your friends and family members from the harmful effects

The Gift of Being "Got"

I often talk about what I think of as the ultimate gift. I call it the ***Gift of Being "Got."*** When someone *"Gets"* you, when they truly understand who you are and what you stand for, that is a very precious gift. It can create an instant **Friendship** and form deep connections.

For someone to truly *"Get"* you, they must first understand themselves. It takes time to figure out who you really are. It takes even more time for the true you to show up front and center in your personality—no hiding, no barricades, no façade—just you, being yourself, for others to see. It is a scary and vulnerable place, but once you are strong enough to go there, the world changes. When the "real you" chooses to ***Step Up & Stand Out*** for other people to see, be prepared for those people who are hurting, to try to hurt you. People in **Pain** distract themselves by dragging others down.

Keep this little tidbit of information in mind. There are people in the world who *"**think**"* they *"Get"* you. They are convinced they do. They think their vision is clear and unobscured. The painful **Truth** is, if they are still hiding behind a façade of **FEAR**, **Insecurity**, or **Resentment**, they CAN'T *"Get"* you.

It's like people who don't love themselves trying to love others. They don't really know how. Pouring everything they have to offer out to someone else will make a person that doesn't yet love themselves feel resentful. Their unconscious motive is to fill their own **Void**. The problem is the **Void** can only be filled with them understanding, accepting and loving themselves the way they are.

Their intentions are often good, but their **Filter** is cloudy, dirty, or marred by their own struggles. It doesn't make them bad or wrong, nor does it suggest that they have ill intentions. But, it is not wise to trust that those who are still in the **Chrysalis of Change**, can accurately see and appreciate who you are. (We discuss more about the **Chrysalis** in *#Christianpreneur*)

They may come from a place of support, but they are not ready to be brought into the **Intimacy Bubble** where you allow people who truly *"Get"* you to enter. I am getting ahead of myself, but in the next chapter we are going to talk about **Intimacy Bubbles** and the danger of a **Bubble Jump**.

Chapter 6
Intimacy Bubbles

---

*"The problem is, when we stop caring what people think
and stop feeling hurt by cruelty, we lose our ability to connect.
But, when we are defined by what people think,
we lose the courage to be vulnerable.
Therefore, we need to be selective
about the feedback we let into our lives."*
—*Brené Brown*

The answer to the dilemma that Brené proposed in the quote above is all wrapped up in this chapter about **Intimacy Bubbles** and your new best friend—**BOBO**.

Have you ever seen the movie with John Travolta called *Boy in the Plastic Bubble*? It is the story of a boy with a rare condition that didn't allow his body to fight off infection, so the family was forced to put him in a plastic bubble to keep him safe from germs.

Intimacy Bubbles are our transparent layers of emotional protection. They keep unwanted negative influences outside of our lives and keep relationships in check. They also keep the most vulnerable parts of ourselves safe. Think of a long set of semi-oval perimeters stretching out from the base, getting longer and wider allowing them to hold larger groups of people the farther they extend.

To help you picture it, imagine a football field. You are located at one end of the field under the goal post. Around you, you have a small semi-oval plastic

Bubble protecting you from the elements outside. It is warm, comfortable, safe, and cozy. It is also clear, so you can see everything that is happening without obstruction. That is your **Personal Bubble**.

Then imagine another clear, semi-oval plastic **Bubble** that is larger and extends in a wider arc around that the first one. That is your **Intimate Bubble**. The pattern repeats, and the next arc is wider and longer than the first two which forms your **Family Bubble**. Additional **Bubbles** continue growing in size and arc until all eight are complete just shy of the end zone on the other side of the field. These **Bubbles** house all the people we meet and the relationships we develop.

The end zone and the surrounding area outside of the chalked off football field represent the **Stranger Zone**. This is an open area that that holds all the people we haven't met yet. The end zone on the opposite side of the field houses the **Restricted Zone** which is guarded by some very impressive protectors.

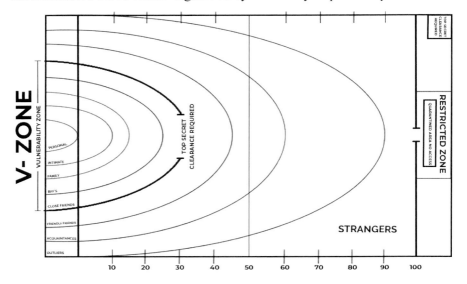

Now that you have a visual on what it looks like, let me explain what it is.

The **Bubbles** are layers of protection against your vulnerability. The outer layers of your **Intimacy Bubbles** are thicker and more durable. The inner layers are still strong, but thinner and provide less protection. The closer we allow people to come to our **V-Zone**, the more susceptible we are to what they have to say and what they think about us.

Vulnerability and the V-Zone

Vulnerability - /ˈvəln(ə)rəb(ə)lədē/-
The state of being vulnerable or susceptible to injury or attack.

Being vulnerable means we expose ourselves to people or situations that can cause us emotional **Pain**. The **V-Zone**, or **Vulnerability Zone**, includes the first five **Intimacy Bubbles** and is the place where we have the biggest threat of being hurt. Consider your **V-Zone** to be a Top-Secret space and only the long term, vetted team members earn access to this area which holds your most valued secrets. (Just imagine NASA allowing someone access to the nuclear launch facility!) That is why we have **BOBO** to help keep you safe.

Meet BOBO

BOBO is the guardian of your **Bubbles** and he is going to be your best friend, if you let him. His job is to make sure each person that comes into your life follows proper procedure and enters your **Bubbles One By One** (thus the name **BOBO**). These sacred spaces can't be taken for granted, and you must insist that those who are allowed entry will treat you with **Respect**. **BOBO**'s job is to guard and protect your **Bubbles**. The only person that can override **BOBO**'s protocol is **you**. So, do yourself a favor and let **BOBO** do his job to protect you so you don't get hurt.

Now that you've met **BOBO**, let's talk about your **Bubbles** and what they are providing so you will understand why we experience, and sometimes create, situations that cause us emotional **Pain**, **Anxiety**, and **Discouragement**.

IMPORTANT NOTE! Before we enter the **Intimacy Bubbles (IBs)**, we must first remember this:

The Intimacy Bubbles don't represent Love
or how much you care for someone,
they represent the level of access
you allow to your emotional vulnerability.

It is important for you to remember that, because it can be confusing to recognize that some family members must be removed from the **Family**

Bubble, the **V-Zone**, or even escorted to the **Restricted Zone** in order to keep you emotionally safe. Not every family member can be trusted equally, so access is earned based on the actions of the participants. If that doesn't make sense to you, I think it will become clearer as you read the next several chapters.

Now, let's enter the **Intimacy Bubbles** so we can understand how they work, why we get hurt, and how to prevent that from happening in the future.

Intimacy Bubble Breakdown

Since **Intimacy Bubbles (IB's)** describe the level of vulnerability you've granted access to, it is easy to understand that allowing someone you just met **BFF** access doesn't mean you want them to be your new best friend. It just means that you overrode **BOBO**'s protocol and ushered them in to your **V-Zone** (Note: This is NOT a good move!) **#TrustBOBO**

<u>PERSONAL Bubble</u> – This is the smallest **Bubble**. This one is just for you, and if you are a Believer, God. It is really a cozy space and is a place of refuge.

<u>INTIMATE Bubble</u> – This is a very private place reserved for you and those you are intimately involved with. Intimacy doesn't have to mean physical contact, it can be any kind of relationship where you feel emotionally attracted to the other person and share deeply intimate details of your life. This is an extremely vulnerable place. Anyone you allow in this space must be worthy of your **Trust**. The people allowed entry in here should be those who have shown strength in virtue and character. You have limited defenses here, so be extremely careful about who enters this sacred space.

<u>FAMILY Bubble</u> –This **Bubble** is reserved for family, or friends you have known so long they are considered family. All immediate family members start here. Then, their behavior will dictate appropriate future **Bubble** placement. NO ONE is GUARANTEED a spot in this **Bubble**. They remain as long as they show they have your best interests at heart. Our children start out here. Once they have grown, if they become abusive, manipulative or disrespectful, their access will be denied. Just a reminder, the **Bubbles** don't represent how much you **Love** them, it is your protection against people who overstep their boundaries. Family will always be family, but they don't all deserve access to your vulnerability.

<u>BFF Bubble</u> – This space is for your true **BFF**(s). The one or ones who are truly devoted to you and your relationship. They know you, you know them, and there is a bond that is deep and meaningful. You **Trust** these people to know everything about you without sharing your secrets. This bond is almost

as strong as the **Intimate Bubble,** but it is not a romantic kind of **Love**. It is a deeply respected and admired relationship that should be cared for and nurtured.

CLOSE FRIENDS Bubble – This section is for the people who know you, care for you and you enjoy spending time with. You invite them to parties and events and share parts of your life with them. You call on them when you need something with the understanding that they can do the same. It is a mutually beneficial relationship. You tend to share sensitive information about relationships, situations, and concerns with this small circle, and you are careful about who you allow into it.

FRIENDLY FRIENDS Bubble – This area houses a larger circle you call friends. These are people you know better than an acquaintance, but you may not hang out with them often. You have no trouble picking up the phone to call and know that it is likely they will make time to chat. You may hang out on occasion, but there is no expectation of commitment or closeness.

ACQUAINTANCES Bubble –This holds a much larger group of people. These are people you have met at events or been introduced to by other friends. You would feel comfortable saying "I know them." You might feel comfortable picking up the phone to call, yet you may need to remind them where you met.

OUTLIERS Bubble –This is a place for the people you "know **of**" and they may, or may not, "know **of**" you (like **Livestreamers,** actors, or radio personalities for instance). You may have seen each other on a broadcast, a speaking circuit, heard of each other, and/or are familiar with each other's work, but have never actually been introduced. There is familiarity, but you could only comfortably say, "I know **who** that is." not that "I know them."

STRANGER ZONE – This area surrounds all the **Intimacy Bubbles** and represents all the people you don't know and have no relation to. They are not in any **Bubble,** they are on the outside looking in.

RESTRICTED ZONE – This zone is **Quarantined**. These people have shown themselves to be unreliable or untrustworthy and have been banned to the **Restricted Zone**. When people have been escorted here, they need to show their intentions are for your benefit before they can **Apply for Re-entry**.

Intruder Alert!

Now that you understand what healthy **Bubbles** look like, you need to understand that you have an intruder that causes problems and prevents you from **Bubble Bliss**. Let's revisit something important.

Your **Personal Bubble** includes your inner thoughts about who you are and what you *Believe* about yourself. The problem is that the **Bully** lives in your head, which means, he occupies this space with you relentlessly hounding you day in and day out. Your **Personal Bubble** should be your "Safe Place," but since the **Bully** has taken up residence there, it has become a space where **Abuse** can visit, and **FEAR** has been invited to stay.

You may not want to hear this part… so **Pull Up Your Bootstraps #PUYB.** Often, the **Bully** residing in your head drives you to find companionship to distract you from the negativity he constantly bombards you with. His reminders may get so loud that you run outside to find someone and drag them back into the **Intimate Bubble** in a desperate attempt to drown him out. We do this so that we can feel close and connected to someone. It is a hollow attempt at quelling his judgmental voice. The truth is it only amplifies the sound.

The repetitive nature of this experience often germinates an entirely new **Bully in Your Head**. One that tells you that you are worthless and that no one would want to be in an intimate relationship with you, which the **Bully** tries to make you *Believe* is the reason people keep leaving you. In reality, your **Bubble Jumping** is what is causing the trouble. Now, it's time to look at how to navigate your **Bubbles** and how to properly identify the occupants of each one. Your first safety lesson is to get comfortable with the **Bubble Bump**. It's time to talk **Bubble Ology**.

Chapter 7
Bubble Ology

"Guilt can prevent us from setting the boundaries
that would be in our best interests,
and in other people's best interests."
—Melody Beattie

In case you don't know, **Ology** basically means the study of... so this chapter is about understanding your **Intimacy Bubbles**, thus, **Bubble Ology**—the study of **Intimacy Bubbles**. (Yes, that is a **Fitchism!**) I need to give you a quick lesson on **Bubble Talk** before we dive into how it affects you, so get ready to learn the **Bubble Bump!**

Bubble – A transparent, but very secure place where we categorize our relationships. Each **Bubble** is a protective layer to our vulnerability and they are meant to be moved through one at a time. Think of it as an evaluation checkpoint. **BOBO** will check their credentials before allowing entry into the next, more intimate **Bubble**.

Bubble Bouncer – A **Bubble Bouncer** is someone who tries to freely move through your **Bubbles**. They may share their intimate secrets with you one day, and act like they barely know you the next. These people cause emotional **Confusion** because they are typically confused about their own feelings, which causes them to do the **Push-Pull**. They **Pull** you into a **Bubble** and then **Push** you away. Although not typically bad people, they are often a bit unstable and rarely know how to provide any depth to a relationship. They will likely hurt you regardless of whether that is their intention or not. Do yourself a favor and **Bubble Bump** the **Bouncer** before they **Bounce** through your **Bubbles** like a pinball wreaking havoc wherever they go. (That is your tongue twister test!)

Bubble Boundaries – These refer to the expectations of what you will and will not accept in each of your **Bubbles**. When your **Bubble Boundaries** are violated, a **Bubble Bump** MUST occur.

Bubble Bump – This is a backward movement that sends people who haven't used good judgment to a less vulnerable **Bubble**. (Think of this as the "Hip Check") You just swing your hips and "**Bump**" them to their new location. Your resistance to performing this **Bump** can cause long term negative effects. **#GetYourBumpOn** (If you want to see my virtual **Bubble Bump**, go to (**www.VickiFitch.com/ETB**)

> **Example:** A person in your **Close Friend Bubble** shares confidential information with other people in your social circle. This is not the first time this has happened and has become a pattern. You need to immediately **Bubble Bump** them outside the **V-Zone**. You may still associate with them, but you will no longer be sharing personal information.

> **Note:** You do NOT need to notify anyone when you perform a **Bubble Bump**. They are your **Bubbles** and you can set the **Boundaries**.

Bubble Hop – This refers to a simultaneous forward movement of two **Bubbles** at a time where you allow someone to "Hop" over a **Bubble** instead of allowing **BOBO** to do his job. This is cautioned against because it can often expose you to unnecessary heartache.

> **Example:** When you meet someone at a party, you are in the **Acquaintances Bubble**. The next natural progression is the **Friendly Friends Bubble**. If you have a lot in common, you may find yourself sharing personal information usually found in the **V-Zone**. If this person doesn't share your **Bubble Values,** they may divulge your private information to others. This can cause you unnecessary emotional exposure and **Pain**. **#NoBubbleHoppers**

Bubble Interloper – This is someone who has been invited into a place that was promised to someone else. If you are married, or in a committed relationship, and you have allowed another person inside your **Intimacy Bubble**, you have a **Bubble Interloper**. They don't belong there. It doesn't matter if you have been physically intimate with them or not, if you are emotionally intimate with them, you have created an easy access panel for the **Bullies** to come and go as they please. We must repair this breach before the Eviction occurs or they will be able to come back in any time.

Bubble Invader – This describes someone who is insistent on entering a **Bubble** they were not invited into. They sometimes aggressively attempt it by pressuring you and putting a strain on the elasticity of the **Bubble** itself. They may also use **Guilt** as an escort, if you are susceptible to her charms. These people are often innocent and just a bit needy. They desperately want to connect with someone and if they keep pressuring you, they need a **Bubble Bump**, or even possibly an escort, all the way to the **Restricted Zone** until they learn to behave.

> **NOTE:** In the case of the **Bubble Invader**, you need to take a hard look at yourself and identify if your words or actions are encouraging this behavior. Are you continually allowing **Guilt** or **Pity** to convince you to invite them back into places they don't belong? If so, you need to adjust that behavior immediately. You are responsible for doing any necessary **Bubble Bumps**, to stabilize your own **Bubble Balance**.

Bubble Jacker – The **Bubble Jacker** is vivacious. They often come into your life with a splash and before you know it, they are inside, but you are not sure how they got there. It is all a blur. **Charisma** and **Charm** escorted them in and you need to be VERY CAREFUL because they have the ability to confuse your **Bubble Values**. This happens when relationships move too fast and you forget to use **BOBO** as your guide. You are most susceptible to the **Bubble Jacker** when you have a **Bubble Void** you are trying to fill. When your **Bubble** gets **Jacked**, you need to do an immediate **Bubble Bump** to clear your head before you forget to protect yourself.

> **Example:** You are introduced to someone by a mutual friend and you enjoy a conversation. The next day, your favorite dessert shows up at work with a note from your new friend. You feel valued and heard. You then get a call about concert tickets they have to your favorite band and of course, you are going! The cycle continues. You realize your time blocks are full. This person you barely know is sharing things about their life and you find yourself reciprocating. However, you also recognize that you have no experience with this person. Although you were caught up in the fun, you should NOT be giving out **BFF** level access to a person you just met no matter how much fun you are having. Step back, do a **Bubble**

Bump, and emotionally ground yourself. It doesn't mean you can't have fun or spend time with them, but, they must earn access to the **V-Zone** via **BOBO**, one **Bubble** at a time.

The **Bubble Jacker** often shows up in physical attraction, too. If you have a **Bubble Void**, you want to fill you could end up inviting them into your **Intimate Bubble** even when they don't deserve access there. Beware the **Bubble Jacker**, their intentions may or may not be honorable, but they tend to swoop in and swoop out when it serves them which could leave you feeling broken hearted.

<u>**Bubble Jump**</u> – This is a simultaneous forward movement of MORE than two **Bubbles** at a time. Where the **Bubble Hop**, "Hops" over one **Bubble**, the **Jump** can be a record setting long jump, especially if you are **Lonely**. This is a DANGEROUS way to fill a **Void** and often results in an emotional disaster.

> **Example:** Take the same scenario as the **Bubble Hop**. This time, you immediately start sharing intimate details of your life, the areas of deep **Pain**, or your emotional **Triggers**. Doing so would catapult this **Acquaintance** far into your **V-Zone** And if your **Bubble Values** are different, you are leaving yourself exposed. People must EARN access by showing us they are safe and trustworthy over extended periods of time. **#ProtectYourself #NoBubbleJumpers**

<u>**Bubble Predator**</u> – The name says enough. We won't be talking about them much, but know they are there. This is a person who does not have honorable intentions.

<u>**Bubble Stalker**</u> – A **Bubble Stalker** is usually someone who's had a long-term **Bubble Void** they want to fill. They believe their level of commitment to the person or the relationship warrants access to the **V-Zone** and they are determined to prove it. **Bubble Stalkers** are typically innocent. However, you need to be careful of the persistent ones that keep trying to sneak in after they have been **Bubble Bumped** and are not accepting the change.

Understanding the Bubble Stalker:

If you are clearly outlining the parameters of the relationship and the **Bubble Stalker** is not honoring your **Boundaries**, don't be afraid to **Quarantine** them in the **Restricted Zone**. This may be temporary, or permanent. You don't have to make that decision right away. You just

need to remember to stick with your best buddy **BOBO**, and let them earn their way through consistent, respectable behavior. Your priority needs to be to protect your **Bubbles**. If you don't, you are allowing the **Bully in Your Head** to access ammunition that can make you feel defeated time and time again. Think of **BOBO** as your personal emotional security guard.

> **NOTE:** Although we are making light of it here with our fun analogies, **Bubble Stalkers** can have an unhealthy attraction or relationship with you. Walking people through the **Bubbles** one by one will certainly create some preventative measures to avoid having an uncomfortable situation on your hands. #BOBOKnowsBest

Bubble Trust – **Bubble Trust** is what you feel toward everyone you let into your **V-Zone**. You expect them to **Honor** the parameters and sanctity of that **Bubble**. When someone violates the basic premise of your **Bubble Values**, they get **Bubble Bumped** and lose access.

Bubble Values – These are the activities that you allow in each **Bubble**. Your **Bubble Boundaries** are your expectations, but your **Values** are what you are committed to.

> **Example:** If someone you meet allows intimate physical contact in the **Acquaintances Bubble**, and you reserve that type of contact for your **Intimate Bubble**, you have conflicting **Bubble Values**. It can be an emotionally difficult situation when you invite someone in to your **Intimate Bubble** and realize they have you at an emotional distance, outside their **V-Zone**. This can create a **Void** for you if you were looking for an emotional connection. It doesn't make them wrong; you just have different **Bubble Values**. This is why you need to remember that **BOBO** won't lead you astray.

Bubble Void – A **Bubble Void** is twofold.

> **Bubble Void 1** – A Bubble that:
> a. Is empty and has no other participants.
> b. Has occupants but the owner feels that **Bubble** needs additional participants. The feeling of "lack" in this area causes a **Void** and a longing to find someone to fill it.

> **Bubble Void 2** – When someone has a desire to be included in someone else's **V-Zone Bubbles**. Not being included creates a feeling of emptiness or loss, thus creating a **Void** to be filled. This is often where **Bubble Invaders** and even **Bubble Stalkers** start.

Vulnerability Zone (V-Zone) – These are the first five **Bubbles** (from **Personal** to **Close Friends**) where we are more susceptible and sensitive to what others think, say, or do.

Bubble Balance

So now that you are getting into the groove of my **Fitchism** lingo, it is time for us to actually look at your **Bubbles** and do a quick analysis.

Fill in the chart with names of people currently residing in your **V-Zone Bubbles** in the spaces provided. (You can download additional copies at **www.VickiFitch.com/ETB)**

If there is no one in that **Bubble**, put a zero with a line through it to signify that it is empty.

    1.) Fill in the **Bubble Balance Chart** – who resides in these **Bubbles**
        a. The **Personal Bubble**
        b. The **Intimate Bubble**
        c. The **Family Bubble**
        d. The **BFF Bubble**
        e. The **Close Friends Bubble**
    2.) Should any of those people receive a **Bubble Bump**?
        a. What **Bubble** or **Zone** do they need to be moved to?
    3.) Do you have a **Bubble Void**? (Are any of the **V-Zones** empty?)

Now that you have been indoctrinated into **Bubble Ology**, it is time to really understand the different types of people that may be inside your **Bubbles**, and to see if you are carrying any of those traits yourself. Remember… **Truth** is the only way to **Neutralize**, so it's time to "Burst your Bubble."

Bubble Balance Chart

Insert names of people in each Bubble

Bubbles and Occupants	Needs Bubble Bump	Where should they be Bumped?	Are YOU?
1. Personal Bubble (Include Bullies)			
2. Intimate Bubble			
3. Close Family Bubble			
4. BFF Bubble			
5. Close Friends Bubble			
Do you have a Bubble Void?			
Bubble Invaders			
Bubble Jackers			
Bubble Stalkers			
Bubble Interloper			

Chapter 8
Burst Your Bubble

"Being a nice person is about courtesy:
you're friendly, polite, agreeable, and accommodating.
When people believe they have to be nice in order to give, they fail to
set boundaries, rarely say no, and become pushovers,
letting others walk all over them."
—Adam Grant

I was never a fan of when someone said, "I don't want to "Burst your Bubble" but…" That is exactly what I am about to do. **#PUYB** because you may not like this next part.

In this case, I DO want to "Burst your Bubble" if you are hanging out in one of the **Danger Zones**, so let's talk about these people specifically. We will also be taking a look at ourselves to see if we are culprits of the same behavior.

We are going to fill in more of your **Bubble Balance Chart** in each section, so be prepared to have it handy under the **Questions to Ponder**.

Remember, this is all to help you become the best version of yourself. I am here to support you, and not let the **Bully** get another foothold when he shows up to discourage you. Remember **"Not today, Bully. Not today."** Take on your **Super Stance** and keep on reading. This is where the rubber meets the road.

Welcome to the Danger Zones

We need to dive a little deeper into some of these **Bubble** personas to provide the best support possible. That doesn't require you to make any changes right now, but you need to be honest with yourself. No one else will know if you aren't, but it will hinder your growth and provide the **Bully in Your Head** additional ammunition to use against you.

Bubble Bouncers

In the last chapter, we discussed these people who are stuck in the **Push-Pull** pattern. Since you now recognize their behavior and know that they aren't healthy for you to be around, it is important that we figure out who they are and work on putting them in the appropriate **Bubbles**.

The **Bubble Bouncer** is typically full of energy. A bit like Tigger bouncing from place to place and person to person, but inside, the **Bubble Bouncer** is **Lonely**. Their history of relationships is unfulfilling, and they find it difficult to connect with people on a deeply meaningful level. They desire relationships but have probably not been very successful at them, so the muscle that has been exercised is one of moving on, not communicating and creating depth in a relationship.

Don't be fooled. A **Bubble Bouncer** may have been married for a long time, that doesn't mean they have a deep and meaningful relationship with their spouse. They are desperately looking to find something to fill their **Void** and have plenty of excuses outside of themselves for why that hasn't happened.

Bubble Bouncers tend to leave us feeling that we did something wrong. We feel that we somehow were **Not Good Enough** for them to stick around. In reality, they are typically afraid others will leave, and it is less painful for them to just move on first. That is no reflection of you and soon you will learn how to become comfortable with who you are and how to really find your **Tribe**. We just need to #EvictTheBully first.

Questions to Ponder: (Fill in your chart)

- Who are the **Bubble Bouncers** in your life?
- Are they actually bringing value to you?
- Do they need to be **Bubble Bumped** or escorted to the **Restricted Zone**?

Are you a Bubble Bouncer?

- Do you do the **Push-Pull** in someone else's **Bubbles**?
- Do you Hop into one **Bubble** and then withdraw your time, attention, or support without notice?
- Do you then show back up again to reclaim the **Bubble** you were previously in?
- Upon re-entry, do you make excuses for why you pulled away?

It might be hard for you to admit that you may be a **Bubble Bouncer.** You may not have even realized you do the **Push-Pull** until reading this book. If this is you, let me help you understand why.

Bubble Bouncers are usually insecure about who they are and what they bring to the relationship. They have been hurt before by others and are afraid to get hurt again. So, they open up and then they **Pull** back when they can't handle the emotions or the **FEAR** of the relationship. It is easier to **Bubble Bounce** where they can't get hurt, than it is to be seen for who they are and leave themselves exposed. They forgot to use **BOBO**, so their **Hot Spots** are raw, and their **V-Zone** looks like **Bubbles** that were shredded by shrapnel and were sewed, taped or glued back together.

If that is you, then forgive yourself. Recognize the **Bully in Your Head** is the one that is influencing your **Bubble Bouncing**. Then, commit yourself to finishing this book and following the **Eviction Process**. It will help you free yourself of this empty way of developing relationships.

Bubble Invaders

The **Bubble Invader** worms their way into a **Bubble** that you really don't want them in or aggressively pursues access to a different **Bubble** than the one you invited them into.

Some of these people are very well meaning. Their intention is to show you that they meet the criteria for the **Bubble** they are trying to gain access to. They tend to be very persistent and wear down our resistance. It is kind of like the neighbor that keeps knocking on the door late at night, until you feel so guilty or uncomfortable that you finally open it and somehow invite them in. I want you to know that **Guilt** is one of the **Bullies** that resides in your **Headspace**. Recognizing that is important for the **Eviction** and **Bubble Bumping** process.

If you are uncomfortable about someone being in a specific **Bubble**, you need to remove them. They are YOUR **Bubbles**; the only one who needs to feel comfortable about who is allowed access to each one is YOU.

IMPORTANT NOTE: This is something we need to teach our children as well. They need to be able to **Bubble Bump** friends and relatives they are NOT comfortable with. You will recognize the importance of this when you get to **Uncle Ichabod**.

Removing someone from a **Bubble** via the **Bubble Bump** is really a painless and non-confrontational process. There is usually no need to announce that a **Bubble Bump** has occurred. You just need to change the access allowed.

Questions to Ponder (Fill in your chart)
1) Who are the **Bubble Invaders** in your life?
2) Are they actually bringing value to you?
3) Do they need to be **Bubble Bumped** or escorted to the **Restricted Zone**?

Are you a Bubble Invader?

Are you trying to wiggle your way into someone else's **Bubbles** without the proper invitation?

Take a good look at yourself to see if the **Bully in Your Head** has caused you to become a **Bubble Invader**. The more insecure we are, the more assertive we might become in our quest to restore **Bubble Balance** and fill a **Bubble Void**.

If you realize you are a **Bubble Invader**, take the initial step to **Bubble Bump** yourself and watch the other person for clues on when the relationship should be moving forward. Remind yourself that you "*Don't know what you don't know, until you know it.*" Now, you have the ability to recognize areas where you might be stepping over the line so, you can adjust course before it becomes more emotionally challenging.

When you are done with the **Eviction Process**, things will be a lot clearer, so relax and remember, you are learning. Stay determined to make a change.

Bubble Stalkers

Bubble Stalkers are usually **Bubble Invaders** that have progressed to the next level. When the **Bubble Void** has been there for a long time, they fall out of **Bubble Balance**. Thus, they feel a very strong desire to fill the need for connection. **Bubble Stalkers** are so eager to feel validated that they can become overly assertive. They can even become quite obnoxious. They tend to get jealous of other relationships you have and may want to make sure EVERYONE knows they are your friend, or that they know details about your life. To them, this is just proof that they deserve a closer position to you. However, this just reminds you that they have lost **Perspective** of the connection and it has become more about filling their need than it is about the relationship with you.

Questions to Ponder (Fill in your chart)

1) Who are the **Bubble Stalkers** in your life?
2) Are they actually bringing value to you?
3) Do they need to be **Bubble Bumped** or escorted to the **Restricted Zone**?

Are you a Bubble Stalker?

Are you trying to fill a **Bubble Void** and insisting your commitment level warrants greater access than what you've been granted?

I am not suggesting that everyone who is trying to connect has **Stalker** tendencies. We do, however, lose our way sometimes, especially with romantic relationships. If you are convinced you found "the one" and then realize that the commitment levels are different, it can cause a difficult adjustment period. You might want to prove to them that you can be less needy or that you won't get jealous. Your efforts to prove this may traverse into the **Bubble Stalker** zone.

Don't be embarrassed. Just recognize this is what you have been doing and **Bubble Bump** yourself out of the situation. **Dignity** and **Respect** are waiting to be reclaimed. You are better than this. Once we #**EvictTheBully** that infected you with **NES**, you will heal, and your **Bubble Balance** will be restored.

Bubble Jackers

There are several different types of **Bubble Jackers** and they can be slick. Let's talk about them and put them on your radar. Remember, you can substitute the masculine for the feminine where it suits you. The important thing is you need to understand the situations.

Rico Suave – You probably heard this term before. This is the person who comes into your life and romantically sweeps you off your feet. He comes in hard and fast and you don't know what hit you. He will compliment you, adore you, and make you feel special... all in an effort to **Bubble Jump** his way into your **Intimate Bubble**, and he is willing to put on a full court press to get there.

I'm not making excuses for Rico, but he has a **Bully** in his head, too. This **Bully** tells him that he will be "successful" when he conquers that which he does not have. If you follow **BOBO**, Rico will probably get bored before he makes his way through seven layers of protection. You need to prepare yourself for this. Your **Bully** will try to tell you that you are **Not Good Enough**, but that is a LIE. You are **Good Enough** to VALUE yourself enough, to allow the time you need to connect with people and verify their intentions are honorable. It will save you a lot of **Pain** and heartache if Rico stays where he belongs and doesn't sweet talk his way to your **V-Zone**.

Charismatic Cathy – On the outside, Cathy looks like she is a bundle of **Confidence**. She is exciting to be around and everyone around her gets caught up in her personality. She loves to be the center of attention and needs to know people admire her. She can come on strong with gifts and trips and parties and places. She knows a lot of people and she is a lot of fun to be around.

On the inside, Cathy is actually insecure. She covers it up by buying gifts and trying to connect with you in multiple ways. She feels valued when you are in awe of her talents, abilities, or the places she gets you into. She is the life of the party, but only because she doesn't want anyone to see **Behind the Curtain**. Inside her is the scared girl who is struggling to find people who really like her for who she is. Name dropping or reminding you of her skills and importance highlight her **Insecurity**. However, many see it as her success, so they are fooled.

Cathy will bring you into her crazy fun life for a while. Remember that she is a **Bubble Bouncer** at heart. She wants to know you will share your most intimate secrets, because that fills her **Bubble Void**, but she will only share with you the ones she can handle you knowing. The true emptiness she feels is buried deep inside her **Personal Bubble**, where her **Bullies** live.

Cathy NEEDS this book and she needs to #**EvictTheBully** in her head so she can become the person she always wanted to be. It has been so long since she thought that was possible that she may have given up. If you recognize Cathy in yourself, know that it is not only possible but inevitable if she reads this book and learns the **Eviction Process**.

Questions to Ponder (Fill in your chart)
1)   Who are the **Bubble Jackers** in your life?
2)   Are they actually bringing value to you?
3)   Do they need to be **Bubble Bumped** or escorted to the **Restricted Zone**?

Are you a Bubble Jacker?

Can you identify with Rico or Cathy? The scenarios may not be quite so obvious, but are you trying to earn favor with someone through your generosity or attention? Have you used this as a way to get the emotional connection you want without considering the needs of others?

I don't want you to be embarrassed or guilty, I want you to recognize it and start the **Eviction Process**. I understand that you have been hanging out with these **Bullies** for so long, you don't even know what your life would be like without them. Understand those **Bullies** are controlling you and it is time you asserted your power and your strength for something good— something that will serve you well now and in the future.

When you learn the **Eviction Process**, you will have the tools you need to reclaim the person you are and to grow into the person you want to become.

Before we talk about our next culprit, I want to prepare you for the complexity and sensitivity by helping you understand the **Danger Zones**.

High Risk Danger Zones

Bully Eviction is emotional work, so prepare yourself, forgive yourself and be prepared to forgive others.

If this next section hits a little too close to home, remember the ultimate goal is **Bully Eviction**, not **Bully Vacation**. It requires a bit of **Honesty** to ensure that you don't leave a side door for him to sneak back in once we have officially removed him from the premises.

Loneliness - In an upcoming chapter, we are going to address the **Bullies** by name. This way, you can identify who they are and call them out on their lies and the troubles they are causing. I wanted to introduce you to this **Bully** first, since she is relevant to our topic of conversation.

>**Loneliness - /ˈlōnlēnəs/**
>**Sadness because one has no friends or company.**

It is said that more than 70% of the population experiences **Loneliness** on a regular basis and since we now know about **Bubble Voids** and how powerful the desire is for people to fill them, we can hopefully recognize why **Loneliness** is a particularly difficult **Bully** to overcome. She haunts you with thoughts that you are incomplete and lacking. She seeks attention, which is where the **Tide of Temptation** drags us into the **Danger Zones**. If you accept the attention, she then engages her **Bully Buddies, Guilt** and **Overwhelm** to keep you immobilized.

If we don't **Evict** this **Bully**, we may fall prey to the sweet-talking words of the **Bubble Interloper.**

Bubble Interloper

Before we talk about the **Bubble Interloper**, please remember that my goal in writing this book is to help everyone **Evict** the debilitating **Bullies** that occupy their **Headspace**, so they can get back to becoming the best version of themselves.

Please let me remind you that I am not judging you. If you know someone else this has happened to, you have no right to judge them either. **Loneliness** is a hard **Bully** to resist. Read this chapter and reach out in **Empathy** to someone who has stumbled into this unfortunate trap.

If you are feeling upset, angry or frustrated right now, I understand. This is a **Hot Spot** and you feel vulnerable. I want you to feel understood, and at the same time I want to share some **Truth** with you, so we can **Neutralize** this vulnerability.

I know that some of you are saying things like,

- "You don't understand! My husband or wife emotionally abandoned me a long time ago. He/She doesn't care about me."
- "We have an open relationship, and this is what we do."
- "We are just friends, nothing is happening."
- "We are just talking online; there has been no true intimacy."

If you are really OK with those answers, this chapter of the book won't make you feel uncomfortable. Again, I am not judging your circumstances or your situation. You are free to continue living your life as you have in the past. If you are content with that life, my words on this page will not strike a nerve with you because you won't *Believe* them to be true, and what you don't *Believe*, you won't *Receive*.

If my words are bothering you, let's take a look **Behind the Curtain** and see if the **Bully in Your Head** has been trying to deceive you and keep you tethered to the **Misery** of feeling as if you are **Not Good Enough**. Or by accepting the sloppy seconds of being someone's back-up plan.

I know that hurt some of you too, and I'm sorry. I wouldn't be serving you well by pretending that isn't a **Bully** trying to **Control** you.

Loneliness is a very deceptive **Bully**. When this siren calls your name, she will be hard to ignore. She will remind you of what you are missing in a companion and friend and lure you with false promises of someone who will love you unconditionally and accept you for who you really are.

When **Loneliness** has her grip on us, we become prime targets for the **Bubble Jackers** of the world. They pop into our lives, dangling possibilities in front of us while we wrestle with the struggle in our current relationship. Then when you are worn down, she invites over some of her **Bully Buddies** like **Selfishness** and her pal **Pity**. They remind you that you deserve to be happy and try to convince you that you aren't really doing anything wrong. Your need to fill that **Bubble Void** becomes overwhelming with the help of this **Bully Brigade**! Their mission is to provide you with all the excuses you need to justify a **Bubble Breach**.

- "If she would have paid attention to me, this wouldn't have happened."
- "If he wouldn't work so much, I wouldn't have noticed that person."
- "If he/she hadn't done this, I wouldn't be doing it now."

No matter what, those are all excuses. I know that hurts to hear, but it is the **Truth**. You have a choice.

You have a choice to invite whomever you want into your **Bubbles**. They are your **Bubbles**. However, **Headspace Heroes** like Integrity, refuse to live in the same location as the **Bullies**, so they can't take up residence with **Selfishness**, **Pity** or **Adultery**.

Think about this for a minute. You may think you can handle the **Bubble Interloper** situation, but if **Integrity** is still close by, she will be a gentle reminder that you promised this space exclusively to someone else. If you have changed your mind about your mate, deal with that first. Then you can start a new relationship without the **Bully Baggage**.

Again, I am not judging. If you are uncomfortable with what I am writing here, then you have some unresolved issues. **Guilt** has probably joined the journey which means **Anger** and **Shame** are usually close by. The only way out of this is to **Evict the Bullies**. Once you have served the **Eviction** notice, you can remove the **Bubble Interloper** and bring all the **Headspace Heroes** back to get your bearings.

I know if you think you are in **Love**, this will sound excruciating, impossible, or infuriating, but if you want your life to change so you can grow, it is time to **Step Up** and take responsibility for yourself and your actions if you want to find true **Joy** and **Happiness**.

Questions to Ponder (Fill in your chart)

1) Who are the **Bubble Interlopers** in your life?
2) If you want to grow… they need to be escorted to the **Restricted Zone**. (No Detours)
3) Would you encourage someone you care about, like your children, siblings or best friend, to be in a relationship like the one you are in?

Are you a Bubble Interloper?

If you are hanging out in the **Intimate Bubble** of someone else who has promised that space to another, you are the **Interloper**. I know you could say to yourself, "It isn't my responsibility. I can't **Control** them." You are correct. You can't, but you have a choice on participating. As I've said before, I'm not judging. My goal is to help you **Evict the Bully** and these excuses about why it is OK are simply stumbling blocks to your growth.

- "They are getting a divorce."
- "He doesn't really love her."
- "We are soulmates."

Let **Integrity** guide you. When you insist on keeping that **Headspace Hero** around, she will help protect you from the **Bullies** that are waiting right around the corner to pounce.

> If they are getting divorced, let them get a divorce. Give that person time to heal before allowing them access to your **Bubbles**. I know you probably don't like this, but **Truth** is simple, not necessarily easy.

> If he doesn't really love her, let him break it off with her before taking the journey through your **Bubbles**.

> If you are soulmates, then you both want to keep **Integrity** in your **Headspace**. That way, you can keep yourselves on solid ground without the **FEAR** that if your relationship hits a snag, that you might be open to another **Interloper**.

We have one **Danger Zone** that we need to talk about but that no one wants to speak of. I understand the hesitancy in discussion, but we must in order to heal those who have been hurt and to help those who haven't met them, yet. We need to talk about the **Bubble Predator.**

Bubble Predator

To make this conversation easier, we are going to name our **Bubble Predator—Uncle Ichabod**.

> **Uncle Ichabod** represents any relative that wants to get intimately close to you or your children. You may have already had an experience with him that created one of your own original **Bully Births**, and if that has happened to you, I am so very sorry. I know this may be uncomfortable for you, but I am willing to bet that you wouldn't wish it on anyone else, so if we can expose it here, we may be able to keep others safe.

> We can't change the past, but we can change the future and teach those we care about to **Bubble Bump** ANYONE, including a relative, if they are uncomfortable for ANY REASON. **#ProtectYourBubbles**.

> We also need to teach our children to tell us if they want to **Bubble Bump** someone, so we can help them process information or feelings when necessary. They may not be able to express why they want to stay away from that person, but you need to listen. Better to have a child that others

think is rude or disrespectful because she won't love on grandpa than to find out later that a **Predator** took advantage of your child.

You may have guessed by now that my **Uncle Ichabod** was my step-grandfather, my maternal grandmother's second husband. We will talk about him in a later chapter, but for now I pray you are hearing me loud and clear. **TRUST YOURSELF** and **TRUST YOUR KIDS!** Teach them the **Bubble Bump** early and give them the **Confidence** to **Bump** ANYONE that doesn't feel right. It doesn't mean you don't associate with that person and it doesn't mean you accuse them. It means you **Respect** your intuition and keep your **Boundaries** clear.

If you have had an encounter with **Uncle Ichabod**, tell someone. If you are an adult, the **Bully** named **Shame** may be trying to stop you. We will get to her **Eviction** soon, but keep in mind that talking about it helps. If you are child, tell a trusted parent or adult. Here is also a hotline for people who need someone to talk to.

National Sexual Assault Hotline
800 656 HOPE (4673)

You are going to heal, and you are part of the next generation of people that are going to protect others from the **Uncle Ichabod's** of the world. I hope you will join the **#YouAreEnough** campaign where we continue to *Heal the Human Heart* of brokenness.

Are you Uncle Ichabod?

If you have been the **Uncle Ichabod** in someone else's life, and you admit it, then you know you need professional help. Any trusted resources I have will be posted to the website **www.VickiFitch.com/ETB**. We want you to get the help you need. to get the help you need, and we also encourage you to keep reading this book. You have **Bullies** that need **Evicting,** so you can start healing and making amends, too.

I know you may be feeling a bit sensitive about the last section. It is an emotional topic and if it happened to you, it can be overwhelming. Be sure to contact the resources you need and keep following the steps to help you get through. Remember **#YCDI (You Can Do It)** & **#YANA You Are Not Alone!**

Now that we have outlined the players vying for the attention of your **Intimacy Bubbles**, we are ready to understand **Hot Spots** & **Landmines**.

Chapter 9
Hot Spots & Landmines

D o you ever wonder why certain words or phrases bother you more than others? Have you ever been hurt by words that might seem perfectly innocent coming from most people, but when said by certain people, they hold so much power over you? They are in direct relation to the **Bubble** you have allowed them access to and how active your **Hot Spots** are. Remember, the **Bubbles** represent how vulnerable you are to what those people say or think. The closer they are to your **Personal Bubble**, the more power and influence their words have on you. Let's look a little closer…

Words are Powerful

In **DS 101** I shared with you the impact Jim Rohn had on me by sharing the true power of the words we use. They affect our subconscious as well as the other people around us. The key principle here is:

What you BELIEVE, you will RECEIVE

In other words, what you *Believe* to be true about yourself becomes your reality. That is why it is critically important that we keep our **Bubbles** protected.

Assigning Value to a Word or Phrase

If a word that is used to describe you has no negative value currently attached to it, you will not likely be offended. We have to know, or accept, the negative connotations of the word in order for it to make us feel vulnerable.

For example, if someone from the **Outliers Bubble** says,

"You are PURPLE."

Your mind would autonomicly go searching for the meaning of the word PURPLE. Since PURPLE is a color, it would unlikely have negative connotations attached to it, so you would probably dismiss the comment as irrelevant. Therefore, you did not *Receive* it, because you do not *Believe* it is true. Or, you don't identify it as something negative, so no **Hot Spot** has formed.

If someone from your **BFF Bubble** says,

"You are PURPLE."

You still have no negative connotations attached to the word, but because of your relationship inside the **BFF Bubble** you would probably ask for clarification.

You value their opinion, so you will seek out a meaning, so you can identify if it is positive or negative, so you can store that information away for future use.

Once we assign value to a word, we either *Receive* it or reject it. That is why it is extremely important to remove the *negative* influences in your life and to replace them with *positive* ones. The **Bully in Your Head** wants to keep you under his **Control** by making you **Doubt** yourself and your abilities. He wants you to *Receive* the negative information, so you will *Believe* it to be true. He is hoping that you will stay submissive to his constant insistence, that you are **Not Enough**.

Once we *Believe* something negative about ourselves, it becomes a **Hot Spot**.

What is a Hot Spot?

As we discussed in earlier chapters, your **Intimacy Bubbles** are your protection from many types of **Pain**. The **Bully** residing in your **Headspace** has left so much debris around that your **Filter** is dirty. The **Filter** that sees you as beautiful, handsome, special or fantastic may even be cracked or broken, distorting the image of the real you. After a while, you accept that the faulty image the **Bully** describes is the real you, and you are left with **Hot Spots** of acidic feelings about yourself that cause you to withdraw and feel **Lonely**.

Hot Spots (which are also called **Triggers**) are places that are particularly vulnerable for you. They are places that are so sensitive, you have a hard time looking at them or dealing with them. You may avoid them whenever possible by pretending they aren't there or that they don't bother you. You may even **Blame** them on someone else or run head-on into them. It is often an effort to fool everyone, including yourself, that they aren't bothering you. When all you are doing is refusing to deal with them. (Yes, this is the voice of experience talking.)

The closer someone is to our vulnerability, the more **Pain** that we feel when our **Hot Spots** are aggravated.

Understanding WHY We Get Hurt by Others

Since being overweight is a very common **Hot Spot**, let's use that for a moment to try to make my point.

If someone from the **Stranger Zone** is walking by you and says, "You're fat!" You will likely respond with either the "*Fight or Flight*" reaction. *Fight* meaning to retort in a sarcastic or flippant tone, or *Flight*, meaning to withdraw by ignoring it, or looking down and feeling embarrassed or ashamed.

Because you *Believe* it to be true, your **Hot Spot** will be activated.

If someone from your **Intimate Bubble** said that to you, because of their proximity to your vulnerability, that reaction would be amplified and would penetrate deeper and last longer. This is another reason to recognize the value of **BOBO** and let him protect that sacred space.

Sometimes you may unknowingly stumble upon a **Hot Spot** of your own, or someone else's, and feel flummoxed about how a compliment could be taken as an insult. These unknown **Hot Spots** are sometimes the beginning of the end of friendships, relationships, and even employment opportunities. Understanding your own **Hot Spots** is imperative but if you really want to make it to **Success Island** you will become a student of watching for other people's **Triggers** as well. Instead of dismissing them as being crazy or ridiculous, the new you will remember that you probably just tripped over a **Landmine**.

Landmines

A **Landmine** is a **Hot Spot** that is engaged by a word, phrase, or situation that is generally considered neutral or positive to most people; it **Triggers** a negative or hypersensitive response from the other person.

For example, if your friend just got a perfect score on her math test and you tell her, "Girl, you are so smart!" and she flares up at you telling you "shut up" or insisting she isn't smart, you may have stumbled on a **Landmine**.

Somewhere along the line, she has associated the word *smart* as an insult or something to be avoided. You might wonder how that could be, let me give you an example:

Smart Girls Stay Single

Myrna was a very smart girl. Straight A's in school while she was growing up. She mastered most classes and was finished early enough to help her fellow students with their work all through grade school. Some kids called her a "nerd" or a "geek" but Myrna didn't care. Her parents were proud of her and her friends liked her help.

In middle school things changed a little as she started to recognize boys. By high school, she was like a typical teenager with a crush, wishing that special someone would ask her out. She was in the locker room with her best friend Becky when Petra overheard her conversation about the boy she hoped would ask her to the dance.

Petra was a perpetual underachiever in school and struggled with many things. She had a myriad of undiagnosed learning disabilities that made school exceptionally difficult for her and she was jealous of Myrna and how easy school came to her. What she did have going for her was being attractive to the boys at school, which made her very popular. Petra always had a date and used her looks as a way to have some of the boys at school help her with her homework. When Petra heard Myrna, she laughed out loud.

Myrna turned with a start, shocked that anyone was listening to her private conversation, and embarrassed that someone now knew her secret. She felt extremely vulnerable and exposed to the mocking laughter.

*"He will never ask you out!" Petra mocked, determined to destroy Myrna's **Confidence**.*

*"He hates smart girls. Boys hate smart girls. You will never get a date if you act smart. Don't you know that **smart girls stay single**?" Petra continuing to laugh hysterically as she left.*

Myrna cried after Petra was gone.

*The final phrase indelibly seared into Myrna's brain created a **Hot Spot**.*

Smart girls stay single.

*Being smart was no longer a good thing. In that one moment, Myrna **Believed** what the pretty, popular girl said was true and she **Received** it. She filed smart away, instead of keeping it on the shelf of compliments; it was now a **Hot Spot**. Further, it turned into a **Landmine** since most typically consider being complimented on one's intelligence a positive thing.*

Sometimes it is difficult to understand **Hot Spots**, so let's think of them like acid indigestion. They are a bubbling cauldron of emotion that makes you feel sick to your stomach. Your whole body reacts negatively when the **Hot Spot** is activated and the only way to stop it from being reactive is to **Neutralize** it.

What is the Neutralizer?

Now that we understand **Hot Spots** and **Landmines**, we need to learn how to **Neutralize** them. Let's start by thinking of your **Hot Spot** as vinegar. When it is just sitting there, not being touched, it doesn't react. It will remain dormant until you add something to exacerbate it, but that **Trigger** can be traumatizing, so it is best to **Neutralize** it as quickly as possible to minimize the effects.

Exposing **Truth** to the **Hot Spot** is like adding baking soda to vinegar. The goal is to balance the pH, so the solution will stabilize, but the initial reaction is volatile causing it to bubble furiously. It looks like it will explode or spill out of the vessel. The more **Truth** you add in, the less explosive the reaction is, and the **Hot Spot** will stabilize and become neutral again. The important thing to remember is that you must accept that there will be a severe reaction to start the process. We have to *embrace* it, not *evade* it.

If you want to visually see this in action, I've included a recipe for your own experiment or you can check out the link to a video on my website at **www.VickiFitch.com/ETB**.

Visualizing & Neutralizing your Hot Spot

Step 1

Gather the items you need

1 Large, clear glass

3 Tablespoons of White Vinegar

1 Tablespoon of Baking Soda (you may want to have a few tablespoons on hand to continue with the experiment)

Step 2

Add 3 Tablespoons of Vinegar to clear glass

Step 3

Add 1 Tablespoon of baking soda. See what happens? It starts to bubble violently and starts rising to the top, threatening to overflow onto the counter or floor.

After it calms down, repeat Step 3 until the solution is completely neutral. That happens when it is no longer reactive to the baking soda.

Bully Bleach

Remember from the beginning of this chapter when I said what you *Believe*, you will *Receive*? If you *Believe* what the **Bully** has told you is true, you will *Receive* it as truth, but the **Bully's** version of the truth is just another lie. When you listen to him, as you have in the past, it is like adding bleach instead of baking soda to your **Hot Spot**. You will get a reaction, but it is one of toxic fumes, which will continue to keep you feeling sick.

You may even find those lies and the toxic fumes it created were mimicking some kind of demented security blanket. I understand that change feels different and different can be scary. That is why I am walking you through this process step by step and sharing my own stories with you at the same time.

Do yourself a favor and step out of the toxic fumes long enough for your brain and your lungs to clear. At least then you will know the difference and can make your choice.

If you are infected with **NES** and are worried you can't do this, let me lead by example and share my story with you, so know there is **Hope** and **#YANA (You Are Not Alone)**.

Chapter 10
The "bully" in Your Home

Bullying is never fun,
it's a cruel and horrible thing to do to someone.
If you are being bullied, it is not your fault.
No one deserves to be bullied, ever.
—Raini Rodriguez

I think the most difficult part of writing books is sharing the part of my **Personal Bubble** that holds my vulnerability. I recognize that I have an incredible support system of people who love my content and **Believe** in my mission. However, exposing the parts of me and my past are still scary because I have to relive them, too.

We all find that little place we tuck away the trials and the struggles that we have overcome. But, writing a book about the **Eviction Process** means having to remember all the personal attacks I endured during the **Bully Births**. I also have to remember all the betrayals and heartbreaks I went through that brought me through the **Ocean of Overwhelm** and sometimes into the **Depths of Discouragement**. Life is hard but when you find the right **Tribe** to go through it with, things are a lot easier.

Was There a "bully" in Your Home?

In every child's life, there is a draw to have a special relationship with the parent of the opposite sex. Little boys want to protect and marry their

Mommies and little girls want to be Daddy's Princess, or at least to have their Daddy adore them.

My Dad was a twenty-two-year career military man who had some strict ideas about families, children and life, in general. Before I go on, I want to say that I loved my Dad even though we didn't always get along, and I learned to understand him when I got much older. I believe our relationship was partly responsible for this book being written and am extremely grateful for the trials we faced because they formed the person I am today.

As this story unfolds, there will be times when you aren't going to like my Dad much. He might be that **bully** in the story we mentioned earlier that you "*love to hate*" until you glance **Behind the Curtain**. I will be honest, I never did find out what was "behind that curtain." My father was a very private man, but everything in me tells me that his story was much worse than mine. I truly believe that my parents, being products of their own environments, did the best they could. That doesn't mean I think they did it correctly all the time, but I think they did their best and that is all we should ever ask of anyone.

We do what we can, with what we have,
and what we know.

HHH

That is what they called my Dad. **HHH** stood for "*Horrible Hollerin' Hank*". He really wasn't *Horrible,* and he wasn't always *Hollerin'*, but his name was *Hank*. His guarded exterior was part of his personality… unless he was drinking. Unlike many people who get mean when they drink, my dad was actually pretty jovial. The truth is he was in a much better mood when he drank. It seemed to be the only thing that allowed him to let down his guard and just be himself.

My Dad, being a career military man, believed in **Control** and that meant the children, too. He certainly didn't know what to do with an extremely bright, feisty young girl that believed she could do anything she put her mind to. Now when I look back, I guess I can kind of understand how challenging I was for him. I started reading in preschool and couldn't stop asking questions and looking for new material to consume.

I tried to master every activity I was offered and pursued each new task with fervor. It was exciting for me. To be honest, most everything came easily to me. Reading, dance, sports, school… I admittedly caught on to things quickly and was always seeking additional things to learn, just because I could.

I got bored, and always looked for new things, new conversations, and new adventures… including catching bees. Did I mention I am seriously allergic to them? Yes, I wasn't the easiest child to handle.

My father needed to **Control** his environment, since that is what he was taught. Whether by the military or by his own family, I am unsure, but I know that compliance was mandatory to gain his **Love** and **Respect**. Compliance, however, was not my greatest strength although I did take on some of these traits later in life as I tried to **Control** the chaos in my own life.

Now, please understand that especially as a young child, I WANTED to please my dad. I wanted him to **Love** me and appreciate me for who I was. Unfortunately, I didn't know how to meet his expectations. I felt so **Overwhelmed** by the prospect that no matter what I did, I was **Not Enough**.

I was really smart… but I was **Not Smart Enough**.

I was really good at sports… but I was **Not Good Enough**.

The most challenging part for me was that I had no idea what the measuring stick was. It was an ever-changing gauge that left me feeling so insignificant that eventually, I gave up.

My Momma don't like me… and she likes everyone

My mom was a lovely woman and everyone enjoyed being around her. She was typically happy and positive and always ready to help someone in need. This included opening our home during the holidays to anyone without someplace to go.

When I say she didn't like me, I don't mean that she didn't **Love** me. However, when I was a teenager, she reminded me on an almost daily basis that she didn't like me. Her quote was,

"I love you, but I really don't like you."

It used to absolutely crush my spirit to hear her to say that. As an adult, I now understand what she was trying to say was "I **Love** *you*, but I do not like the way you are acting." That is an entirely different thing and reemphasizes the power of words and why we need to exercise our ability to really articulate what we are trying to say. It is one of the reasons I'm so passionate about my speaking and writing. I want to provide **Hope** and remind people there is a better way. One that doesn't leave emotional scars behind.

There were a lot of other quotes and ditties she used that were just as damaging, but I know she loved me and that only proves my point:

"We are a product of our own environment."—Dr. Phil

We learn what we know and when we make mistakes, we have to acknowledge them and move on. We can't change the past, but we can let it serve as a beacon to guide our way.

Now that I have kids of my own, I understand that teenagers can be difficult to handle. Having a child that feels completely misunderstood by others, unloved by her father, and tolerated by her mother probably made for a moody young lady. I am certainly not laying the **Blame** on them. I still believe they were doing the best they knew how. The same goes for you, be sure to recognize what you want to change with our punishing yourself for what you didn't know.

Dr. Phillip C. McGraw (Dr. Phil) reminds us that children have an inherent ability to take on responsibility for the actions of others. They tend to **Blame** themselves for what happens to their parents, their families, or themselves. They seem to find a way to accept responsibility for things that were not in their **Control**. So, before we go any further, I need you to remember…

It's NOT YOUR FAULT!

As you know by now, the **Bully in Your Head** came to you via a **Bully Birth**. The most common places for **Bullies** to be born is from someone in our homes. I am not suggesting that your family is intentionally trying to make you feel insignificant, although I suspect some of you reading this book are thinking exactly that.

"What happened to me was intentional! He/She is evil and deliberately made my life terrible."

That is absolutely possible. In some cases, sadly enough, even probable. But, if this book teaches you anything, I want it to be that you must look beyond the awful circumstances that happened to you and recognize:

It was NOT YOUR FAULT.

Read that again. **It was NOT YOUR FAULT**.

I don't care what you did or said as a child. **It was NOT YOUR FAULT** that someone mistreated or hurt you. You were a child, you learned from somewhere, and were doing your best to figure out who YOU were, while trying to navigate the **Abuse** that was around you.

You need to forgive yourself and forgive them.

I know you may not want to exercise **Forgiveness**. I know they may not deserve it. They may still be in your life, challenging you and frustrating you. Sometimes you may feel like they are sucking the life right out of you. I want to be perfectly clear, those people need an immediate **Bubble Bump** or an escort to the **Restricted Zone** if you haven't already done that. You do not need to keep yourself in proximity to your abusers. When you forgive what they have done and look at them with **Empathy** about what must have happened to them, it will help YOU heal. This is not about them. It is about you and the **Bully in Your Head** that wants to continue holding you captive to avoid **Eviction**.

Think about it for a moment. As a general rule, people that are able to be so incredibly unkind had to have had something happen to them to produce those reactions. Some of them may have even been convinced that the things they are doing, that you consider cruel, are actually a way to express **Love** or affection.

I know it sounds incredulous to some of you, but **Abuse** starts somewhere and if you were told your entire life that you ridicule people you **Love**, (i.e. "I only tease you because I love you.") that is what you will do.

I would like you to consider the possibility, not necessarily accept, but at least consider the possibility, that if your tormentor was someone that was supposed to **Love** you, that somewhere along the line, someone else could have convinced them that the behavior they were exerting was a sign of caring.

I know it may not be accurate, and that it might be hard to believe, but acknowledging the possibility frees you up to let go of some of your **Pain**.

For example, we have a close family friend that used to flick my toddler on the cheek when he came over. I got really angry and told him if he did it again, I was going to flick him in the face. He looked incredibly hurt and said that was a sign of affection.

In his home, your father flicking you in the face was a sign of **Acceptance** and **Love**. The action was wrong, but the intention was good. We need to try to investigate what is **Behind the Curtain** and understand intention, before we exercise **Judgment** on other people.

Please don't get me wrong. Just because someone has good intentions doesn't mean you allow the behavior to continue, but without having a discussion, I could have **Bubble Bumped** him right out of our lives simply because of a **Dirty Filter**.

In *Direct Selling 101*, I discussed the **Lens**, **Filter** and **Dirty Filter** analogies extensively but in case you haven't read that book yet, a **Dirty Filter** is caused by the debris of life that has been left on the way you view your circumstances and surroundings.

As you continue to read please remember, this book is all about YOU and how to help the scared little boy or girl inside **Stand Up** and **Evict the Bullies** that are terrorizing you. I am on your side. I am not sympathizing with your tormentor, I'm asking you to allow for a different style of thinking. It will serve you better than holding onto **Anger** and **Resentment**. You have every right to feel those emotions, but you are reading this book because you are tired of the **Bullies** in your head being in charge and running the show. It is time to take back your life and stop allowing people to convince you, that you are **Not Enough**.

Chapter 11
I am NOT Enough

"Rough diamonds may sometimes be mistaken
for worthless pebbles."
—*Thomas Browne*

Who told you, you were Not Enough?
I lived my life as a child feeling like I was **Not Enough**.
Not Good Enough, Not Smart Enough, Not Pretty Enough, Not Thin Enough, just **Not Enough.** The **Pain** was excruciating because it was no longer outside sources telling me. It was the **Bully** in my head reminding me of it every day, and it manipulated me into doing some things I'm not really proud of.

Let me share a bit about my trials with you and see if you can relate. Remember, the goal here is to find *Profit in the Pain*, not to wallow in it.

Not Pretty Enough

As I mentioned before, every young girl wants her Daddy to adore her and think she is beautiful. He is often the center of her world. He is Prince Charming, and her Gladiator all rolled up into one. Imagine (some of you don't have to imagine) instead of him telling you how lovely you are, he shares what he thinks is wrong with you.

As a young girl who was quick-witted and inquisitive, I spent a lot of time at the adult table. I was interested in basically… everything. I wanted to understand the world, and my mind was busy trying to gather the plethora of information available to me. I learned about politics, people and places. I asked questions and absorbed the answers like a sponge soaking up whatever I could before I was shooed away.

I watched the adults and how they acted and became aware of the nuances of adult conversation. I listened to what they said, and how they said it. I became very adept at understanding body language and recognizing when people were lying, or bluffing, as they played poker, and sometimes when they shared "stories."

When they were drinking, which was most of the time, I got to stick around a little longer as long as I didn't ask as many questions. I was the "beer runner" who got up and ran to the garage refrigerator whenever they ran out. I was happy to do it, because it gave me more opportunities to learn.

One day, when I was around 10 or 11, my father and his friends were playing cards and drinking beer. After one of my beer runs to the garage, my father, who was as they say, "three sheets to the wind," said in front of his friends,

"Hey Vicki, when are you going to Fredericks to buy some falsies?"

He was referring to the store called "Fredericks of Hollywood" where they sold lingerie and apparently bust enhancing items that I wasn't even aware of at the time.

All his friends looked at me and of course assessed the situation. I felt their eyes looking at my body like it was an object that needed to be evaluated for deformity. I remember one of his friends cocking his head to the side as he eyed me up and down. He had a half smirk on his face, as if to say, "Not bad." It was like I was a piece of meat from the butcher he would be willing to "settle" for.

I don't want to give anyone the wrong impression that my father or his friends were the lecherous type. That was not the case and I never felt that in any way. We already know from *DS101* that the brain autonomically starts formulating the answer to a question that is posed. Add excessive drinking into the mix and your brain might forget to filter out the assessment phase, thus the evaluative stares. I hold no ill will towards them; however, it didn't change the fact that I felt like I was being judged and that I didn't measure up.

I chuckled as I sat down and crossed my arms over my chest to cover the area they were referring to. For many girls my age, including me, we hadn't even reached puberty yet, but I still felt humiliated and wanted to crawl under the table. From watching them, I had learned to hide my emotions and pretend like a knife hadn't just been stabbed into my heart. That was the day my **Self-Image Bully** was born. My father and his friends left me with the impression that I was **Not Pretty Enough**.

I remember excusing myself a few minutes later to my room where I sobbed in my pillow for what seemed like hours. I was heartbroken. I remembered thinking, given the way they looked at me, that getting male approval was critical in this world. Those **Bully Birthing** moments are often remembered in intricate detail. I am crying as I am writing this because recalling emotional **Pain** is difficult. Even after the **Bullies** are **Evicted**, they tend to leave some residue behind that can catch you by surprise.

Before you start hating my Dad, let me remind you of a few things.

They were drinking, and likely drunk, at this time. You will soon learn about a whole host of **Bullies**, and one of them is **Alcoholism**. I didn't know it at the time, but my father was certainly an alcoholic. He was high functioning and he never drank while he was working. However, he was a six to twelve pack a day kind of drinker. If you are still under the impression that drinking that quantity of **Alcohol** is normal, I suggest you consider investigating that. **Addiction** is a very strong **Bully** that hangs out with a host of cohorts. They ALWAYS travel together, so you need to be aware of them, too. We will talk about them in another chapter.

I may have been 11, but I honestly looked much older than I was. I was 5'6" in the 5th grade, slender, had a small waist, and a curve in my hips that couldn't be ignored. I may not have been busty, but in the right clothes with some make up on, I could have passed for 20, especially since I had spent so much time with adults. I knew how to act mature. I wasn't allowed to wear make-up at this time, so I certainly wasn't looking older at this moment, but knowing this will make a difference when I share more about this particular **Bully** and how she continued to hurt me.

If this were the only reminder about my appearance, I may have grown out of that **Bully** and been able to **Evict** her without additional help. Unfortunately, the critiquing didn't stop there. The older I got, the more my father reminded me about the different ways I didn't measure up.

I was still a little girl at heart and wanted to be pretty. Of course, watching television made me want to emulate beautiful women. One such woman was Daisy Duke on the show *The Dukes of Hazzard.*

When I was 12, *Dukes of Hazzard* hit the scene. Daisy Duke was pretty, tough and respected by her family. She was fiercely loyal and wasn't afraid to own who she was. She was a bit of an idol to me and sometimes, pretending I was someone else, made my life feel a little less painful.

My friend, Ally, and I decided to play Daisy Duke one day. We dressed in our shorts and our little sandals (no heels, just a wedge sandal, but I did have a little mascara and blush on since we were playing dress-up). I put my long hair up in a ponytail on the side of my head and was walking over to Ally's, who lived across the street. When I got to the middle of the street, I felt someone grab my ponytail and start dragging me backwards. I started to panic and thrash about until I heard my father's voice.

"Where do you think you are going you little floozy?"

I didn't even know what a floozy was, but I knew I was in trouble. He literally dragged me to the house by my ponytail, humiliating me in front of all my neighbors and friends. Daisy Duke would have punched him, run off and jumped in the General Lee with her cousins who were waiting there to save her. But I was 12, and scared, and sad.

He started yelling at me, telling me that I looked like a tramp as he berated me. I was so confused and upset that I went to my room and cried again for what seemed like hours. Something was wrong with me. I didn't know what it was, but I knew it had to do with my looks. The **Self-Image Bully** was getting bigger and stronger, reminding me once again that I was **Not Enough**.

Not Thin Enough

As I continued to get older and started to mature, my father started addressing other parts of my body in ways that made me feel judged and insecure. One of my least favorites was whenever I wore a bathing suit, he would call me "Thunder Thighs." As I look back on photos, it would have been difficult for me to be any thinner than I was. But, when I would walk down the hall, sometimes I would hear him yell… "Thunnnnderrrr!" I knew it was for me. I smiled a mock smile each time he did it, recognizing that my body was "not right." I had long legs, a thin waist, and still wasn't very busty. I was **NOT Thin Enough**.

I remember doing bust enhancing exercises, swimming more, and dieting. At one point, I started eating one meal every three days to try to adjust my weight. No matter what I did, I was **NOT Thin Enough**. I didn't know what to do with that information, so I just tried to tuck it away in a place behind a steel wall. That way, it couldn't hurt me. Each time he said something, I tried to pretend that it didn't break my heart, make me feel self-conscious, and remind me that I was **NOT Enough**.

When I was in Jr. High, my mother sent me to modeling school. I was 5'10," wore a size five, had a twenty-two-inch waist and was bold. I don't know exactly why she did it. It may have been to help me combat what my father was saying, or so she could live vicariously through me. I am not sure. I knew she really did think I was pretty and that I could make it in modeling or acting if I wanted to pursue those things. In either case, I learned some things about beauty.

I learned how to apply make-up and cover blemishes and inconsistencies. I learned that when I was behind the camera, I had to pretend that I thought my body was perfect. My mother used to remind me that "Twiggy" was a very popular model back when she was younger, and she wasn't busty either. She tried to encourage me where my father had shaken my **Confidence**. Although I pretended on the outside that I was fine, on the inside, I was felt broken. I felt that I would never measure up to other women's bodies.

So now that you know how my father inspired some **Bully Births** in me, you might ask, "Why?" and my answer is, "I don't know."

- I don't know why a man would objectify his daughter in front of his friends.
- I don't know why a father would humiliate his daughter in front of the neighborhood and call her names that she didn't even understand.
- I don't know why he thought it was OK to isolate body parts and laugh and mock like it was funny.

What I do know, like I mentioned before, was I looked twenty when I was twelve. I think his dragging me back in the house was, in some twisted way, him trying to protect me from being a victim in the world. I choose to **Believe** he was trying to protect me, maybe from myself. Maybe he wanted to knock my **Confidence** down a notch or two because he thought it would get me in trouble. Maybe he did it to make himself feel better. Maybe that is the way his father treated his sisters. I truly don't know. Truthfully, it doesn't really matter.

Things were said, I *Believed*, so I *Received*. My belief that they were true and started living my life with their lie. The **Truth** is, I am beautiful just the way I am. You don't have to think so. Vogue magazine doesn't have to think so, and the general public doesn't have to think so. The person that needs to **Believe** it is me. Just me.

I will be honest, I didn't used to **Believe** that. I pretended because it was the only way I knew how to protect myself. It wasn't real protection of course, it was just a façade guarding a carefully hidden secret. I've written this book to give you the **Courage** to come out from behind that façade and face the world as yourself. It may take some time, but I am confident that **You Can Do It**! When you get to *OWN IT! How to Step Up and Stand Out*, I will share more about how I overcame those challenges and how you can, too.

The good news is I really do love myself and my body the way they are. I'm not saying I don't want to tone up or lose a little weight sometimes. What I am saying is that when I want to make a change, it is because **I want** to change, not because I falsely *Believe* that I am flawed because someone else thinks or says so. That is a huge difference. Wanting to make changes for yourself is fine. They are goals you can decide on and work towards. Wanting to change for someone else or because you are under the false impression that you are **Not Enough** the way you are is the problem. I want you to recognize the value of you, just the way you are. It doesn't matter what others have told you, it is time to find your real **Truth**, your real life, and your real friends. They are out there, and they want to find you too.

I have learned that most people who spend time assessing other people's "flaws" are trying to avoid their own perceived flaws and think it will help them feel better. The problem is, the **Bully's** judgmental voice in their head is so loud, they can't drown him out no matter how hard they try.

Now they have a better way. An actual solution to the problem, that doesn't include creating **Bully Births** in others… That solution is **Eviction**!

I never said this process was going to be easy, but what I did say is that I am here with you. I am leading the way by sharing my stories with you and showing you if I can do it, you can, too. I am also providing a safe environment for you to share your **Bullies** and help you walk through the **Eviction Process** with a **Tribe** that will **Love** you for who you are. (For details on the community go to **www.VickiFitch.com/ETB**)

So now that I shared some **Bully Births** with you, I want you to take a trip with me over to an Island in **Fitchipelago** that we haven't been to yet. You are going to learn a lot there! Let's set sail for **Nough Nation**.

Chapter 12
The Noughs & the Nots

> *"Complaining is finding faults,*
> *Wisdom is finding a solution."*
> —*Ajahn Braham*

There's an island on the Southeast side of **Fitchipelago**, called **Nough Nation**. Running right through the center of the island you will find a huge and glorious mountain range called **High Ground** which is surrounded by two lush valleys. Each one is the home of a specific clan—the **Noughs** and the **Nots**.

The **Noughs** lived on the west side of **High Ground** in a beautiful valley full of gorgeous greenery, flowing rivers, delectable fruit, and abundant vegetation. It was also home to the most beautiful and fragrant flowers anywhere. Deeply inhaling their rich scent provided a daily sense of peace and tranquility for the **Noughs**. They were a **VERY HAPPY** clan.

The **Nots**, on the other hand, were a miserable bunch. They lived on the east side of **High Ground**. Even though they had an abundance of all they needed, they constantly complained about the sun being too hot or there not being enough shade. They mumbled and grumbled about everything and made each other miserable.

Both lived on a stunning island with the perfect climate, but one clan could **Not** see the beauty or the opportunities. They were focused on what they did **Not** have. This is the story of the two clans.

The Story of the Clans

For generations, the **Not Clan** chose a new leader every four years. All clansmen were in rotation to be leader. Each new leader was expected to **Step Up** and lead the clan in its traditions and enforce its rules as those before had. It was almost time for the next transition. The clan's custom was for the next in line to provide a gift, offering, or discovery to the clan to prove they were worthy of being the leader.

The **Not Clan** had always felt they had been taken advantage of by their brethren clan, the **Noughs**. History told that the **Noughs** had taken the best parts of the island for themselves and that their side of the island had better food, supplies, and resources. The entire clan was resentful about it, but no one up to this point had ever tried to do anything about it. That was going to change.

Not Good E. Nough

Not Good E. Nough, who was next in line to lead the **Not Clan**, decided it was time to address the unfair division of the island of **Nough Nation**.

The entire town knew the story of how **Big E** had forced the **Nots** to the other side of the island, so he could keep all the prime real estate for the **Noughs**. **Not Good E. Nough** was going to demand they give the **Nots** their due. His plan was to demand land on the **Noughs** side of the mountain, since the **Nots** were given fewer resources than they needed for their people.

The ceremony was four days away and that announcement would be the perfect gift to the clan, proving he was worthy of leading them.

The next morning was Winter Solstice and before anyone else awoke, **Not Good E. Nough** packed his things and headed up over **High Ground** to make his way around to **Nough Valley**. They journey was long, and by the time he reached the other side, it was dark, and getting darker by the minute. As he looked down, he noticed a beautiful glow in the **Valley** below that shone bright. As he got closer, the path was clearer because there were lamps and candles lit everywhere!

"What a wasteful place!" he muttered to himself as he walked down the winding road to town. "There is so much abundance here. They waste wax and oil to burn lamps all night! They truly have taken more than their fair share if they can afford this type of luxury."

The townspeople greeted him cheerfully and walked out toward the road with their lanterns bright to greet the stranger. They smiled, and he found himself wanting to smile back, but he felt suspicious of their kindness. He had been conditioned to believe these were a selfish people that wanted the best for themselves.

He was tired and hungry and ready for a good night's rest. He wanted to be prepared for the difficult negotiation he would have tomorrow to demand what his clan was owed. When he finally made it to the middle of town, he saw an Inn that looked comfortable. As he stepped in, he saw more smiling, happy faces of people enjoying each other's company. The Innkeeper greeted him with a bright, warm smile and a welcoming attitude. He couldn't help noticing that she was beautiful and somehow looked familiar to him. She prepared her best suite and served him a delicious meal. He then settled in for the evening mentally preparing for what he would say the next day.

The next morning, he awoke to the sun shining brightly through the window and was reminded of his mission—to get what was due the **Not** people. He would not leave without getting their fair share. He just needed to have some breakfast and then find the leader of the **Nough** clan to make his demands.

As he walked downstairs to the dining area to get some breakfast, he was greeted by the Innkeeper with the same smile and beautiful countenance as the night before. He found himself a bit smitten. Why did she seem so familiar?

He sat down to eat at a small table in the corner of the room. As he opened the menu, he started reading the story of **High Ground** and how **Nough Nation** was actually separated into the **Noughs** and the **Nots**. It was a fascinating story that had never been shared with him before. He was mesmerized, and even a bit perplexed, at what he read.

The Story of Nough Nation

Long ago, **Nough Valley** and **Not Valley** were part of the same community called **Nough Nation**. The founder of **Nough Nation** was **Big "E" Nough** and he was proud of the people and the land. He led them with a kind heart and a gentle spirit. The community was so grateful for all **Big E** had done that it became customary for everyone born there to be given the middle initial **E**. People considered it a badge of honor.

Big E. Nough had a very distant cousin who also lived in **Nough Nation**. His name was **Naught Nough**. *("Not" for short)*. He was a big man and although he was helpful, he didn't have the same kind disposition as his cousin. He was jealous of **Big E** and wanted people to honor him with their names as they did with his cousin.

As **Not** started his own family, he created his own tradition. It became the custom of the **Not** clan to add his name, preceding their given name, of all family members as they were born. His first three children started the tradition.

Not Brave E. Nough
Not Sure E. Nough
Not Quite E. Nough

Not felt pride that his family was growing and wanted it to be larger than **Big E**'s.

Year after year, **Not's** bitterness grew as he continued to compete with his cousin for the love and affection of the community. One day, his grumbling led him to a very rash decision. He went to **Big E** and demanded that his family be given their own land, so they could have their own separate community.

Big E tried to convince **Not** that they could work things out, but by this time **Not's** negative attitude was so deep seated there was nothing **Big E** could do. Although he was disappointed, he offered them the **Valley** on the other side of **High Ground**. It was a lush and beautiful land with flowing rivers, peaceful groves, and wild growing food. The berries there were the sweetest, most delicious things **Big E** had ever tasted. The lakes and streams were packed with fish and would provide well for his cousin and the entire **Not Clan**.

The town was sad to see them leave but wished them well. They hoped that someday they would be back, and **Nough Nation** would *once again be united together. Every year since then, the entire town would light candles during the Winter Solstice to make sure the path was clear and bright in hopes that their brethren from **Not Valley** would come back and reunite the towns.*

He closed the menu stunned and stared off in the distance trying to make sense of it all.

This was not the story he had been told his entire life. The way his relatives had relayed it, the **Noughs** were a greedy and selfish clan and the **Nots** were taken advantage of and basically run out of town.

As he was pondering what he had just read, the Innkeeper approached him to take his breakfast order. He ordered bacon, eggs, and coffee and while he was waiting he read the story again.

He looked deep in thought when the Innkeeper arrived to deliver his breakfast, so she carefully laid it down with the check beside it.

As he finished eating, he turned the check over and read the note on the other side.

Thank You!

Your entire stay has been paid in full, compliments of the management. Feel free to turn the menu over if you want to hear more about our story...

Intrigued by this kind and thoughtful gesture, **Not Good E. Nough** proceeded to turn the menu over to read the story of how the Inn came to be.

Nough Nation Inn

*If you are visiting from **Not Valley**, thank you for coming and please know you are welcome here. The stories we were told have been changed through the years and may have given you a different view of **Nough Valley**. Here is our story of how this Inn came to be. Just as we were cared for on our first visit, you will be cared for on yours...*

*A long time ago, before the **Noughs** and the **Nots** split, generations of our family had lived together in **Nough Nation**. Having some members from both clans that had married, our Great-Great-Grandparents had to decide on where to live. Due to the pressure* *from the **Not** clan, they moved to **Not Valley** but insisted on sharing stories of the old days and how wonderful they were from generation to generation.*

*The longer we stayed in **Not Valley**, we noticed the bitterness and hostility that was being passed down and had a desire to reunite the **Nation**, inspired by the family stories, which were told nightly by the fireplace.*

*Recognizing that there was nothing physically keeping us from exploring the possibility of reconnecting the clans, we decided to take a trip to **Nough Valley**.*

It was dusk by the time we got to the top and it was getting dark, which made it dangerous on the way down. As the people in the town saw us heading down the hill, they came out with their lanterns to light the path and help us find our way. We felt welcomed and cared for.

*Having never had visitors from **Not Valley** before, there had been no need for an Inn, so a local family offered to allow us to stay in their home for the evening and provided us with a hot meal, a warm fire, and friendly conversation. We were convinced that we needed to make our home here and share what we experienced with the rest of the **Not Clan**.*

*Although our clansmen rejected the idea of reuniting, we settled here, committed to the positive environment and hoping to be the catalyst for others. We opened this Inn to welcome the people who did make the trip, so they would feel as welcome as we did. We hope you felt this warmth as well and will share it with others. It is our deepest wish that others will join our effort in reuniting **Nough Nation** once again.*

All of this was so contrary to what **Not Good E. Nough** had been told his entire life, but these people seemed genuine and he was eager to understand and speak to someone about what he had read.

He thanked the Innkeeper for her hospitality and asked if it would be possible to speak to the owner of the Inn and she hurried off to find him.

When she returned, she led him to a room with large couches and a huge fireplace, then directed him to a gentleman with a gleam in his eye. He seemed somehow familiar although he couldn't put his finger on why.

He introduced himself, and the gentleman assured him he knew who he was.

Not Good E. Nough looked surprised as the man continued.

"I'm not surprised you don't remember me, but I remember you. My son and daughter used to play with you in the forests of **Not Valley** when you were very small. Your father and I were the best of friends, and your mother and my wife were nearly inseparable. We used to joke with one another that you and **Not Ever E. Nough** were to be married someday so we would be family. When we took this journey to **Nough Valley**, your father was furious. He forbade your mother to speak to my wife again. The women were heartbroken."

"Over the years, we tried to reach out and invite your family to come visit, but, my requests came back void. Losing your father as my best friend was the most painful thing I had ever had to deal with at that point in my life." He sounded choked up.

The memories started flooding back of the times running in the forest and swimming in the creek with his neighbors. How had he forgotten? It had been so long ago, and he had been so young, but those were such joyful memories!

Then suddenly it struck him. That was what was missing from **Not Valley** – Joy. That is why he felt so welcome here.

They sat and talked a while longer and **Not Good E. Nough** recognized that as the leader, it would be his responsibility to try to reunite the clans. He was perplexed as to how to make it happen, so he asked for help.

"How did you do it?" **Not Good E. Nough** asked.

"It was easier than you think." He stated in a matter of fact tone. "**Remove the NOTS**."

Startled, **Not Good E. Nough** gave him a raised eyebrow, and a curious look.

"You want to remove us?" he asked a little concerned.

"No! Wait a minute!" the gentleman said with a chuckle. "That isn't what I meant." he said to assure **Not Good E. Nough**.

"Removing the word **NOT** from the way we speak changed our perspective."

"We realized the **NOTs** in our life were keeping us from doing the things we wanted to do. They were stopping us from believing we were capable and clever and resilient. When our family used to sit around the fireplace and talk about what an amazing place **Nough Nation** used to be, whenever someone would mention trying to reunite, we would always fall back on what we knew.

*"We can **NOT** break tradition."*
*"We can **NOT** make peace."*
*"This is **NOT** possible."*
*"This is **NOT** the family way."*

Then one day, one of the children piped up with a simple question that changed our perspective.

"Shouldn't someone try?"

As we all looked at her in amazement, we recognized that she was right. We had been so stuck in our thinking. We were stuck in **NOT Valley**. Not physically; there was nothing truly stopping us, it was the limiting belief of the word "**NOT**" that was holding us back.

We wrote the objections on a piece of paper and simply crossed out the word **NOT** on each line.

*"We can **NOT** break tradition.*
*"We can **NOT** make peace."*
*"This is **NOT** possible."*
*"This is **NOT** the family way."*

It was such a simple thing to do, and this was after the result.

"We can break tradition.
"We can make peace."
"This is possible."
"This is the family way."

We were struck by the simplicity and wondered if the answer had really been as simple as removing the word **NOT** from the equation. Our entire community had been formed upon it and expected it. It was so deeply entrenched in our culture for generations that we hadn't seen it until the innocence of a child reminded us to look for the solution. That is when we posed a new question.

"How can we?"

We brainstormed possible solutions and recognized the first thing we needed to do was take a trip to **Nough Valley**. When we came here with the question, "**How can we**?" instead of the definitive statement "We can't.," everything changed. We recognized the weight of the word and that it was dragging us down with negativity.

Then we expanded it to removing the **NOT** from our names. The meanings changed, and we all felt a sense of relief. Let's do it with a few of your family members.

"I am **Not Good E. Nough**."	Became	"I am **Good E. Nough**."
"I am **Not Smart E. Nough**."	Became	"I am **Smart E. Nough**."
"I am **Not Strong E. Nough**."	Became	"I am **Strong E. Nough**."
"I am **Not Pretty E. Nough**."	Became	"I am **Pretty E. Nough**."

"Can you imagine if everyone in **Not Valley** started believing they were **E. Noughs** again?" his voice trailed off and a smile spread across both of their faces.

Not Good E. Nough could clearly see the value in what was being shared and recognized he had some work cut out for him, but he knew as the clan leader, it was his responsibility to share this with his people. He wanted them to find the **Joy** again, and he believed reuniting **Nough Nation** again was the best way to serve his people.

His initial reaction was

"This is **NOT** possible!"

Recognizing the value of the lesson being shared, he implemented the **Remove the NOTS** philosophy and came up with

"This is possible!"

He knew teaching the clan to **Remove the NOTS** was the right solution and would help him become a far better leader than he had ever imagined. More importantly, it was the best gift he could provide to the clan because it would create possibility thinking.

Now the challenge would be getting the **Clan** to see what he saw.

There was strength in working on a problem with other people who were committed to the same goal. They just needed a plan.

"So," continued **Not Good E. Nough**… *"How can we…"*

Moral of the Story

Recognizing that negative self-talk prevents you from being the best version of yourself is critically important to your growth in business and in life. When we are repeatedly told we are **Not Good Enough, Not Smart Enough, Not Strong Enough, Not Pretty Enough, Not Thin Enough, Not Rich Enough, Not "Whatever" Enough**, we start to *Believe* it. Each time we accept it as **Truth**, it feeds the **Bully** and allows him to grow bigger and stronger, which is why it is critical that we cut off his food supply and start recognizing our own value.

#RemoveTheNots

It is important that we **#RemoveTheNots**, or the excuses, that are holding us back from excelling. We need to recognize that replacing the statement, "I do **NOT** know how." with the question, "**How can I**?", creates possibility thinking and a positive mindset.

This is an important step, as we work on the **Bully Eviction Process**, and it is something you will have to practice. The **#RemoveTheNots** philosophy will be like sealing off those tiny crevices where the **Bullies** will try to work their way back in to your **Headspace**.

Now that you understand the damage that can be done by these **Bullies**, it is time to introduce you to **Freddie**.

Chapter 13
Meet Freddie

> *"Sometimes the most dangerous thing for kids*
> *is the silence that allows them to construct their own stories.*
> *Stories that almost always cast them as alone*
> *and unworthy of love and belonging."*
> —*Brené Brown*

The **Bully in Your Head** comes in all shapes & sizes. Male, female, gender neutral, it doesn't matter. They all have super powers that range in degree of intensity, so I thought I would start out by sharing a story about **Freddie**.

When **Frederique Enrique Alejandro Rodriguez** was a young man, his family called him **Freddie,** and everyone loved him. He had a bright smile and a kind heart and was adored throughout his community. **Freddie** had an uncle, his Mother's brother, whom he was named after. He was proud of his uncle and wanted to be just like him. He walked like him, talked like him, and tried to copy his stance, his expressions, and his demeanor. He was so much like his uncle that everyone started calling him Jr.

Freddie has a sad story. His father left his mother as soon as she got pregnant. He said he had no interest in children and more specifically, "Didn't want no stinkin' kid around." His uncle moved in with them just after **Freddie** was born by convincing his sister that he was there to take care of things and provide a strong role model, like a father. It sounded like a good idea at the

91

time, but Uncle Freddie made sure Jr. was reminded that his own father didn't want him.

Uncle Freddie was the closest thing he had to a father so like most kids, **Freddie** mimicked his role model. He developed the same strut, the same attitude, and the same demeanor. He started squinting his eyes and smiling less, just a little to look tougher. Uncle Freddie said smiles made him look like a sissy. Like many young children, **Freddie** started imagining a world where he was the king.

For years, he watched his uncle order people around and tell them what to do and **Freddie** started mimicking that behavior in preschool and then kindergarten. The children were afraid of him and followed his directions. **Freddie** liked the feeling of being in charge and started demanding more things of the kids when he got to elementary school. He used the scowls he practiced from watching his uncle and dropped his tone of voice and people did what he said.

If he wanted a ball on the playground, he demanded it. If he wanted something else to eat, he insisted on having it. The more he acted like his uncle, the more power he had at school. If his dad could see him, he would be sorry that he left.

He watched how his uncle handled adversity. If someone didn't do what he wanted, he made a quick forward motion to scare them and people jumped. Uncle Freddie would just laugh. If they still didn't listen, he punched his fist in his hand with a head nod, like they were going to "get it" if they didn't comply. And that stare… that cold blank stare would petrify anyone.

If that didn't work, Uncle Freddie would resort to pushing, shoving, or physically restraining people. He always got what he wanted, and Jr. was determined to have that power, too.

He kept practicing his attitude, his **Intimidation**, and his stare. The children at school did whatever **Freddie** told them. They were afraid. When his uncle witnessed that, he congratulated **Freddie** and told him he was acting like a man, which encouraged him to continue with the same behavior.

By the time **Freddie** started the 4th grade, he noticed changes in his uncle. He was getting angrier and meaner with people. When he didn't get what he wanted from others who were bigger or stronger, Uncle Freddie would take it out on **Freddie** and his mother.

Uncle Freddie would call Jr. names push him around and tell him he was worthless. Sometimes, just to be cruel, he reminded **Freddie** that even his own father didn't want him, adding additional Pain by telling him he was broken, stupid, and would go nowhere in life.

Each time he heard these things, he was more determined than ever to have the kids at school **Respect** him to prove his uncle wrong. He insisted on being first in line, first to be chosen and first to eat. Even if that meant taking other kids' food. He became more difficult to deal with and harder to please. The kids who didn't want to be the victim of his **Abuse** became his "friends", a mini 4th grade posse, just like his uncle's. **Freddie** felt powerful because he was in charge.

By the time he was in 7th grade, he was taking kids' lunch money, homework, or whatever else he wanted. He started getting physical by shoving and even hitting others if he didn't get what he wanted. His group of followers continued to grow.

His uncle started drinking and got meaner. He started ordering **Freddie** and his mother to do his bidding which made **Freddie** angry and determined to prove that he could take care of himself and his mother. The **Frustration** inside of him grew every day. He wanted to have power over his circumstances. No longer was his uncle his idol. He became his nemesis.

As Uncle Freddie's drinking progressed, he became more verbally and physically abusive with **Freddie** and his mother. One day, Uncle Freddie slapped him across the face and **Freddie** came out swinging. He was only twelve years old and didn't have the strength to do much. But, the **Rage** inside of him had his arms flailing, trying to make contact to transfer some of the **Pain** he was feeling. Uncle Freddie just laughed at him and held Jr.'s head at a distance and since Freddie's arms weren't long enough to reach his uncle, he swung in vain until he was worn out. Uncle Freddie made sure to mock him and humiliate him in front of others just to keep Jr. in his place.

Freddie's Resentment grew. He vowed that someday Uncle Freddie would be sorry for treating him that way. Until then, he would take his **Anger** out the only way he knew how, on other kids that he had **Control** over.

As time went on, **Freddie's Anger** grew, and so did his posse.

By the time **Freddie** was in high school, he had a reputation, and everyone was afraid of him. He was "respected" in school—at least what he had mistakenly interpreted **Respect** was from watching his uncle. Kids moved out of the way when he walked down the hallways. Teachers didn't want to fail him because they didn't know what the repercussions would be. Watching the dread in people's eyes when he and his posse walked into a store at night was priceless.

After a long day of controlling students at school and causing chaos with his posse at night, **Freddie** went home to see his uncle yelling at his mother. He was in her face, telling her that **Freddie** was a loser just like his dad and that she needed to make him go get a job to help support the household. Uncle Freddie didn't work. He was "the man of the house" and he forced **Freddie**'s mother to support them all.

She didn't have the strength or **Courage** to argue with him, but she agreed to get a third job, so **Freddie** could stay in school. She asked if he could buy his own liquor and cigarettes because it was hard to pay the bills and feed the three of them with the limited budget she had.

Uncle Freddie had already polished off his nightly six-pack, so he had no reservations about drawing his hand out and backhanding her across the face with such force it knocked her into the wall.

This was the last straw for **Freddie**. He was 17 now and big enough to defend himself and his mother. **Freddie** ran at his uncle and knocked him into a wall as he slapped, punched, and insulted him. Freddie, now 6'2", towered over his Uncle, who stood at 5'10. He felt powerful as he looked down into his uncle's eyes with the cold hard stare he had become so familiar with. His mother sat in the corner cowering during the altercation. She had learned through years of conditioning that any intervention on her part would be met with mental and physical **Abuse**. She just watched and continued to feel helpless.

Freddie's Rage turned to satisfaction when he saw **FEAR** on his uncle's face for the first time. The tables had turned and now his uncle was afraid of him.

Freddie ordered his uncle to get out of their house reminding him he was no longer needed there and was not welcome to return. With **Freddie's** posse outside, there would be no arguing. His uncle gathered a few things and left.

That momentary feeling of contentment quickly subsided as **Freddie** realized that his biggest challenge in life had just been handled, and he didn't feel any better about it. Inside, he was still angry, lonely, and empty. He couldn't help but recall the list of things his uncle had reminded him of his entire life.

- He was so worthless, even his own father didn't want him.
- His mother didn't care, she didn't **Stand Up** for him or protect him.
- He didn't have any real friends, only a posse that was afraid of him.
- He would always be a loser, so he should quit school and act like a man.

He had learned to *Believe* those statements his whole life, so it was natural that he *Receive* that as his truth and decided it was time for him to take on the role of "the man of the house." He ordered his mother to get dinner ready and told her he was dropping out of school. There were plenty of opportunities for him to get what he wanted.

This was a new day and it was time for a new name. He no longer wanted to be associated with a weakling like his uncle. He decided to use his initials and changed his name:

__F__rederique __E__nrique __A__lejandro __R__odriguez
would now just be called FEAR for short.

This is how **FEAR** came to be. How long he stays is up to you, because the **Eviction Process** is simple, and **Freddie** and his posse won't know what hit them. Speaking of his posse, I think it is time for you to meet them and his **Bully Buddies** that are either hanging out in your **Headspace** or are trying to get in.

Chapter 14
Meet the Bully Buddies

"My Bully is charging me rent now…"
—Adam Migacz

NOTE: Some of the **Bullies** may require professional help in conjunction with the **Headspace Heroes**. Help is available for you and your loved ones from the Substance Abuse and Mental Health Services Administration.

SAMHSA's National Helpline
1-800-662-HELP (4357)

<u>ABANDONMENT</u> – This **Bully** does double duty. He hangs around with **Distraction** and quietly persists at eating away your **Dreams** by encouraging you to abandon them. At the same time, he infects you with **NES (Not Enough Syndrome)** so when your relationships change you believe it is your fault. He is tricky and heartless and often drops you off at the doorstep of **Despair**.

<u>ABUSE</u> – This big burly **Bully** is a powerhouse. He can turn the strongest person you know into a whimpering child or a raving lunatic. He thrives on the distance he can create between you and the people you care about. When you see him, **Anger** is usually close by.

<u>ADULTERY</u> – This little vixen is often the unfortunate love child of **Loneliness** and **Selfishness**. **Loneliness** is so desperate for attention and interaction that

Adultery creeps in without any direct dialogue. The attention that fills the **Void** is so important that **Loneliness** is like a sitting duck waiting to get picked off by the first hunter that comes along. **Selfishness**, on the other hand, tends to be a willing participant and has difficulty seeing anyone's needs but his own.

<u>ADDICTION</u> – This is another **Bully** that brings his own posse. This crowd sticks together like glue, so when you encounter one of them, the others are nearby. Don't let them fool you. They lurk in the shadows where **Loneliness** lives, but these villains aren't quiet. They are loud, vocal, and insistent on getting their way. This is one of the most difficult **Bullies** to remove, because they know how to dig in deep. These trenches are triggered by emotions and outside stimuli. They are insistent on getting their way, but don't listen to their nagging.

WARNING! Do not think you can **Evict** only one of the minions here. They are like a neural network of disaster just waiting for you to offer admittance to one and the rest come along for the ride. They move in FAST and you can't always see the other members of the clan, but beware, they are there! If **Addiction** is present, all his minions must go! This needs to be a **Non-Negotiable** in your life if you really want it to change.

> <u>Alcohol</u> – Seems social at first, but as he gets his way, you will be under his **Control**. He will try to convince you that you can keep him around to just come out on weekends or holidays. He is a liar and can't be trusted. **Eviction** is the only option.
>
> <u>Drugs</u> – He has a bunch of little mini minions and is relentless when trying to figure out which one's will keep you under his thumb.
>
> <u>Gambling</u> – This cowboy comes riding in on the white horse of entertainment. However, you will quickly find that the façade fades away and you are left feeling broke and broken. This rodeo-riding adrenaline junkie needs a constant fix.

CAUTION: If **Addiction** is a **Bully** that is plaguing you, be aware of his tricks to persuade these participants to come to the dark side and join the **Bully Buddies**.

> <u>Food</u> – This one hides in plain sight. Since we need her to survive, when **Addiction** turns her to the dark side, we are at a disadvantage. Her power over us can be overwhelming because it is impossible for us to eliminate her, but a **Bully Conversion** is possible.

Sex – If **Addiction** sinks his teeth into her, she tends to hijack your thoughts. She uses her sweet and seductive charm to worm her way through your **Bubbles**, wreaking havoc on your life.

Shopping (Retail Therapy) – She is a flirty little trickster when **Addiction** takes hold of her. She will entice you into believing that you can get away from all the other **Bullies** by hanging out with her for a while. She adds on a bit of southern charm to convince you that a little retail therapy will quiet down the other crew. It doesn't work, and if she has her way, she will keep you shopping until you find yourself hanging out in **Brokeville**, with your **Gambling** entertainment counterpart.

ANGER – He doesn't try to hide himself. He hangs out in your face and pulls together his **Bully Brothers** to keep you stuck. His little brother, **Frustration**, hangs out to learn the ropes. When his older twin brothers **Rage & Fury** jump in the arena, all bets are off. This is a losing combination and this quartet will do whatever they can to stay where they are and take you down with them.

ANXIETY – He is a quieter **Bully**. He gets in the limbic system where he can pull strings in other parts and have you feeling more than just overwhelmed. He leaves you feeling dazed and confused. **Anxiety** is often found trailing his big brother **Abuse**. He doesn't like to stand in the spotlight, which is why he retreats to the **Limbic Lounge**.

APATHY – A lazy and lethargic Bully that is the complete opposite of his twin Empathy. He is essentially numb and has no interest in changing. When he hangs out in your Headspace, he infects you with the same emptiness.

BLAME – A corrosive and sometimes explosive Bully that is afraid to take responsibility for his actions. Instead, he points fingers and provides an arsenal of excuses.

COCKINESS – This is the twin brother of **Confidence**. They are identical so when you see them from a distance it might be difficult to tell, but they are easily recognizable up close by their actions. **Cockiness** insists on everyone looking at him, while **Confidence** doesn't need attention to define who he is.

COMPARISON – The oldest of the **C Sisters**, she is sometimes subtle and often docile at first, encouraging a little healthy competition. Her sisters **Criticism** and **Complaining** often jump on her proverbial band wagon which begs **Judgment** and **Envy** to come along for the ride.

COMPLAINING – The youngest of the **C Sisters** she spends a lot of time with **Judgment** and can find fault in anything that is happening.

CONFUSION – The cousin of **Doubt** finds himself lacking the ability to make decisions. He is often found hanging out with **Distraction** which keeps him moving on from idea to idea or project to project. These two are the creators of **Shiny Object Syndrome**.

CONTROL – A king that must have things his way. He sometimes manifests himself as OCD (Obsessive Compulsive Disorder), which drives you to try to find his daughter **Perfectionism**. His son is **Pride**, and they all feed off each other which creates a vicious cycle. This family is responsible for creating many **Bully Births**.

CRITICISM – She is the middle of the **C Sisters** whose main purpose is to badger you into believing that you are **Not Good Enough**, **Not Smart Enough**, **Not Strong Enough**, **Not Pretty Enough**, **Not Thin Enough**, **Not Rich Enough**, and **Not Whatever Enough**. She is the most rampant **Bully**, charging from person to person, as you pass her on, by criticizing others.

DEBT – This **Bully** lurks around where you either owe money, or just feel you have a lack of it for what you want and need. When your finances aren't where you think they should be, this rambunctious **Bully** will try to convince you that **Broke** means **Broken**. He is insatiable and spends a lot of time with **Envy** and **Greed**.

DECEIT – The estranged brother of **Truth**. He spends his days with **Resentment**. Together, they infiltrate the front lines to create an opening for the other **Bullies** to enter.

DEFEAT – Although he sounds like a big **Bully**, he is actually a tiny little guy who likes to hang around with a group of **Bullies** and pretend he has power over you. In reality, he is just a **Stepping Stone** and should be treated as such.

DEPRESSION – He can be an elusive **Bully** that you aren't sure is there, until you feel him dragging you down or sometimes choking you with the weight of his **Bully Buddies**, **Guilt** and **Shame**.

DESPAIR – This meandering **Bully** is the estranged brother of **Hope**. Because **Hope** is a **Headspace Hero**, they do not run in the same circles and he is unable to find her. Thus, some refer to him as **Hopeless**, because he is without his sister, **Hope**. She would gladly return to his side if he were committed to changing his ways. but he prefers his sullen life.

DISCOURAGEMENT – A distant cousin to **Courage**, this **Bully** hung out in **Dis**, a small town in **Not Valley** and chose a much different path. He spends a lot of time with **Depression** and **Loneliness**.

DISTRACTION – Misdirection and redirection are two of the tools this **Bully** uses. Keeping you moving from one thing to another, he can prevent you from achieving your **Dreams**. Since he enjoys hanging around with **Confusion** and **Overwhelm**, you often find yourself choosing **Abandonment** because he seems like an easier **Bully** to handle.

DOUBT – FEAR, **Shame**, and **Doubt** are the **Big 3 Bullies** to watch out for. Although **Doubt** is small in size, he packs a powerful punch. Always unsure, **Doubt** hangs out like a scared, quivering child that never makes decisions on his own. **Doubt** is dangerous. He is a **Flip-Flopper** that lives in a constant state of flux about what to do, where to do it, and who to do it with. His position is never stable because anyone with an idea can sway him and anytime he tries to **Step Up** and make a decision, his big sister **Regret** confuses him, making him start all over again.

ENVY – She is a vindictive **Bully**. She wants what others have and never feels satisfied even when she gets it. There is always something more **Envy** wants.

FAILURE – **Failure** is a fraud who is part of **FEAR**'s posse. He threatens you and often enlists the help of **Shame** to hold you back from pursuing your **Dreams**. On the outside he looks like one of the scariest **Bullies**, but in reality, he is a molehill pretending he is a mountain.

FEAR –**F**rederique **E**nrique **A**lejandro **R**odriguez (See Chapter titled *Meet Freddie*) He is one of the **Big 3 Bullies** and tends to hang out with **Intimidation**.

FRUSTRATION – This is the youngest of the **Bully Brothers** and he wants to grow up to be more like his brothers **Anger**, **Rage** and **Fury**. He tries to keep you focused on the things you **CAN'T** do and tries to infect you with **NES** by keeping you in a perpetual state of thinking you are **Not Enough**.

FURY – When this **Bully** takes over, you lose complete control. He is dangerous and needs to be avoided at all costs. He hangs out with his younger brothers **Frustration** and **Anger**, but the party gets really heated when his twin brother **Rage** shows up. They are a tag team that pushes you from one **Bully Brother** to the next.

GREED- This is an ugly **Bully** who rounds up **Envy**, **Selfishness** and **Deceit** and is blinded by his desire to have whatever he wants.

GUILT –She skulks up and down looking for new victims to drape herself over. She leaves you overwhelmed and unable to move with the heavy load she lays on you. She tends to spend time with **Depression** and **Shame** and is hard to get rid of if you let her settle in.

HATE – This is the 350lb Linebacker of **Bullies**. He is big, bold, and aggressive and can hold a grudge like a dog with a bone.

HUMILIATION – She is complicit in keeping her sister **Shame** stuck in your head. She is loud, obnoxious, not easily hidden, and uses her sister to remind you of your inadequacies.

INSECURITY – This **Bully** tends to be timid, uncomfortable and is constantly looking for confirmation that he is OK. He tends to hang out close to **Anxiety**, **FEAR** and **Failure**.

INTIMIDATION – This is a thug **Bully** who often hangs out with FEAR as one of his many posse members. His size alone can immobilize you.

JEALOUSY – Often found with **Envy** and the **C Sisters** (**Comparison**, **Criticism** & **Complaining**), this **Bully** will do anything to be the center of attention.

JUDGMENT – Stern and critical, this **Bully** feels he has the right to pass his judgment on others. He looks down on you from his lofty bench, identifying all the things you should change about yourself.

LONELINESS – Her nickname is **Lonely**, and she is a quiet carrier of **NES** suggesting that you are **Not Enough**. She lurks around in the shadows, not being noticed and only feels validated when you are alone. She enjoys attending **Pity's Parties** because she can always find a new victim there.

MANIPULATION – This deceptive mastermind pals around with **Deceit** to get what he wants. He is a chess master, moving other **Bullies** into place to force your move.

MISERY – This **Bully** loves company and she surrounds herself with any **Bullies** who attract a crowd. Her goal is for you to get stuck in the **Weeds of Wallowing**.

OVERWHELM – This abuser creates the kind of chaos that you can't get away from. No matter which way you turn, he is there to crush you underneath his rolling waves of anguish. He is often accompanied by **Defeat**, and **Depression**.

PAIN – Coming in softly or like a roaring lion, this **Bully** is relentless and can cause you to think you are going crazy. He talks constantly and eventually, if that is all you can hear, you often fall into the waiting arms of his little sister **Pity**.

PERFECTIONISM – This Princess has a desire for things to be perfect. Her brother **Pride**, encourages her to continue her quest for perfection which is an illusion that keeps her in a perpetual loop with her father **Control**.

PITY – **Pity** is a party girl. She likes to throw **Pity Parties** and invites everyone to come along. If you know her big brother, **Pain**, you've probably met her. She is never too far away from him because he provides a lot of guests for her little soirees.

POPULARITY – Also known as **Pop**. She is desperate for everyone to notice and marvel at her. She tends to hang out with **Envy** and **Criticism** being sure to drag everyone else down.

PRIDE – He is a prince that wants to be the king and remove his father **Control** from the throne. He is arrogant and spends a lot of time frustrated when he isn't noticed. He and **Cockiness** tend to fight for attention.

RAGE – He is the younger twin brother to **Fury**, who is the oldest of the **Bully Brothers**. **Rage** is the more unpredictable of the two and must be watched closely. He tends to blind his opponents leaving them helpless.

REBELLION – This teenager is defiant and always looking for a contrary way to do things. He thinks his way is right, but even if it isn't, he will proceed, just to prove a point, no matter where that leaves him.

REGRET – This relentless **Bully** is always prepared with the **Woulda Coulda Shoulda** attack. If you **Would** have done that, you **Could** have done this, and you **Should** have done that. **Regret** is never satisfied with the way things turn out no matter how great they are. They always **Coulda** been better. She befuddles her little brother **Doubt** with this special attack and keeps him in constant torment.

RESENTMENT – This is the indignant **Bully** who always believes she has been treated unfairly. She has a hard time seeing the other side of the situation. She gets **Stuck in her Stubbornness**. She is a cancer that will eat away at the fabric of who you are.

<u>**SADNESS**</u> – She is a fairly innocent **Bully** that comes and goes, but if you leave her in your **Headspace** she will invite her big brother **Depression** over to stay.

<u>**SARCASM**</u> – He is a nasty **Bully** with a sharp tongue that will cut you like a knife.

<u>**SELF**</u> – This **Double Agent** starts out neutral and can go either way. If **Self** is raised by the **Bullies**, multiple negative personalities will emerge. **Self-Righteous**, **Self-Deprecating**, and **Self-Loathing** to name a few, Of course this also produces a negative turn on **Self-Image**, **Self Esteem**, **Self-Respect**, **Self-Control** and becomes very **Self-Conscious**, just to outline a few.

<u>**SELFISHNESS**</u> – He is part of **Self** but is so focused on himself that he insisted on staying separate. His name says it all. He wants to have it all and he wants it NOW. He is extremely convincing and can be a formidable foe.

<u>**SHAME**</u> – One of the **Big 3 Bullies**, this one is the deepest penetrating, by infiltrating every fiber with her liquid like persistence. **Shame** is like liquid. She permeates every crack and soaks every fiber, leaving a residue wherever she goes. She is hard to remove and constantly reminds us of our past with scrapbook like clarity. Her sister **Humiliation** loves to tag along and often drags **Depression** around to make things worse.

<u>**SPITE**</u> – This red-hot viper gets tangled in messes with all the **Bullies**. She spends a lot of time with her sister **Vanity**. Together, they spew derogatory things at you to make you cry.

<u>**VANITY**</u> – Lovely on the outside and hollow on the inside. She spends time with her sister, **Spite**. Anyone not passing compliments to her, will feel her sisters' wrath. She will resort to almost anything to fill her emptiness.

<u>**WORRY**</u> – This **Bully** is like a perpetual storm cloud that hovers over you pointing out everything that could possibly go wrong. As part of **FEAR's** posse, when they are together, you can become immobilized by the negative possibilities.

Now that you have met a few of the **Bullies** that reside in your head, along with the cohorts and comrades they hang out with, you might start to understand that when they take up residence in your **Headspace**, their damage starts immediately.

One of the **Big 3** deserves a chapter of her own and I call her... the **Bully of Bullies**.

Chapter 15
The Bully of Bullies

"Shame is a liar and a story stealer."
—Brené Brown

Now that you are familiar with some of the **Bullies** and their **Buddies**, I want to highlight a very sneaky and dangerous **Bully** that has the ability to permeate your defenses if you don't know about her. Her name is **Shame**.

Shame is the Bully of Bullies
because she is often the root cause of their existence.

Shame was the catalyst for **Freddie** becoming **FEAR**.
- **Freddie** felt **Shame** because he was not wanted by his father.
- **Freddie** felt **Shame** because his uncle pushed him around.
- His mother felt **Shame** that his father didn't stay with her.
- His mother felt **Shame** that she didn't protect her son.

Freddie was surrounded by **Shame** which is an ever present yet elusive **Bully**.

Shame is like liquid. She infiltrates every crack and crevice. She is also absorbed into every fiber, leaving a residue wherever she goes. Even when you think she is gone, you find remnants of her clinging to the other **Bullies**

hanging around in your **Headspace**. She enslaves us by reminding us of a past that we don't want to remember.

When **Shame** is present, she is never alone. She is always surrounded by an arsenal of **Bullies** that will locate every vulnerable place you have and attack them all at once.

If you want to understand this, take a moment to privately think of something you are truly ashamed of. Not that time you cheated on a test when you were in 6th grade, although I understand that might still haunt you a bit, but something you are truly ashamed of.

Have you ever:

- Betrayed the trust of a friend or loved one?
- Cheated on your spouse or significant other?
- Intentionally hurt someone or damaged their property?
- Lied about something you don't want anyone else to know?
- Done something that is morally or ethically against your values?
- Stolen something or borrowed something you "accidentally" never returned?
- Had something awful happen to you that you have convinced yourself is your fault?
- Blamed someone for something you did, or allowed an innocent person to be blamed?

Maybe something else came to mind, or maybe this section made you really uncomfortable. You may have hidden that secret in some dark dungeon that is locked tight and you didn't want to think about it. That is **Shame**, and she has a hold on you.

You can pretend you don't remember those things, but if they happened, **Shame** is in your **Headspace**. You may think you have her tucked away, but she is fluid. That door doesn't stop her or keep her confined. She can seep out and permeate any space she wants to. The only thing that will remove her is facing her head on, so you can **Evict** her. I know she is scary and you might consider just keeping her under wraps, but that is not a solution and it won't work.

If we successfully **Evict** all the other **Bullies** but leave **Shame**, she will serve as a prop keeping the door wide open for all the **Bully Buddies** to come back in. She may allow them access one at a time, or she might have a **Shaming Slam** and invite them all back at once.

We need to *Evict the Bully in Your Head* and allow the **Headspace Heroes** to do their job.

We all have a past and all of us feel **Shame**. It is what you choose to do with it, that makes the difference in who you are and who you will become. Remember, the **Headspace Heroes** aren't going to take your past away, they will help you accept who you were in the past, while growing to become someone stronger in the future.

I don't want you to be a slave to **Shame** anymore, so I am going to share a story with you of how my sister taught me to "**Let it in.**"

Life Lessons in a Convertible

I have lived in California since I was in 3rd grade. The weather here is beautiful, and sunny is a word that accurately describes most days. However, that doesn't mean it is always warm. As a matter of fact, at night, it can get downright cold. If you head down to the beach, the temperature drops even more. (For those of you reading this in cold weather climate, I recognize that our cold is barely a chill for you. However, I promise the analogy will still work, so keep reading.)

For my sister Sue's 16th birthday, she got a light blue 76 VW Convertible. One of the thrills of having a convertible is driving with the top down... just because you can. I remember many nights heading down to the beach during winter with the top down and the heater blasting to keep warm. I'm laughing out loud at the absurdity of it, but we LOVED IT and it was part of who we were!

As we traveled down the road, wind whipping through our hair, blankets piled high and heater blasting, I remember my body slightly convulsing because of the cold.

"I'm freezing!" I would say, as my teeth chattered to a familiar song, my body shaking violently as I tried to fight off the cold.

My sister, who was driving, never seemed to be as cold as I was. I remember her saying one day...

"Let it in."

"What?" I asked with an incredulous tone in my voice.

"Let it in. Don't fight the cold, just let it in."

Still perplexed, I wondered what in the world did that meant. Take off the blankets and freeze myself so I was numb and couldn't feel it anymore? That sounded crazy.

She could tell I was still confused, and she continued to explain until I finally understood. I was so busy "fighting" the cold that it had control of me. It had my body moving to its rhythm instead of washing over me.

> *When I fought the cold, it would always win. No matter how hard I tried to fight it, I was still cold; my teeth would chatter uncontrollably, and my body would shake. When I stopped fighting it and let the cold "in," I stopped shivering. It was still cold, but I was free from the grip it had on my body. The more I practiced feeling the cold and not fighting it, the easier it became.*

> *It was incredibly freeing, and I recognized it as a viable solution to other situations in life.*

If you have experienced the difference between "fighting" the cold and "letting it in," you will recognize dealing with **Shame** is the same way.

The key was Feeling instead of Fighting.

Fighting it is like pretending there is nothing to deal with. It's more like stuffing it. Just like your body reacts by shivering when you try to fight the cold, your body will react to stuffing your **Shame**. You may feel dizzy, get cold sores, break out with acne, feel stressed out, or even get sick. When you allow yourself to stop fighting the **Shame**, just like with the cold, it loses its power over you.

Feeling it reminds us to let it flow over us while we deal with the emotions. When you feel the **Shame**, just like you feel the cold flowing across your body, you are not validating it. You are acknowledging that it was there while you expose light to any area that was previously cloaked in darkness.

When we turn the light on it, we often find it isn't as scary as we thought. We have just been hiding from it for so long that we forgot how to handle it and we may have forgotten how strong we really are.

I try to apply this same "Let it in" philosophy to any of the **Bullies** who infiltrate my **Headspace**:

When I am confronted with a **Bully**, I accept how I am *feeling*, and let it wash over me, so I can move forward. If I choose to *fight* it, I get stuck in the **Weeds of Wallowing**, reliving the **Pain** which doesn't serve me well and it won't serve you well either.

My Shame

I will share more details about this story in an upcoming book in the **#12Books12Months** series, but I wanted to give you a brief summary of a time when I felt **Shame** to make my point.

I was married for a very short time when I was 21. I made the unfortunate choice to marry an alcoholic/drug addict, which you may realize, significantly complicates a relationship.

One day, my husband came home and to make a long story short, he basically said this:

"I don't love you anymore."

"I'm not sure I ever did."

"I had an affair…"

"…and I want a divorce."

I was shocked to say the least. I thought we were happy… OK, I thought he was happy. I knew I was a stressed-out mess. Never sure where he was or what he was doing was difficult, but when he would come home late I would **Worry**. It wasn't a fun place to be, but I thought I could "handle it." After all I had put up with and all I had done to make him happy… … I was being dumped… by a drug addict.

Please don't get the wrong impression here. I was a very accomplished 21 year old homeowner/entrepreneur with a serious case of **NES,** so my **Self-Esteem** hit bottom. My pursuit of being the "perfect" wife, to someone who desperately needed me, didn't even work.

To add to the story, he also charged up all my credit cards and depleted our bank account before he left.

It felt like a replay of my childhood. The **Shame** of feeling like I was **Not Enough** came flooding back and hit me like a tidal wave.

I felt **Shame** that he left.

I was **Not Good Enough**.

I felt **Shame** that he cheated on me.

I was **Not Pretty Enough**.

I felt **Shame** that he took my money and charged up my credit cards.

I was **Not Smart Enough**.

Shame's message was like a blast from my past. She was reminding me of what I had been running from… that **I was Not Enough**.

This breach in trust caught me so off guard that it left an unobstructed path for **Shame** to allow her **Bully Buddies** to show up in **Brigades.**

<u>First Wave</u>: **Pain, Humiliation, Anxiety,** and **Overwhelm.**
<u>Second Wave</u>: **Anger, FEAR** and **Resentment.**
<u>Third Wave</u>: **Discouragement, Depression, Despair** and **Loneliness**

I didn't intentionally allow them in, I just didn't have the strength to keep them out because I was too busy *fighting* and hiding my **Shame** instead of *feeling* it and letting it flow over me.

I lost weight, couldn't eat, couldn't sleep, and I was too proud to tell my parents or my staff what was happening. I would sit in my office all day with the door closed crying. I was engulfed in **Shame** about a situation that I accepted **Blame** for even though I had no control over it.

That was a very dark time that I wasn't sure how to get through. With the help of a good friend who allowed me to stay with her while I regrouped, I was able to dress those wounds and embrace a new **Perspective.**

I was ready to face **Shame** head on and replace her vindictive lies with the **Truth** of the **Headspace Heroes**...

Chapter 16
Headspace Heroes

> *"A Hero is an ordinary individual who finds the strength to persevere and endure in spite of overwhelming obstacles."*
> —*Christopher Reeve*

Who are the **Headspace Heroes**? They are the superheroes of the mind that come in and rescue you from the **Bullies** in your head. They keep your **Headspace** in check and provide positive reinforcement to keep your mind free from the **Bully Brigade**. Let me introduce you to some of these **Heroes**. Let's start with the **Captain** of the team:

CAPTAIN:

<u>CONFIDENCE</u> – **Captain Confidence** is the leader of the **Headspace Heroes**. He is strong, but like any muscle in your body, he needs to work out every day. **Confidence** has an estranged twin named **Cockiness**. Although they are identical, it is easy to tell them apart because **Confidence** does not feel the need to call attention to himself. His best friend is **Corporal Courage** and the two of them typically deliver the **Eviction Notices**.

CORPORAL:

<u>COURAGE</u> – **Corporal Courage** is powerful, but when he is teamed up with **Captain Confidence**, trying to get in their way is like trying to stop a tidal wave of

support. His purpose is to empower you and the **Headspace Heroes** to face the **Bully Brigade** head on, so he and **Captain Confidence** can deliver the **Eviction Notices**.

VOLUNTEER ARMY:

<u>ACCEPTANCE</u> – This **Hero** enjoys spending time with her big sister **Love** and her best friends **Understanding** and **Empathy**. **Acceptance** chooses to embrace everyone for who they are, not what others think they should be.

<u>BELIEF</u> – She is a strong and focused friend, not letting anything sway her. She follows in the footsteps of her older brother **Courage**, and gravitates away from her estranged little brother, **Doubt**.

<u>COMPASSION</u> – Although this **Hero** is often confused for being weak or gullible, she is actually very strong. She spends a lot of time with her sister, **Kindness**.

<u>DETERMINATION</u> - This burly **Hero** is built like a Mac Truck. He charges at things with his strength and is usually found with his fraternal twin, **Drive**, or protecting his little sister, **Persistence (Persi)**.

<u>DIGNITY</u> – She encourages you to always hold your head high and to know your value. She spends most of her time with her sisters **Respect** and **Grace**, and with their brother, **Honor**.

<u>DRIVE</u> – As the slightly older twin, **Drive** is often leading his brother **Determination** and coaching his little sister, **Persistence**. **Drive** is a speedy little **Hero** that moves around like a Ferrari consuming rocket fuel.

<u>EMPATHY</u> – She has a twin brother **Apathy** who mistakenly refers to her as weak. The truth is **Empathy** has incredible strength to see through the cruelty of others and recognize the **Pain** that influences their behavior. **Empathy** teams us with **Forgiveness** to keep your **Headspace** clear from the **Bully Buddies**.

<u>ENCOURAGEMENT</u> – This **Hero** is a cheerleader who constantly reminds you that "**You Can Do It.**" When **Encouragement** and **Belief** are together, they keep you moving toward your goals!

<u>FAITH</u> – Lighthearted committed, focused, and true, **Faith's** goal is to strengthen the core of who you are. Her cousin is **Belief** and her best friend is **Hope**.

<u>FORGIVENESS</u> – She is one of the most powerful but sometimes forgotten of the **Heroes**. Just like a muscle, if you don't exercise **Forgiveness**, she will become weak. She needs her strength because she frees you from carrying the

Bullies like **Anger** or **Resentment** around. **Forgiveness** is best friends with **Peace** and together they are the **Headspace Cleaning Crew**, removing all the debris, to make the space inhabitable for the **Headspace Heroes**.

FRIENDSHIP – This is a rare **Hero** that some have rejected because of imposters pretending to be her. You can identify **Friendship** by the other **Heroes** she hangs out with like **Belief, Acceptance, Kindness** and her best friend, **Loyalty**.

GRACE – Quiet, confident, and always ready to give someone an opportunity. **Grace** is the **Hero** we all look for when we have made a mistake. She often spends time with **Acceptance** and with her sisters **Dignity** and **Respect**.

HAPPINESS - He is the life of the party and perpetually reminds you of the **Bright Side** of things. **Happiness** is a bundle of energy that celebrates everything, so he can get worn out fast. He loves his sisters, **Peace, Love, and especially wants** to grow up to be just like his oldest sister **Joy**.

HONOR – This tall, proud soldier is the brother of **Dignity, Grace,** and **Respect**. He spends most of his time with **Truth** and will stand guard over any **Hero** and protect them with his life.

HOPE – She is recognized as one of the most powerful **Heroes** of all time. **Hope** is sweet, her spirit is contagious and inoculates people infected with **NES**. A shot of **Hope** can rejuvenate a crushed spirit and revive any **Hero**. Her best friend is **Faith** and she has an estranged brother named **Despair**.

INTEGRITY – This frontline **Hero** spends time with **Truth** and **Honor** and this trio is always ready to defend. If you forget to engage these **Heroes**, you may win your battle, but you will lose the eventual war.

JOY – This **Hero** is rarely without her sister, **Peace** or her best friend **Kindness**. When things feel chaotic, turn to this trio and they will guide you through any challenge.

KINDNESS – The sister of **Compassion** and a sweet girl who enjoys spending time with **Friendship**. She loves to do random things for others. She spends her days looking for ways to make other people feel better about themselves. She is often found spending time with her best friend, **Joy**.

LOVE – The oldest sibling of **Peace, Joy,** and **Happiness,** she provides guidance and direction for all the **Headspace Heroes**. Although she is not physically the strongest **Hero**, she is the most powerful and generous **Hero** there is.

LOYALTY – Her best friend is **Friendship** and the two they often team up with **Honor** to defend you when the **Bully Brigade** tries to attack your character.

MOTIVATION – **Motivation** looks deep inside you to find what matters most and keeps that in front of you like a beacon of **Hope**. He fans the flames of your fire to keep you moving forward. He is susceptible to the negative influences of the **Bully Brigade** and needs the other **Heroes** around to keep him on track.

PATIENCE - Her best friend is **Empathy** and they spend a lot of time together listening, to help people work through difficult situations. Her twin brother called **Impatience** who tries to tag along wherever she goes and is always upset because he is not allowed to hang out with the **Headspace Heroes**.

PEACE – Although she seems like a docile **Hero**, **Peace** is incredibly strong and doesn't' allow cruelty to affect her. Her best friend is **Forgiveness** and together they clean up the debris left after the **Eviction Notices** have been delivered. Her sisters are **Joy** and **Love** and her brother is **Happiness**. They are a close family that brings strength wherever they go.

PERSISTENCE – Also called **Persi**, she is the little sister of **Drive** and **Determination**. Her source of strength is spending time with **Belief** and her cousin, **Faith**.

PERSPECTIVE – **Perspective** has been around almost as long as **Wisdom**. The two often sit and discuss things to help the other **Heroes** grow and continue to become stronger. They can maintain conversations that continually benefit each other and the rest of the **Heroes**.

RESPECT– She is strong and bold, yet quiet and demure. She is a support system that reminds us: **Don't Accept Unacceptable Behavior**. She is a steady source of comfort and support to her sisters, **Dignity** and **Grace**, and is proud to lead the way for her brother, **Honor**.

SELF – This is a **Double Agent**. **Self**, starts out neutral and can go either way. If raised by the **Headspace Heroes**, you will see a positive **Self-Image**, healthy **Self-Esteem** and honorable **Self-Control**, but if the **Bully Buddies** raise him, things go downhill fast.

TRUTH – Close companions with **Honor**, the two create a support system that fortifies and strengthens. **Truth** is soft, transparent, and tempered with **Love**. She is never harsh or brutal, like her estranged brother **Deceit**.

UNDERSTANDING – She is often called weakness by those who are confused about how powerful this **Headspace Hero** is. She spends time with **Empathy** and **Compassion** and provides clarity to others.

WISDOM – Preparing the **Heroes** for the inevitable battles that are coming, **Wisdom** is a sage that provides guidance and reminds them of how to stay committed to becoming the best version of themselves even when the **Bully Brigade** tries to derail them.

I hope you can see the power of engaging the **Heroes**. and how they can defend your **Headspace** against the **Bullies** that have already hunkered down inside. They are strong and committed to protecting you.

There is so much more I want to tell you now that you understand these rivals. For now, I want you to look at your life just in case the **Bully in Your Head** wants to keep you quiet.

Chapter 17
The "bully" in Your School

> *"If you've witnessed bullying or if you're being bullied,*
> *tell somebody you trust. Tell mom and dad.*
> *Tell your counselors or your coaches.*
> *Tell your teachers. Tell an adult who you trust."*
> —*Stephanie McMahon*

Now that you have met some of the **Headspace Heroes**, we can now address some potential pitfalls that could prevent you from participating in the **Bully Eviction** that we will soon be conducting. I want to take a look at some things that might be occurring in your life that you may not be sure how to handle.

"bullies" in your Life

No matter your age, preteen to senior citizen, there are **bullies** that can infiltrate your life. I've committed this chapter to discussing them, understanding them, and supporting you in your next action steps. For those of you experiencing actual **bullies** in school, home, work or life in general, I want to talk to you directly, about handling the stigma attached to it, and the **Eviction Process**. Let's start with school.

Children and School

Age is not a determining factor in being bullied or becoming a **bully**. **Bully Births** can happen at any age, so pretending very young children aren't contributing to the problem is naïve at best.

Toddlers have been seen bullying other kids on playgrounds or in daycare. It is possible they have been subjected to an older sibling's controlling behavior, or perhaps they are just trying to learn the basic skills of sharing, conflict resolution, and patience. The reasoning behind the aggressive or abusive behavior is less important than the commitment to immediately correcting it.

There will always be differences with children learning how to share and navigate friendships, but it is imperative we notice what is happening with our children by asking questions and verifying the answers. There is no need to be paranoid, but you should trust your instincts and investigate any behavior that seems odd.

Your research may turn up that your child has learning disabilities, **Asperger's** or another condition preventing them from feeling successful in school. As we will discuss later, you may even find that a teacher, family member, or authority figure is causing your child to struggle.

You may discover that people are teasing your child about something they are sensitive about like wearing glasses, having acne, their weight, or perhaps a scar or birth mark. Children that are insecure, or are being bullied by someone else, will usually pick the next most vulnerable target on the social food chain to start tormenting. They have the false impression that this will relieve some of the pressure they are feeling. That means your precious child could start emulating that behavior as, well to relieve the **Pain** they are experiencing. We want to remind them:

"Hurting others doesn't heal you."

Elementary, Middle, and High School

Moving into each level of school presents its own set of unique challenges. Kids are constantly trying to figure out:

- Who they are.
- What they like.
- Who their friends are.
- Who is safe and who is not.

Children will naturally start to segregate themselves.

- The socially awkward kids will typically gravitate toward being alone or toward other children similar to them.
- The socially aware children who have learned to mimic others, or who have **Confidence**, tend to flock together as the "popular" kids.
- The largest group of kids in the middle, just trying to fit in somewhere. They want to belong, and once they are accepted somewhere, they don't want to lose their place.

As children progress in school, they try to find their "**Tribe**." If they end up with the wrong group, they might find themselves harassing the socially awkward kids to act "cool" or to keep up with appearances. Since differences are not usually embraced in school, children who are deemed "different" often become targeted and bullied. Kids can be cruel and in the children's world of "survival of the fittest," even some of the nice kids participate in some acts of bullying.

Dealing with Differences

Physical differences are visually obvious just by looking at them. Color, race, height, weight, and abilities can all be targets. It is our role as parents or leaders to train our children to see that differences can be fascinating instead of a reason for exclusion.

Unfortunately, we as parents or leaders may be partly responsible for what is transpiring.

As a parent, do you ever find yourself commenting about another person in front of your children? Do you talk about their weight, height, fashion sense, haircut, attitude or other characteristics?

When we do that, we are inadvertently setting an example for our kids. You may not realize it, but your judgment of others' attitudes and behaviors in some way validates the behavior they see at school, and subconsciously emphasizes that it is OK to treat others in that manner.

Remember, I am not judging you, I am simply trying to help you see all the ways the **Bully** can infiltrate our **Headspace**. He will encourage those thoughts that run through our minds and influence them to tumble out of our mouths.

I understand that sometimes you are responding to someone else's conversation, and that it is meant in jest. The problem lies in the fact that they are very impressionable, and you are, As Dr. Phil says, "Writing on the tablet of who they are."

The **Bully in Your Head** may try to convince you that this behavior is harmless fun, but it isn't. It continues to give the **Bully** a foothold in your **Headspace** and may cause a **Bully Birth** in someone else. It may also be a sign of you trying to overcompensate about some inadequacy in your life, which as we discussed is a symptom of **NES**.

I told you, the **Bully** is powerful and has one goal: to stay firmly planted in your mind where he can continue to **Control** you. So, forgive yourself if you have acted that way in the past. Commit to no longer participating in that behavior and focus on the **Eviction Process** so you can be free of the **Bully Brigade** and their destructive behavior.

Visual Differences

Did you have any differences as a child that others brought to your attention?

- Did you wear glasses or have braces?
- Were you really tall or short?
- Did you have any big or small features that were noticeable?
- Was school either very easy or incredibly difficult to you?
- Were you uncoordinated or clumsy?
- Did you have a speech impediment or other noticeable difference like a facial tick, a lazy eye, a gap in your teeth, or a limp?
- Was there anything about yourself, your surroundings, or your situation you wished you could change?

I am betting you answered "yes" to at least one of those questions. For those of you who have already graduated from high school, I want you to think back to your middle to high school years for a minute. We ALL have differences, and most of us during those formative years are uncomfortable about what they are. It is how we handle them that determines how others will react.

For instance, if you had braces you may have been self-conscious if someone jeered at you and called you "Brace Face" or "Railroad Tracks." If not you, perhaps you had a friend that experienced this. My point is that there were probably popular kids in your school who had them, too. Dental alignment is a common thing during adolescence and it doesn't segregate by any type of popularity boundaries. The difference between these two groups of children is one of the **Headspace Heroes…Confidence**.

One of the greatest strengths and anti-bullying measures you can initiate with yourself, and teach to your children, is Confidence.

When **Confidence** is around, it doesn't matter what insecure people say. This **Headspace Hero** isn't swayed by comments and negativity. He stands strong and **bullies** don't typically harass confident people.

Mental or Emotional Differences

Now that we explored some of the physical attributes people notice, let's understand the unseen ones.

Learning Disabilities or Challenges

Although the medical field calls them disabilities to provide resources to people that are affected, I personally see them as "differences", not disabilities. Although the way information is processed is not standard and often considered "quirky", that nonlinear thinking is often what is needed to solve a difficult problem. I think **#QuirkyIsCool!**

> **Learning Disabilities** are present in approximately ten percent of the population and people often struggle with certain subjects or situations. We can't externally see what is going on inside their brains, but we know something is different. We may notice them getting anxious or overwhelmed if they need to participate in an activity that will highlight an area they feel weak in. That hesitation could have them labeled as "different" and opened the opportunity for the bullying process.

> **Dyslexia** for instance is an alternate style of thinking. The brain views and interprets data differently which can cause a disruption in reading and receiving information. The students level of intelligence doesn't change. The child with **dyslexia** is just as smart other children but will struggle to learn things in the traditional manner.

> My son is dyslexic, and one of the unique things I've noticed is that he sees puzzles and problems differently. I think in a linear format to come up with conclusions and he comes up with brilliant "out of the box" solutions that I may never have thought of. It is important to recognize differences and embrace them as a contributing factor to who we are, not shun them as inappropriate, or irrelevant. This is another reason we must **Evict the Bully**, because his lies will infect you with **NES** and can falsely lead you to believe that you are broken, when the **Truth** is, **#YouAreEnough** just the way you are.

Famous people with Dyslexia: include, Tom Cruise, Orlando Bloom, Jim Carey, Walt Disney, Chef Jamie Oliver, Steven Spielberg and Shark Tank's Daymond John.

ADD and ADHD

Both **ADD** (Attention Deficit Disorder) and **ADHD** (Attention Deficit Hyperactivity Disorder) create noticeable differences in ability of students to focus or pay attention to specific tasks or duties. Due to this, and the inability to sit still without fidgeting, they are sometimes labeled hyper or the "Class Clown" because they use humor or the chance to entertain as a way to hide their distractibility instead of embracing it. This groups tends to move quickly in mind and/or body. Once they recognize and harness their differences, they offer amazing contributions.

Famous people with ADD or ADHD: Sir Richard Branson, Will Smith, Justin Timberlake & Jim Carey.

Autism Spectrum Disorders (ASD)

Note: Although in 2013 when the 5ᵗʰ version of the Diagnostic Manual was published, many of these terms were changed, I am going to use the previous terms due to my own familiarity with them as well as the fact that many organizations and groups still use them today to provide more clarity.

You may be familiar with the **Autism Spectrum** which encompasses varying degrees of differences. It is widely believed that people on the **Spectrum** have above average intelligence but struggle with delivering the information they want to share or asking the questions they need to ask. The conclusions people with **ASD** come to, and the way they get there, are often completely different than the average person but the answers are sometimes superior to the standard style of thinking. Because their brains receive and process the data differently. they may have difficulty sharing their thoughts and are often labeled as "weird," which offers other children the opening to make fun of, tease, or torment them.

Asperger's Syndrome is a very high functioning title on the spectrum. They are often incredibly intelligent, but they lack the ability to cognitively share the information they are producing in a way that is simple for others to understand. This leaves **Aspies** at a communication disadvantage.

They are more notably different for the following reasons:

- They are typically challenged with making direct eye contact.
- They also don't enjoy as much physical contact.
- They have difficulty reading social cues.
- They are less aware or unaware of spatial boundaries and proximity to others.

- They have a tendency to focus on topics of interest in an overzealous manner called **Perseverating**.
- They tend to have a concrete literal style of thinking which some can interpret as sarcastic or rude which can get them again labeled as obnoxious or "difficult."

Example: If a child asks the teacher, "When are we reading our story?" and she replies, "This afternoon." It would not be uncommon for a child with **Asperger's** at 12:01pm to say, "It's story time!" In effect, 12:01pm is **after** *noon* and therefore in a concrete literal style thinking, he/she is correct. Since typical vernacular suggests, afternoon is any time after 12:00 PM. A teacher might consider this behavior disruptive and rude. It may even upset the other children because the child was wrong and inadvertently got them excited about the activity.

The **Asperger's** child starts to feel insecure because he has made a mistake... but, he doesn't even know how or why one was made.

That can make things more challenging for those supervising because these children navigate the world a bit differently and require explanations and patience that aren't usually required in a classroom setting. If we teach our children to be aware of differences and guide them to reach out in **Compassion**, we will start changing the world, one interaction at a time.

Many of the differences in **Aspies**, have to do with creativity and expression.

Famous people with Asperger's: Dan Aykroyd, James Durbin and Courtney Love
Famous people suspected to have had Asperger's: Mozart, Michelangelo, Abraham Lincoln, Thomas Jefferson, and Albert Einstein.

Developmental Delays

Some situations deal with both the physical and emotional communication and that puts this set of individuals in the crosshairs of the bullies as a release for some of their frustration.

Down's Syndrome, for instance, has obvious details that manifest on the outside such as facial features, speech patterns, etc. These differences often make these children the super targets. If you are the victim of bullying, it is easy to redirect the **Abuse** to an easier target, like someone with Down's Syndrome. A child with Down's is even less likely to be prepared to handle the abusers.

It doesn't mean that your child is deliberately mean. We have to recognize the other children are just trying to survive as well. It is our responsibility to train them to engage the **Headspace Heroes** and teach them to strengthen those muscles, so they can stand strong with **Confidence**

As a parent with a child that has experienced excessive bullying, I understand the emotions and the instinct to defend your child. We are called to protect them, and we should. My point is that we can protect them AND make a difference without blaming others or being resentful of the children who are tormenting ours. I know that sounds difficult and with the voice of experience I can tell you it is. But, when you choose to **Evict the Bully** and engage the **Headspace Heroes**, we can support our children while setting an example on how to handle these situations.

Remembering the chapter called The **Art of Empathy**, we should peek **Behind the Curtain** to see if we can help the child who is bullying as well as correct their **Unacceptable Behavior**. Showing **Empathy** for their circumstances in no way makes us tolerant of the behavior. The behavior must stop immediately and there should be consequences. Those consequences should require the **bully** to get counseling if necessary and participate in supervised opportunities for them to understand the child they have injured.

Teaching someone Empathy
is a much more effective way to change their behavior,
because it changes their heart.

#QuirkyIsCool

We talked about kids being quirky and now we need to embrace the #**QuirkyIsCool** philosophy. That means we not only need to recognize, but embrace the differences in ourselves, our friends, and our children. When we allow ourselves to be authentic, we will find our **Tribe** and connect with people who instinctively understand who we are. I have an entire book coming out about that later in this series called it *OWN IT! How to Step Up and Stand Out*: (#**QuirkyIsCool** & Normal is so…*Yesterday*.)

For now, just remember that you can't please everyone, and neither can your children. Allow them space to explore their differences to figure out who they are, and we will have generations of happy, well-adjusted adults raising children who are accepted for who they are.

It is time to embrace your uniqueness and remember… #**QuirkyIsCool**.

We will talk about solutions in an upcoming chapter, but for now we need to expand upon the other **bullies** we experience in our day to day lives.

Chapter 18
The "bully" in Your Life

"The people who are bullying you,
they're insecure about who they are,
and that is why they're bullying you...
They desperately want to be loved
and be accepted, and they go out of their way
to make people feel unaccepted so that they're not alone."
—*Madeline Petsch*

Now that we understand what happens with bullying at school, it is important to recognize that although the children can be incredible cruel, they are not the only ones that are causing the problem...

Unhappy Teachers create Bully Births

Hindsight is of course 20/20 and if I have taught you anything so far, it is that you have to forgive yourself for things from the past. You can use them as **Stepping Stones** for the future to grow yourself and to help someone else. You cannot allow the **Bullies** of **Judgment**, **Doubt**, or **Regret** to plague you. I recognize that is easier said than done, so I wanted to share my own story with you to give you **Hope** and **Encouragement**.

When my youngest, Elijah, was in kindergarten, we went to a Parent-Teacher-Child Conference where the kids got to share with us what they were learning in school. There were specialty stations set up as different centers where we could experience a "Day in the Life" of our Kindergartener. Elijah was so proud to show us what he was learning. When we got to one of the tables, his teacher walked up to the table and stood over us, observing the interaction. I watched my son freeze and sit there with wide eyes and nervousness as he looked up at her, praying for approval.

I was perplexed by what I was seeing. I tried to encourage him to show us what they were working on. He hesitated and kept looking up at his teacher, who was now staring down at us. She was tapping her foot impatiently with her arms crossed. The next words out of her mouth were, "We do this every day, Elijah…" and she sat there staring at him like he was incompetent.

He looked at her and then looked at us back and forth. I didn't know it at the time, but I was watching a **Bully Birth** right in front of me. I intervened and started asking questions about the items on the table to distract him from her gaze. He was then able to reengage with us and finish the explanations of the center. When we left the classroom and got in the car, he started slapping his hand against his head saying, "I'm so stupid! I'm so stupid!"

At that moment, my heart broke. I recognized that this was obviously not the first time the condescending gaze, the foot tapping, and the reminder that he wasn't doing something "right" had occurred. This had to have been going on for some time because today was the day, after hearing that, you are **Not Good Enough** message repeatedly, that he *Believed* it and so he *Received* it as truth. There was nothing I could do to stop it. The **Bully** was born.

Just as I can't beat myself up for what transpired there, you can't beat yourself up for what has happened in your child's life or your own life for that matter. We can only move forward and do better in the future.

Authority Figures

Remember not to let the **Bully** of **Judgment** start running the show in your head. I'm not proud of what I am going to share with you, but there is a saying:

"You don't know, what you don't know until you know it."
—Unknown

Well, that was the case for me, "I didn't know what I didn't know." either.

Doctors

When Elijah was very young, he was showing signs of being left-handed. During one of our routine visits, the doctor told us to encourage him to be right-handed. "This is a right-handed world we live in. You need to do him a favor." He proceeded to tell us to remove the spoon from his left hand and put it in his right. I told you… don't judge.

I now know that not allowing my child to develop the skills and abilities that were natural to him was not the best course of action. I would have done things differently if I had been older, wiser, or more experienced in this situation.

In my defense, remember the quote "We are a product of our own environment." from Dr. Phil in a previous chapter? My left-handed sister almost flunked kindergarten because she was unable to cut with her right hand. (I know… go figure!) Knowing that and how difficult it had been for her (they didn't have lefty scissors back then), I was more inclined to trust that this person, with a degree in medicine and a specialist in children, would know more than I would.

When we look at the **Bright Side**, my son has developed some incredible talents when it comes to sports. He shoots a basketball with his left hand, throws a baseball with his right, kicks a football with his left, can bat both ways, plays golf like a leftie…in other words, no one can figure him out. He is a bit of an anomaly on the field, which makes him unique.

It doesn't do me any good to wonder if things would have been different had I not listened to the doctor. It serves me well to see how fantastic he is doing now. I choose to look at the **Bright Side** and continue filling my head with the **Headspace Heroes**, not leaving room for the **Bullies** who are anxious to set up shop in my head again.

Other Authority Figures

We train our children to be respectful of authority figures like the police and firefighters. That is what we were taught, and we pass that down as respect and good manners. Most of the time, it is a positive thing. Teaching them that these public servants can assist them is a good baseline. It is necessary to give them a sense of right and wrong and to give them clarity about the rules.

What about administrators, bosses, and political leaders? We know that respecting authority in these places is important, but what if these leaders want you to violate your ethics or moral code? Are we teaching our children it is OK to say "No" when faced with these dilemmas? Do we accept the behavior ourselves?

What if it is a celebrity, sports hero, or a person you've admired from afar? Does your desire to connect or please them cloud your moral compass?

For me, violating my moral or ethical standards is a DEAL BREAKER no matter who you are.

It is easy to make decisions on what to do when you engage the **Headspace Heroes**. When you ask **Integrity**, **Truth**, or **Honor** about engaging in something that is flagged by your internal radar, their answers will be definitive. When you try to filter it through the **Bullies**, like **Greed**, **FEAR**, or **Intimidation**, your answers will be skewed. We need to make it easy for ourselves and our children to make the right decisions without having to ponder whether the authority figure in question should be trusted.

I know it is easier said than done but if you have been exercising the **Headspace Heroes**, your natural inclination will be to follow their lead and choose to say "No" to inappropriate or unethical behavior or requests.
The next question is, how do you handle it?

- Do you quietly slip away, never to return again?
- Do you make a scene and storm out like a martyr?
- Do you ignore the request and just move forward pretending nothing ever happened?
- Do you report the behavior to people who are in a position of authority that are able to do something about it?

The answers to these questions should become clearer as you engage the help of the **Headspace Heroes**. I shared with you before that your **Heroes** need to work out to stay strong. If you aren't using **Integrity** very often, she will be weak. If **Confidence** and **Courage** haven't been called on, they will not be at optimal strength. So, start practicing now in your everyday life.
Try this exercise: (You can download a **Headspace Hero Journal** (**HHJ**) at **www.VickiFitch.com/ETB**)

Read the list of **Heroes** every morning and engage your active thoughts to strengthen them. Read them again at night before you go to bed and make a note of which ones you used today and which ones you are struggling with.

The harder part of that exercise is to see which **Bullies** were present during the day, but you should make this a nightly practice. Which **Bullies** got to you today and which **Headspace Heroes** will be the most helpful with the **Eviction**? Make a conscious effort to engage these **Heroes** the following day.

This may sound silly to you, but it is part of the steps to **Evict the Bully** and it is a very effective tool. You need to know your friends… and your foes.

You have probably heard the phrase, "What you think about, you bring about." So, if you think about **Honesty**, **Integrity**, **Kindness**, **Confidence**, and **Courage**, do you think it will have a more positive effect on you than **Doubt**, **Anxiety**, **FEAR**, and **Frustration**? The answer should be obvious. In case it is not, do an experiment. Focus on the **Headspace Heroes** one day and only hang out with them. Then, the next day, focus on the **Bullies** like **Jealousy**, **Envy**, **Resentment**, **Pride**, and **Shame**. Note in your **HHJ** which day you felt better. I think you know the answer but writing it down will help you remember.

Family

What do you do if the authority figure in question is family? This person could be an older sibling, a parent, cousin, or grandparent. We teach our children to listen to their elders, which includes older siblings that might be guiding them or babysitting them. There are plenty of family members who have some form of authority over a child and most of the time, it is acceptable and safe.

Sometimes, it is not.

From an emotional perspective, it can be difficult to see the **Truth** because we don't want to believe that family members could have a different agenda or have a different **Bully** calling the shots. If you have been living with your own **Bully** for so long that your **Filter** is dirty, and you are having a hard time discerning **Unacceptable Behavior**; or if you feel concerned but are afraid to say something or stop a situation for **FEAR** of offending someone who is innocent, let me stop you right there. "**It is better to be safe than sorry!**" especially when it comes to your child's safety, or your own.

You need to be more concerned
with trusting yourself, your friends, or your children
than you are with offending others.

If you are afraid to get in a car with an older relative, **Trust** yourself and don't get in. If your natural inclination is to believe that others are good, I applaud that, but only if you listen to yourself when you feel something is wrong. Let me share a story with you...

Grandpa's Lovin'

When I was very young, and all the girls in my family were in single digit years, we used to go visit my grandparents on the east coast. My step-grandfather used to give me the **Heebie Jeebies**. I didn't know why, I just knew I wanted to stay away. My mother used to make us go and kiss our grandparents and it was always fine for me to kiss my Nana, but Grandpa made me feel uncomfortable.

He used to make us sit on his lap and then he would say, "Give Grandpa some lovin'." Being obedient, I would run over, give him a kiss on his slobbery wet lips, and run away. If I didn't, he would press his lips against mine and wiggle them back and forth. He would hold me too tight on his lap. I had no idea why I hated it so much or what exactly I didn't like, I just knew I didn't like it. I didn't feel good around him and avoided him whenever possible.

When I was in my late twenties, it finally came out that my Grandpa wasn't a nice man. My sister admitted that he wanted her to pose nude for him while we were staying there at their house. She had kept this secret for over twenty years! She only shared it because my grandmother was in the hospital and we found out that he had left her for her best friend. My sister thought it would make her feel better to know that he was a creep.

We MUST TELL and teach our kids and friends to tell, too. It is better to be embarrassed by a misunderstanding than to allow a **Bully Birth**, or worse, have bad things happen to you, your friends, or your children!

I'm not suggesting that on a slight suspicion, you destroy someone's reputation or call the police. If you have a feeling, talk to someone you trust. If appropriate, have them discuss it with the third party. If it is regarding a minor, decide on what your next action should be.

It is critical here to engage the **Headspace Heroes** and not allow the **Bully** to make the decisions for you. Using the threat of telling to intimidate someone is wrong. Sharing the information that you have without a vendetta and with a desire for the **Truth** should be your objective.

Understanding the power of the **Headspace Heroes**, it is time to recite the mantra we've been weaving throughout this book. **Don't Accept Unacceptable Behavior**.

Chapter 19
Don't Accept Unacceptable Behavior

"We must always take sides,
neutrality helps the oppressor, never the victim.
Silence encourages the tormentor, never the tormented."
—Elie Wiesel

By now, you have started to understand the "**Don't Accept Unacceptable Behavior**" concept. There are a lot of different types of **Unacceptable Behavior** and we are only discussing a few of them here in this book. Just keep in mind, no one has the right to treat you disrespectfully, to yell, scream or demean you, to tease you or taunt you, to touch you without your consent, to try to encroach on your values or morals, or to take things that are not theirs.

Some of these behaviors simply require you to remove yourself from the situation. Then, you just need to do a **Bubble Bump** or escort some of them to the **Restricted Zone**. On the other hand, some of them require a stronger approach.

The ONE VOICE Philosophy

In the last decade, we have seen a rise in people with the strength to stand up for themselves and ban together within our communities. They have raised their voices against oppression, abuse, and injustice. Every movement, no matter where it started, has had something in common—**ONE VOICE** having the **Courage** to make itself heard.

At the end of 2017, the #MeToo movement spread like wildfire. Although it started back in 2006, it caught the attention of the world via social media when multiple people chose to share the difficulties they had experienced in the workplace, specifically addressing people that had sexually harassed them. We need to recognize that victims often "stuff" their feelings of **FEAR** of not being believed or being blamed for what happened. Those stressors encourage silence. That is another important reason we have to share the #**YouAreEnough** campaign around the world. We need to expose **Abuse** where it exists, so we can prevent these **Bully Births** from happening in the first place.

Many consider speaking out a futile effort, and the #MeToo movement gave a voice to millions of people around the world. That **ONE VOICE** gave others the strength to follow suit and share their own stories. Still others recognized they weren't alone and broke their silence. Some reached out for counseling or help, while others followed through with actually reporting the behavior.

The point is, that it only took

- **ONE VOICE** to **Step Up.**
- **ONE VOICE** to **Stand Out.**
- **ONE VOICE** that had the **Courage** to say, I will stand alone if necessary, but I am going to do what is right. I will tell what I know and relieve myself from the burden of carrying this secret. I **Hope** that someone will listen, but I will stand strong with the **Headspace Heroes** even if they don't.

The **Bully in Your Head** doesn't want you to share your secrets. My years in **Al-Anon** taught me,

"You are only as sick as your secrets."

The **Bully** wants you to hold onto them as long as possible because it is his leverage against you. Every time you start to feel courageous, the **Bully** can "put you back in your place" by reminding you of your past mistakes, issues, traumas, and stumbles. It is ammunition to stop you from growing, starting, or continuing the **Eviction Process**.

In this case, that **ONE VOICE** is you. Each time you take your **Super Stance**, flip that wrist and utter the words "**Not today, Bully. Not today!**" You are the **ONE VOICE** in your own life.

Each time you have the **Courage** to **Stand Up** to an injustice in the world done to you or another person, you are acting as that **ONE VOICE** that others may find **Hope** in.

When you recognize that you have value and share this book or these concepts with someone else who is obviously struggling, you are the **ONE VOICE** that is shedding light on the darkness.

It isn't easy being a trailblazer. The terrain is often unknown, but YOU ARE AN EXCEPTIONAL HUMAN BEING! Yes, I was shouting that at you in case the **Bully** tried to plug your ears with his endless prattle about your being **Not Enough**. Remember: #YouAreEnough just the way you are.

I know that growing into the person you want to be looks a little scary, but it is necessary for us to grow so we can thrive. It is your time to become the best version of yourself.

To Tell or not to Tell

All too often, this **Unacceptable Behavior** turns to bullying. It can happen at home, at work, at school, out in public, or in private. Bullying comes in so many forms that certain types of it seem to be "swept under the rug" and never really dealt with. Sometimes, we choose this because it is less of a hassle, less embarrassing, or because we aren't 100% sure that someone will believe us and that would just make it even more humiliating.

We have seen many cases of the **FEAR** of reporting incidents with professional athletes or celebrities. Bill Cosby was one of America's sweethearts. No one wanted to accuse him of the heinous crime of drugging and raping women and yet, after one came forward, more than 59 others followed to claim they too had similar experiences with him. The **Bullies** of **FEAR** and **Humiliation** kept people from telling, and his escapades kept on for over 40 years! Those were some strong, deeply entrenched **Bullies** that were keeping those women silent. This book was written to ensure you become familiar with the **Headspace Heroes** and that you **Trust** them to support you through the process.

We've already been clear throughout this book that the **Bully in Your Head** came from somewhere. It was a birthing process that left a little bundle on your doorstep. You then felt obligated to bring this bundle inside your nice, warm, cozy, and safe **Headspace**.

We've also been clear that the person or people who helped spawn your **Bully**, had some unwanted guests of their own.

Now that we know these things, we need to have a difficult conversation. This is where you need to **Pull Up Your Bootstraps** because standing up for yourself and others takes moxie.

If a person of authority invites, encourages, or insists you do something you don't want to do; or that is against your moral or ethical code, do you just leave and pretend it didn't happen?

What if your boss, teacher, neighbor, relative or public figure wants you to do something and won't take no for an answer? That is bullying or abusive behavior and needs to be addressed.

When someone is abusing you, there is always the dilemma of whether to tell or not.

- There is **FEAR**. What will people say?
- There is **Humiliation**. What will people think?
- There is **Doubt**. Will they believe me? If they do believe me will they now think poorly of me for telling or for "letting" it happen?
- There is **Worry**. Will I lose clients, friends or my job?

If a **bully** at school…

- pushes me,
- threatens me,
- takes my lunch,
- pulls down my pants,
- grabs a part of my body,

do I just take it because the repercussions might be worse? Do I retaliate with mean and ugly words, shake them back, or start yelling at them? Do I just choose to act like it is no big deal and sit in silence?

The **Bullies** have us focus on how others will perceive the information, instead of focusing on what is right. When we engage the **Headspace Heroes** of **Truth**, **Integrity**, **Honesty** and **Love**, the choice is clear. Being a hero isn't always easy, but it is simple. We need to do what is right.

What's Next?

No one likes to be wrong and accuse people of things that were misunderstandings. If you are unsure if you interpreted the feelings, emotions, or objectives of the person incorrectly, you can consult a trusted friend or advisor to get clarity on the situation. We know that we are "A product of our own environment," and therefore subject to viewing everything through our own **Dirty Filter**.

Furthermore, we have existing **Bullies** hanging out in our **Headspace** who will try to twist things and taint them, to make us confused. You are just learning to trust yourself, so it is better to ask someone you know whose opinion you value, instead of ignoring your feelings and just letting it go. So, here are some suggestions to help you decipher the difference and act accordingly.

Step 1: Find a trusted friend or advisor and tell them what happened and how you feel. If you are a child, an adult, needs to stand in the gap to protect you. That is your parents' job. If they are unskilled in this area, there are other resources available. That person should help investigate the situation. Explain what made you feel uncomfortable and try to get clarity to avoid any future misunderstandings.

Please understand this conversation is not meant to decide whether you are right or wrong. You felt how you felt and you have the right to remove yourself from situations where you feel threatened or uncomfortable. You do not have to continue spending time with people who you do not feel safe around. The conversation needs to happen so that an unbiased third party can assist you with the next step if necessary.

Step 2: If it is determined that inappropriate behavior took place, you need to tell the appropriate people, administration, or authorities.

For some of you, the prospect of sharing your concerns or discomfort is overwhelming. This is why I want to help you **Reframe** and look at the situation from a different angle, one that utilizes the **Headspace Heroes**.

We've already determined the reason people **bully** others is because they are housing their own **Bully** and are unsure how to deal with it. In addition, it is very possible that they are being bullied by someone else, which also affects their ability to make good decisions and treat others with **Dignity** and **Respect**. If there is no one who cares enough to intervene, then it will continue from generation to generation. Isn't the right thing to do to share it with someone you trust who can help stop what is happening and prevent future **Bully Births**?

- If you knew a child was being starved, beaten, or abused, would you tell someone?
- If you knew someone was hurt or injured and needed help, would you tell someone?
- If your friends knew that someone was hurting you, would you want them to help you?
- If your neighbors knew a criminal was in your house, would you want them to warn you?

Of course, you would.

You have a desire to help and be helped and we all want friends we can count on.

The first place to start is with you acting like your own best friend. A best friend recognizes your value, speaks kindly, supports you, believes in your **Dreams**, can be counted on to encourage you, and will be there when you need them. Constantly finding your own flaws and then putting them under a microscope so you can point them out in detail is unacceptable. That is sabotage and gives the **Bullies** the opportunity to stay firmly rooted where they are. So ask yourself this question:

Are you treating yourself
how you would want your best friend to treat you?

Next, I want you to look at it from different perspective, as well.

Who is the most important person in the world to you?

Really think about it. Is it a parent? A child? A best friend? A boyfriend or girlfriend? A spouse?

It is important that you think about them for a moment and how much you care about them. If the same thing that happened to you, was going to happen to them, would you stop it if you could? All you had to do to prevent it from happening was to tell someone what happened to you. Sharing other people's inappropriate behavior with the appropriate authority could prevent any future trauma from happening to not only you and the people you know, but others as well.

You would be exercising a host of **Headspace Heroes**, including **Confidence** and **Courage**. That makes you a hero as well.

Protecting others when you can is an important part of **Bully Eviction**. You deserve to be treated well and cared for. You are worth it. This is where I remind you again to be **Part of the Solution**.

The Road to Recovery

I am hoping this book will bring you the **Courage** you need to not only **Stand Up** for yourself, but to inspire those coming after you who are unable to speak up for themselves. This is for the babies in the world who haven't been infected with **NES** yet. This is for the children in the world who are learning to trust their instincts. This is for the adults in the world who are suffering with a whole **Bully Brigade** they don't know how to deal with.

When you bring **Hope** to the party, she can change everyone. She sheds light on the darkness and makes room for the rest of the **Headspace Heroes** to join in. Make a decision today, right now, to no longer accept **Unacceptable Behavio**r... from anyone.

What if the "bully" is YOU?

First, I want to remind you of something that might seem harsh, but it is the crux of this book.

---

*Don't Accept Unacceptable Behavior...
even from yourself.*

While reading, there may have been some parts of this book that upset you and had your feeling upset or uncomfortable. You may have noticed an unsettled feeling or and a recognition that you have participated in some of the unhealthy behavior we discussed here. Some of the stories, examples or questions may have encouraged you to look at little deeper. Now, you aren't sure you like what you see.

There may have been a little gnawing sensation at times, suggesting, even for a second, that YOU are the **bully**, or at least have been in the past.

I know that hurts a little. The first thing I want to do is reassure you that if you have been a **bully** in the past, things can change. You are learning a new way to handle the **Bullies** in your head and if you are continuing to read, you must want to change. That is good news and you need to celebrate that as we set up the new guidelines.

Engage Empathy

If you are the **bully**, let me start out with, "**It's not your fault**." Or perhaps I should say, what happened up until now has been due to your circumstances, but you are now aware of it. If you don't make a change, you are consciously choosing to discard the **Headspace Heroes** and allow the **Bullies** to run free. It is time for you to make the changes necessary to become the best version of yourself, and that doesn't include bullying ever again.

I know there are going to be those of you out there who are not, nor have ever been, a **bully**. You may be yelling at me and telling me that I'm wrong. I am hearing you as well. I know the **Pain** some of the **bullies** have caused you is so monumental that if you could, you would probably reach through this book and **#Fitchslap** me right across the room.

I need to be perfectly clear —I am not in any way, shape, or form agreeing with, condoning, or sympathizing with their behavior. What I am doing is empathizing with their circumstances.

If we knew what the **bullies** in our life had experienced and what caused them to be this way, we might be able to emotionally separate ourselves from the situation long enough to find **Empathy** for them. I know it is difficult when you are looking at circumstances when you've been the victim but try to see it like you do at the movies after you've gotten a look **Behind the Curtain**.

Again, I know this is making some of you upset and after you finish the book, feel free to share your thoughts with me. I am willing to listen, I am willing to hear, and I am willing to change my position, if so warranted. I am simply sharing what I have learned about people and want you to recognize:

"We use Pain as a catalyst for change...
or a catalyst for Blame."

I want to help people use the **Pain** of the past as a catalyst for change. That change is for those that are bullying to recognize their behavior and stop the unhealthy habits; and for those that have been bullied, to let go of the **Anger**, **Blame** and **Resentment** that is eating away at them like a cancer.

"Holding onto Resentment is like taking poison
and waiting for your enemies to die."
—Jen Sincero

Don't take the poison, it is only hurting you. The way to heal, although not popular, is to look on others who have hurt you with **Empathy**. Not as a call to accept **Unacceptable Behavior** but as a way to heal your heart. I understand that there is a time when we need to feel those feelings and work through them. But there is a point where that becomes wallowing, which becomes more of a cancer that can consume you instead of being a defense mechanism to protect you.

Make A Choice

If you have been a **bully** in the past, you were reacting from what you knew. That being said, you have just been made aware of your behavior and where it comes from. Now it's time to make a choice. If you are ready to change, start by saying this to yourself:

I forgive my past mistakes and look forward to my future!

You are now accountable for everything you do, and you need to commit to thoroughly work through the **Eviction Process** and engage the **Headspace Heroes** to be your guide.

Will you make mistakes?

Yes. And if you are part of our **Tribe**, we will try to help keep you in check and accountable. You should apologize to those you have bullied to try to make amends. You also need to apologize to yourself for the terrible way that you treated... YOU.

People who Love themselves, rarely bully others.

I recognize it might be hard for some of you to see where you have been a **bully**. Something is gnawing at you, telling you that this information might be relevant to you, but you can't quite accept it. Just in case that is you, I want to remind you that the **Bully in Your Head** is tricky. He is crafty and cunning. He doesn't want you to believe that the actions you've been taking are wrong, because he wants you to stay stuck, floating aimlessly in the **Sea of Status Quo**. For a moment, I need you to **Step Up** and remember our **Super Stance**.

"Not today, Bully. Not today."

Ask yourself the following questions:

- Do you find yourself yelling at your children, friends at school, or coworkers repeatedly because you had a bad day or are under stress?
- Do you use rude or degrading language toward other people, like calling them, stupid, incompetent, ugly, loser, disgraceful, or any other disrespectful terms?
- Do you visually or verbally judge other people for their race, color, creed, ethnicity, sexual orientation, gender, or differences?
- Do you punish your children out of **Anger** or intimidate them or others with quick threatening movements?
- Do you assert your authority over family, friends, coworkers, employees, or any other group of people you are responsible for, just because you can or to show them "who's boss?"
- Do you find yourself using **Intimidation** as a "weapon," making sure other people know you have either the physical power or authority to do them some sort of harm?
- Do you ever take things from other people without regard for whether they gave you permission or not?
- Do you sneer, eye roll, eyebrow tilt, mock, scoff, or ridicule others in any way to show your superiority, to make them feel bad, or **Doubt** themselves?

None of these, when they take place as an isolated incident, makes you a **bully**. However, repeated behavior, patterns, and others telling you that they feel bullied are good indicators that the **Bully in Your Head** has more **Control** than you might have noticed.

Recognizing your negative behavior patterns is difficult. Please note, we do not want **Shame** to join the **Bully in Your Head**. We want to call on the **Headspace Heroes** like **Determination** to take over and commit to changing that behavior **TODAY**.

As of NOW… as in 5 minutes ago. It is no longer acceptable.

It is time to move in the other **Headspace Heroes** like **Dignity**, **Respect**, **Honor**, **Kindness**, **Love**, and **Friendship**. The **Headspace Heroes** are the solution, not inviting new **Bullies** in to torment you.

What if you can't go on...

Sometimes the **Pain**, pressure or realization of something can put the **Bully Brigade** on a full court press. **Overwhelm**, **Failure**, **Guilt**, **Regret**, **Despair**, **FEAR**, **Doubt** and **Shame** surround you and you feel like you can't handle the pressure.

If you are feeling like you can't go on or know someone who has mentioned this to you, take it seriously. Here is the number for the

National Suicide Prevention Hotline
1 800-273-8255

It is strictly confidential and there are trained professionals there to help you clean your **Filter** and recognize the immense value you bring, just the way you are.

The **Headspace Heroes** are waiting for you. The first one in line is **Hope**. She is followed by **Love**, **Acceptance**, **Faith**, **Forgiveness**, **Grace**, **Peace** and **Understanding** just to name a few. They recognize your value and acknowledge your **Pain**. Give them a chance to help you remember… **#YouAreEnough**.

Chapter 20
#YouAreEnough

"You are absolutely enough, the way you are."
—Laurieann Gibson

#**YouAreEnough**. You might not have heard that a lot during your lifetime. I am betting for most of you, it is more accurate to say that you feel more like the previous chapter, **I Am NOT Enough**, than **#YouAreEnough**. Remember, that doesn't make it true. Forgive the mini soapbox I am about to stand on, but it needs to be said.

You are perfect just the way you are. Not perfect as in flawless, that is an illusion, but you are perfect in the sense that God made you just the way he wanted to. Does that mean all of your previous actions in the past have been exactly what you wanted them to be? No. But it means that your journey through life should be a quest to become the best version of yourself. You should always seek to grow and change to improve, educate, or explore new things - for yourself. Not because someone else or the **Bully in Your Head** thinks you should.

Please understand that last paragraph. The physical attributes and challenges that have been given to you are there for a reason. They are tools in your tool belt to help you become the person you are meant to be.

Before you decide to write me an email that this is contradictory, think about this. When you are born, you have all that God wanted you to have.

The DNA that is included in the one and only you, is there for a reason. You can't stay in that naked, screaming place forever. You have to grow, learn, and explore.

You learn to trust that you will be fed and that you are safe. You learn to explore the space around you. You start to reach, touch and grab. Your physical body starts growing and you learn new skills. You learn to eat by yourself, dress yourself, read, ride a bike, and to communicate with others.

You are constantly changing into the best version of yourself, but **#YouAreEnough** right from the beginning. Are you following me now?

Life is a journey of constant growth. That is where **Wisdom** comes from. If we never choose to expand ourselves beyond where we were, or where we are now, we are doing ourselves a disservice.

#YouAreEnough and I want you to hear it from me. I want you to share it with others! When you see something posted on social media where someone is discouraged, bullied, or struggling, share an encouraging message and use the hashtag **#YouAreEnough** and **#EvictTheBully**. Be part of the movement to help others with the **Eviction Process**. At the same time, you are making our **Tribe** of people that support you, stronger.

If you look back at the **Intimacy Bubbles** for a moment and examine the chart you filled out, there are probably some you may need to rearrange even now. Are there additional **Bubble Bumps** that need to happen? Are there **Bubble Voids** that you want to fill?

One of the reasons we feel so desperate to fill those **Voids** is because inside, **#YouAreEnough** sounds hollow. We mistakenly believe that we need someone in those **Bubbles** to tell us we have value in order to make it true. But, we don't. We need to *Believe* so we can *Receive*.

#YouAreEnough just the way you are.

If you have been watching my **Livestreaming** broadcasts, you already know the song *What Love Really Means* by J.J. Heller, touches my heart every time I hear it. I think it speaks to the wounded child in all of us, who is struggling to understand why we feel empty. The desperate yearning in our heart to embrace the **#YouAreEnough** philosophy is a lack of feeling truly loved by others for who we are, not what we have done, will do, or can do for others.

I will be honest and vulnerable here. This song sings my story. It is my **Pain**. It was my **Bully**. I just wanted to be loved by someone who **Believe**d in me and truly thought that I was "Enough" when they looked at me.
My version of the chorus goes like this:

> *I want you to love **me** for **me**.*
> *Not for what I **have done** or what I **will become**.*

Note: I wanted someone to **Love me,** for **me** (the present). Not for what I **have done** (the past) or what I **will become** (the future). I wanted someone to recognize my value in the present. That is especially hard for others to do, especially when you don't recognize your own value.

If you are somewhere you can get access to the internet, the words are powerful, and I highly recommend you listen to the song. I've provided a link for you on the resources page at **www.VickiFitch.com/ETB**

While you are listening, you might find yourself feeling the same way I did. You may recognize your story. Maybe you will think of how, at some point, you may have given someone else reason to sing this song. **Bully Eviction** is a process. Feel the feelings and use the **Headspace Heroes** to comfort you and ignore the **Bully** and remember #YouAreEnough.

If you have time, click the link on the resources page and listen to the song and ask yourself these questions:

- Did you find yourself in tears while reading or listening to that song?
- Did it mean anything to you?
- Did any of those words or phrases touch or break your heart?
- Did it make you say, "That is me!"

When we have experienced the scenario described in a song, it creates a deeper and more emotional connection for us. If someone else were experiencing it, we would likely feel **Empathy**, and yet for ourselves, we tend to be harsh and judge ourselves instead. We need to treat ourselves with the same **Kindness** and **Respect** we extend to others.

For me, at a certain point in my life, these words rang true with me.

"She's the woman whose husband has run away."

Instinctively, some of us would reach out to comfort her and encourage her during a difficult time. How did she treat herself? Or a better question would be, what lie did the **Bully** try to convince her of?

That if she was thinner, maybe he would have stayed.

She was infected with **NES**. The question we want to ask ourselves is something my dear friend Dale said to me after my husband left.

"Why you wanna love somebody that don't love you?"
—Dale McClain

What an enlightening question to ask.

- Why do we allow our **Self-Esteem** to be controlled by someone else?
- Why does someone else's opinion of us matter more than our own?

The simple answer is **NES**. It seems so easy when you are looking at it from an outside perspective and not from the noisy confines of your brain where the **Bully** is falsely trying to convince you that you are **Not Enough**. Some of us have become very good at caring about other people, but we have completely abandoned ourselves. It is time for us to inoculate ourselves against **NES** and start using the **Headspace Heroes** to influence our thoughts and feelings.

There is a distinct difference between feeling "sorry" for yourself and feeling **Empathy** for the version of you that is either going through this now or has gone through it in the past. If you start feeling sorry for yourself, you will get stuck in the **Weeds of Wallowing**. You may not know this yet, but that location is on the shore of **Fitchslap Island**, which is the place where I get to gently redirect your course when you have gone astray.

When we are under the influence of **NES**, we may allow a full **Bully Beatdown** to occur. If the current version of me, could go back and talk to the younger me, do you know what I would say?

Girl,

Pick your beautiful self up off the floor. Dry those tears, touch up your make-up and look in the mirror. You are smart, talented and amazing. That boy is a fool for letting you go, and he will be kicking himself for the rest of his life. You should be thanking the good Lord for rescuing you from a situation, you may have been stuck in for the rest of your life without His mighty intervention.

Now it is your turn to continue growing into the fantastic woman you want to be. If and when he comes to his senses, you can decide at that time if you are ready to have a conversation with him. That will be on your terms, but for now… you have a glorious life to lead.

No matter what happens, #YouAreEnough just the way you are. You do not need anyone else validating your existence. Be yourself and you will find someone worthy of your Kindness, Love, Loyalty and Friendship. You are the bomb girl!

What man wouldn't want a smart, creative, hardworking partner that knows how to deal with challenges and look for solutions? The skills you bring to the marketplace and relationships are truly noteworthy and it is time for you to start leading the high caliber life you have always dreamed of. The time to start is now!

It is time to rise, to embrace who you are and remember again how to Believe in You!

OK, I am stepping off my soapbox now, but admit it, isn't that the kind of pep talk you need when you are facing trials that feel overwhelming? That is what I call a **Fitchslap**. If you remember from *DS 101*:

A Fitchslap is a public service.
It only comes out when necessary,
it is always done in Love,
and is used to redirect the course
of someone who has gone astray.

Sometimes we need to give ourselves a good **Fitchslap**. It redirects our attention to the good things in our lives instead of allowing us to be **Nudged** off course.

When we start to wallow in our feelings of insignificance or to condemn ourselves for every possible mistake we made in the past, we are encouraging the **Bully Brigade** to stick around while they have a virtual party at our expense. The **Bullies** are up there, keeping score of every move you ever made that didn't turn out the way you wanted it to. They use that as ammunition to attack you at every given opportunity.

Today, I want you to invite **Empathy** to your **Headspace** and forgive the younger you. I don't care if that younger you is from ten minutes ago or ten decades ago. That version still deserves the best you have to offer while we are on our journey to becoming the best version of ourselves.

The ONLY expectation we should have of ourselves and others,
is that we ALWAYS do our best.

Life truly is too short for us to beat ourselves up and echo the insults of our Bully claiming we are **Not Good Enough.** We need to **#EvictTheBully** and remind ourselves and each other **#YouAreEnough**, while we head on over to talk about another bully…the one in our *feed*.

Chapter 21
The "bully" in Your ...Feed

"I am a huge advocate for anti-bullying in our youth.
What I have seen with the rise of social media
is that children are not facing bullying on a playground,
they are facing it on their cell phones."
—Whitney Wolfe Herd

We've talked about all the **Bullies** in your head, the **bullies** in your home, the **bullies** in your school, and the **bullies** in your life, but we need to address another place **bullies** show up… in your feed. We are talking about **Social Media** and **Cyberbullying**.

With all the different forms of digital connection these days, becoming a **Cyberbully** is easier than ever. These cowardly **bullies** can go after you publicly or privately, through social media, texts, email, blogpost comments, or anywhere you might have a presence online.

Since there are literally hundreds of social media platforms, someone can choose to antagonize you at any time, and they can become relentless. Even though you may never meet these people in person, their constant **Criticism** can be a highly effective bullying tactics unless you enlist the help of the **Headspace Heroes**.

Internet

Through this section, it is important that you know that I am speaking from the voice of experience and not from a place of **Judgment**. The online world can be difficult terrain to navigate and I want to help you understand it, so you can make an informed decision on what is best for you and your family. Since it is likely that online, digital, and social media platforms are here to stay, becoming familiar with them, and how to keep yourself and your loved ones safe, is the best remedy.

One of the biggest concerns parents have about allowing their children to use social apps is the **FEAR** of them being bullied, harassed, or victimized by unsavory characters. It is well-documented that bullying can cause people to feel anxious, depressed, and even sometimes suicidal, so it is understandable that parents try to protect their children from the internet and any possible predators.

Since participating in the online space is now considered a social norm, you may be setting your child up for relentless teasing or even ostracization by their peers if they have no access to these social connections. Choosing to stay off the platforms all together, or forbidding your children to get online, can actually make them an even bigger target, since children now use social connection as a primary means of communication. Your refusal to allow them access to their friends may inadvertently encourage their disobedience in a desperate attempt to fit in. If your child chooses to secretly access these platforms, that puts them in an even more vulnerable position.

If something inappropriate happens, or someone is harassing them, they will be far less likely to share it with you aware of the potential repercussions for disobeying. This type of isolation, where children don't feel like they can share the pressures they are feeling, can cause **Depression** and even more drastic thoughts.

When the **Bullies** of **Guilt**, **Doubt**, **Shame**, and **Insecurity** are all attacking your child with a full court press, it creates a lot of emotional pressure. Please understand, I am not suggesting or recommending you substitute my judgment for your own; I am simply trying to share some possible pitfalls for your protection.

Once you recognize that your children are going to learn to navigate the internet with or without you, it might seem prudent for you to consider being involved in the process. That way, you can teach them how to be proactive in learning to protect themselves. Being an advocate for our children oftentimes requires us to move outside of our own comfort zone, which is what joining the digital age may represent for you.

Social Media

A lot of people choose not to participate in **Social Media** for **FEAR** they will make mistakes or that others will make fun of them. Sometimes, they are scared that their opinions won't be popular and therefore will bring them ridicule. Although it is true that there are **Cyberbullies** out there who will choose to be rude, inappropriate, and disrespectful, people also act this way in person. It is important that we recognize the problem is often with the people, not the platform.

Since each social media platform has different nuances, it is recommended that you become comfortable with the social etiquette of each. Understand that it is never acceptable for people to taunt, tease, chastise, or harass you for making a mistake. Only someone being led by the **Bully Brigade** would try to demean your efforts on a platform.

Those led by the **Headspace Heroes** would gently try to help you understand the "Do's and Don'ts" of the platforms. I challenge you to keep that in mind and be a leader in the **Social Media** space that treats others with **Dignity** and **Respect**.

I wrote *DS 301: Using Social Media and Live Video to #RockThatStream* as an easy to understand guide to the major platforms. If you have questions, you can ask them in my Facebook Group, the **Entrepreneurial Rock Stars**. (link to both of these resources at **www.VickiFitch.com/ETB**). We are a helpful group that will try to provide the support you need to have fun exploring the **SM** space.

When you do experience some type of bullying in your feed, you want to recognize there are a lot of hurting people out there looking for a place to vent. There are some simple things to remember to keep yourself off the receiving end of their **Pain**.

1) Learn the **Social Media** etiquette from someone who understands the platforms and can guide you in the right direction. (***DS 301*** and my daily **Livestreams** are a great place to get your answers!)

2) Try to **THINK**, as Alan Redpath suggests, about other people before you post. Use the acronym below:
   - **T** – Is it True?
   - **H** – Is it Helpful?
   - **I** – Is it Inspiring?
   - **N** – Is it Necessary?
   - **K** – Is it Kind?

3) Pose some of your opinions as questions instead of statements, giving others an opportunity to share why they feel the way they do. If it gets heated, you can just say, "Thank you for your perspective. I will think about that." Whether you are thinking positively or negatively about it doesn't matter. You have kept yourself out of the line of fire.

4) Don't engage with people that want to "fight" against your opinion. Some people are "Right Fighters." They only care about being "Right." You will not win with them, so don't try. Just use the quote from #3 above.

5) Don't post controversial, religious, or political posts unless or until you are ready to constructively handle a debate and are OK with the outcome no matter what it is. I don't recommend this step until you are a seasoned pro that is ready to handle the conversation. It is imperative that there are no **Bullies** still lurking in your **Headspace**, because this is exactly the back door, they will be looking for to slip back in.

6) Don't be afraid to report truly harassing posts to the appropriate platform. You have every right to engage in these spaces free from inappropriate behavior, harassment, and bullying.

Social Media platforms are an amazing opportunity for connecting, sharing, and finding a **Tribe** that resonates with you and who you are. When you use them responsibly, you can find a richer, fuller life by experiencing different cultures, perspectives, and opportunities. You may even meet some people that will become truly trusted friends… (ONLY after they have been appropriately vetted by **BOBO** and work their way through the **Intimacy Bubbles** one by one!)

Livestreaming

Livestreaming, also called **Live Video**, is one of the hottest trends in **Social Media**. I broadcast daily on multiple platforms and have built a fabulous following of individuals who enjoy my content and style.

If you are ready to dive in to **Livestreaming**, or if you want to improve your delivery, connection, or conversion, I highly recommend my three-day mini course called **#RockThatStream**. You can get FREE access to it by going to the resources page **www.VickiFitch.com/ETB** and as I mentioned earlier, I have an entire book on **Social Media** and **Livestreaming** as part of the **#12Books12Months** series. These platforms are a powerful place to deliver your message. Learning how to properly engage with your audience will increase your online presence, credibility, and influence.

We also want to recognize that being live is the most vulnerable kind of social media. When **Trolls** can see you, they can point out things you might be uncomfortable with. Having people jump on your platform to tell you their version of how you are **Not Enough** can feel pretty emotional if you are not prepared. It is simply their immature way of trying to get attention. When people are hurting, they look for ways to feel in **Control** of their lives and unfortunately watching others squirm from their cruelty tends to do the trick.

I was really impressed when I saw child actor Lonnie Chavis, do a video on his Instagram channel telling **bullies** who were in his feed to **#FixYourHeart**. They were making fun of the gap between his teeth and was honest that it hurt his feelings but that he could handle it. He went on to remind them that children were hurting themselves over what these **Trolls** were doing. (You can see the clip on my resources page **www.VickiFitch.com/ETB**). His question for them was:

"I can fix my gap... but can you fix your heart?"
—Lonnie Chavis

I applaud his strength of character and his sincere delivery. It was an inspiration. He took a negative situation that was happening to him and used it to take a stand and encourage millions by sharing it on channels.

If you learn how to navigate it properly, **Livestreaming** can not only be a great tool for connecting likeminded individuals, but it can turn into an excellent revenue source, as well. It provides the opportunity for you to find a **Tribe** that cares about you, your cause, your business, and/or your life. With all of this, here are some things I want you to remember on how to handle what I call #TrollPatrol.

#TrollPatrol

In *DS 301* I discuss online bullies, aka **Trolls**, and review their behavior and how to handle them in what I call **#TrollPatrol**. It is basically a way of dealing with their bullying without becoming a **bully** yourself. If you watch my broadcasts, you know that I have also accomplished what I call **#TrollConversions,** where these unruly participants actually become fans and loyal followers – (Jeremy we love you!) Once, I actually received $50 from a **Troll**, so being nice and teaching each other how to be respectful is an important skill.

Until you know how to handle them, you at least need to be prepared for them because putting yourself out there live for everyone to see can be a bit scary. The people who choose to be **Trolls**, don't have the kind of **Courage** it takes to be vulnerable and share themselves, their content and their value with the world. They are so fearful that people will judge them, that they have chosen to stay safely behind their screens playing **Keyboard Coward**. In trying to discourage you, they momentarily feel better about themselves.

Think about how sad that is for a minute. There are actually people out there that have nothing more valuable to do with their time than to spend it hunting for broadcasts where they can try to hurt someone's feelings. When you peek **Behind the Curtain** and engage **Empathy**, it is easier to recognize that they are simply lost, lonely, and in desperate need of guidance and direction.

Sad and insecure people will go to great lengths to feel better about themselves. You should be proud of yourself if you have the **Courage** to **Livestream** and show the world who you are. I have some great tips inside the **#RockThatStream** course to prepare you for going live if you want to be ready. You can also watch some of my previous broadcasts labeled **#TrollPatrol**, or if you are one of my **Entrepreneurial Rock Stars**, post that as a topic you want for the week and we will try to add it in. Who knows, you may even be lucky enough to see a **#TrollConversion**!

Now that we have touched on the numerous types of bullying and how to handle these difficult situations, it is time for us to say "**Goodbye**" to some of the toxic people in your life…

Chapter 22
Dear John...

"You are the average of the five people
you spend the most time with."
—Jim Rohn

You probably know what a "**Dear John**" letter is. In case you don't, it is a letter used to end an existing relationship. The toxic people in your life are not serving any purpose except being resources to the **Bully in Your Head**. It is now time to get our **Bubble Bumps** in gear and execute the first set of **Eviction Notices**.

Let's start with the easiest ones first. Pull out your **Bubble Balance Chart**.

Bubble Stalkers… bye bye!

Bubble Jackers… see ya!

Bubble Invaders… hasta la vista!

As you continue to go down your list this time, you will probably have some additional clarity on who should be moved, escorted, or bumped. Now that you've gotten to know the **Headspace Heroes**, you see what you have been settling for all this time.

The quote at the top of this chapter reminds us that the people we spend the most time with influence who we are and what we do. Jim Rohn made the bold statement that you are the AVERAGE of those five people. If those are high quality people that look at the world with a positive attitude, you are in excellent company. If you are spending time with people who are negative, derogatory, discouraging, needy, and/or foolish, you will find yourself donning a different perspective. I am hopeful that by this point in the book, you are ready to **Stand Up** for yourself, recognize your value and seek out relationships that will help you elevate your life.

After you list out the five people you spend the most time with, ask yourself these important questions:

1) Is this person really adding value to my life?
2) Do I usually feel better about myself after spending time with them?
3) Do I feel uneasy, judged, or **Not Enough** when they are around?
4) Do they typically support my **Dreams** and goals?
5) Do they **Believe** in me?
6) Do they really have my best interests at heart?
7) Do I cringe or roll my eyes when I see them call or send a message?

Don't be embarrassed by your answers. Resolve to make the changes you need in order to support your personal growth. Each of those five people should already be on your **Bubble Balance Chart**, but if not, you should add them now.

The next step is to reexamine your **Bubbles** now that you more clearly understand the process and who you are hanging out with. Is it time to "**Do the Bubble Bump**?"

Maybe you realize that a long-term relationship you are in is not a good fit, but the thought of ending it is overwhelming. Or, what if your best friend is negative and perpetually drains your energy with her criticizing or complaining? I know you may have gotten used to your role as cheerleader, but is it really helping either of you?

I recognize that the thought of **Bubble Bumping** your bestie is a difficult thought and I want to remind you that what you write down doesn't mean you have to execute the directive. It means you are being honest with yourself about the relationships that support you and which ones are not. You may even have to accept the possibility that you are contributing to the dysfunction of the relationship by enabling others.

The purpose of the exercise is to make you aware because,

"You can't change what you don't acknowledge."
—Dr. Phil

To make this a little more palatable, I am going to give you something fun to associate it with. Do you remember a song from the 70's (even if you weren't around then, it is pretty iconic when dealing with anything 70's Retro) by Van McCoy called *The Hustle*? (You can check it out here **www.VickiFitch.com/ETB**.) Anytime you have to take on the unsavory task of removing people from your **Bubbles**, sing that little ditty while you change the words, "Do the Hustle!" to…

"Do the Bubble Bump!"

Listen to the song a couple times and practice your hip check. Then, update your list, get your groove on, and let's **#DoTheBubbleBump** with a good ol' "**Dear John**" letter…

Dear "John"

This is one of the hardest letters I've ever had to write, but I finally have the Courage, so here goes…

This relationship isn't working for me. *I thought it would or could in the past, but you have repeatedly showed me that you either don't want to or are incapable of supporting me. Your Doubt in me and my abilities has started to make me Doubt myself, and that just can't continue.*

I have made a commitment to myself that I will no longer accept Unacceptable Behavior. In my opinion, ignoring me, dismissing me, laughing at me, or talking about me behind my back… is all unacceptable. I realize I may have doubted myself in the past, but that is changing. I have Dreams and I am valuable. Not the way you want me to be, or the way you think I should be, but just the way I am.

Your judgmental eye rolls and condescending sneers are no longer something I am willing to tolerate. I want people around me who appreciate me and think I am pretty, smart, witty, exceptional, lovely, kind, considerate, and loving because I am all of those things. I have been wasting my energy trying to get you to think so, and in the process, I forgot they were already true. I realize I was looking for you to validate who I am, but no more.

I feel better already just by writing this down. I now realize that your lack of caring for me and my feelings isn't a reflection of me; it is a reflection of you. You are allowing Selfishness and Insecurity to dictate your actions. As much as I felt like a victim before, now I recognize those are your Bullies and instead of allowing them to infect me with Not Enough Syndrome, I choose Empathy.

I actually feel sorry for you. It must be lonely where you live, constantly surveying your situation and comparing yourself to others. You were trying to micromanage me because looking at yourself was too painful.

I don't know why I've been afraid to stand up for myself in the past, but I am ready to face my future with clarity that is fresh and clear. This may be difficult for you to understand, but that future doesn't include you in your current state of toxicity. Before you tell me… "You've got it all wrong… I do care for you and your feelings." I need you to know that I don't FEEL valued. You aren't honoring the things that are important to me, and that is no longer a good fit for me.

Right now, you bring Sadness, Discouragement, and disappointment into my life, so I have chosen to revoke your All-Access Pass. You have officially been escorted to the "Restricted Zone." To return from there, you would have to change your ways and become trustworthy, kind, and supportive. It will be a long journey, but if you are committed to it, there is always Hope!

I've been hoping for some time now that you would wake up and realize what a special gift you have in someone like me. Now, I realize that is a bit pathetic. **Why was I giving you my power?** *In all* **Honesty**, *it was ME who allowed you to cloud my thinking* *about who I am. I chose to let you "IN" and now I choose to let you "OUT."*

I choose Peace, Joy, Happiness, Confidence, Courage, Love, and *Believing*

I AM ENOUGH!

So, as mad at you as I was when I started writing this letter, now I simply feel gratitude! Yes, gratitude because without you treating me so poorly, I never would have had the Courage to escort you to the Restricted Zone, so I could develop into the even more amazing person that is waiting on the other side of this letter.

I feel like I have been released from what could have been a life sentence, if I hadn't been inspired by someone to remember that **#IAmEnough** *just the way I am! I now understand that I don't need you to Believe in my Dreams. They are My Dreams, and I'm excited about my journey!*

So, thanks again "John." You have changed the person I am today and who knows, maybe the reason you are the way you are is because you need to write some "Dear John" or "Dear Jane" letters to the toxic people in your life. I have to tell you... it is quite freeing!

So, to recap, I am officially:

- *Taking back my power.*
- *Believing in myself.*
- *Removing toxic people from my life.*
- *Living my Dreams.*
- *Investing in relationships where I feel valued.*

If you want to get to know the new me, you will have to apply for re-entry from the "Restricted Zone." The criteria are much more stringent now, but I am definitely worth it! If you have come to that conclusion too, we might have something to talk about!

I am looking forward to becoming the best version of myself and I Hope that happens for you, too. Until then, it is time we said... "Goodbye!"

This letter was designed to include some of the most common things that happen in relationships that require a **Bubble Bump**. You can add to it, take away from it, or just leave it alone if it accurately represents what you are feeling. The purpose is to state out loud that you are not going to accept

Unacceptable Behavior anymore. Reading it, saying it, and that **Bubble Bump** hip check will engage multiple senses, which you know from earlier in the book helps you internalize the information better.

While you were reading that letter, did you think of anyone else who has infringed on your boundaries in some of these ways? Are you ready to take responsibility for yourself and **Evict** the toxic people in your life?

Remember, if they are just getting a simple **Bubble Bump** and they are not being banished to the **Restricted Zone**, modify it to suit your needs. There is a downloadable and customizable version at **www.VickiFitch.com/ETB** and I want you to print out copies for everyone on your list. The purpose is for you to start valuing yourself enough to make the changes in who you spend time with in your life, especially your **V-Zone**. Although you don't actually have to mail or send them, you do need to start the internal process of standing up for yourself and knowing that **#YouAreEnough** and that you will no longer accept **Unacceptable Behavior** from anyone... including yourself.

If you recognized that there were people that came to mind when you read the letter that you have no way of reaching, or that are no longer here on earth, here is what you do:

- Fill their names in
- Print it out
- Crumple it up
- Throw it in the trash can
- Consider it *Signed, Sealed, and Delivered!*

The "**Dear John**" letter is the **Eviction Notice** for people in your life who need to a good #**Fitchslap** to get back on track. (If you have forgotten what a **#Fitchslap** is, remember to read the **Fitchtionary** in the back!)

Now that you have **Evicted** the toxic people in your life, it is time to get to the real reason you are here... to *Evict the Bully in Your Head*. It's time to board the boat headed to **Bully Bay** called the **Eviction Express**... All Aboard!

Chapter 23
The Eviction Express

Bullying is a national epidemic.
—Macklemore

The **Eviction Express** is a small but mighty part of the fleet that travels around **Fitchipelago**. It makes the daily, island-to-island rounds, picking up the newly **Evicted**, and dropping them off on the dock in **Bully Bay** nestled next to their new home on **Eviction Isle**.

There are going to be times on this journey when giving in looks better than digging in because change is hard. Our natural tilt is to go back to what we know. It is common to withdraw to the familiar, even when we know it is harmful to us. Because of that, it is imperative that you make the commitment to stay the course all the way to **Success Island** and up to **#RockThatDream Ridge**. I want you to be proud of your progress. You must realize by now that you have been held hostage by this **Bully** and it is time for you to face him.

The **Bully**'s goal is to distract you and try to get you stuck in one of the **Sister Seas**. The **Sea of Sameness**, the **Sea of Mediocrity** or his favorite, the **Sea of Status Quo**. You will notice when looking at the map of **Fitchipelago**, that these dangerous bodies of water either drag you to the **Depths of Discouragement** force you into the **Tide of Temptation** or even suck you into the **Ocean of Overwhelm** to keep you away from the **Headspace Heroes**.

If you are used to the **Bully in Your Head** telling you that you are **Not Enough**, it can weaken your resolve to follow through on the **Eviction**

Process. That is why it is time to enlist the strength of your volunteer army that is ready, willing, and able to execute that task on your behalf.

It is time for you to say goodbye to your **Bully** and allow the **Headspace Heroes** to deliver his **Eviction Notice**.

Dear **Bully**,

I realize you have become comfortable in my **Headspace**, but it is time for you to go. I have no use for your daily reminders and incessant utterings telling me I am **Not Enough**. I have a new mantra:

I AM ENOUGH!

Your negative influence, insults, and lies have been packed up and are waiting at the dock next to the **Eviction Express**, which will escort you to your new home.

Since I have been known to allow you to come and go freely in the past, I wanted to make sure you know, the locks have been changed and you no longer have access to the premises. I already have a new set of tenants moving in and they are committed to clearing out the residual debris that you are your **Bully Buddies** have left behind.

This is your official **Eviction Notice**: (Download your customizable copy at **www.VickiFitch.com/ETB**.)

Eviction Notice

To all parties mentioned below, and any friends of the aforementioned, you are officially on notice of **Eviction**. You are no longer welcome on the premises. Should you trespass, the **Headspace Heroes** have permission to remove you by any means necessary. Any baggage that was once here has been disposed of. You have no reason to return.

[Insert Names of your Bullies here]

On this _____ day of _____ you have officially been **Evicted** from my **Headspace** and you may never return.

_____   _____
Signed by: Dated

Enter all the names of the **Bullies** you can think of that currently reside in your **Headspace** and print out the **Eviction Notice**. Print it out and place it somewhere prominent for you to see and recite every day until you are sure they are on permanent relocation.

Take a moment to congratulate yourself on hanging your **Eviction Notice**. It is a big win for you and now it is time to create a fresh, clean environment that is free from the residue the **Bullies** left there. The **Headspace Heroes** are ready to remove everything including the echoes of insults that may be trying to haunt you. It is time to bring in the crew to **Clean your Canvas**.

Chapter 24
Clean your Canvas

"It is a good thing to start fresh."
—Sean Spicer

When I need to clean or organize something, I start with one simple step. I clear EVERYTHING out of the space, so I can see the possibilities. When some things are left, I tend to start organizing *around* what is there instead of prioritizing the things that are going back in by usefulness and frequency of use. When you start organizing your life that way, you become more productive.

Your **Headspace** is the same way. You need to remove all the negativity that you have become accustomed to instead of "dusting around" it. When clearing the **Bullies** from our **Headspace**, you need to wipe the canvas clean. Nothing gets left behind. Your **Bully** saved every negative feeling and emotion you've ever had and packed it into the dresser drawers. He tucked each **FEAR** into the nightstand to taunt you and your secrets in the closet to haunt you.

He repainted the walls with toxic words that made you feel sick. The insults he threw at you were piled so high you didn't see that his creepy friend **Resentment** was lying in wait on the floor among the debris. Upon a closer look, you find little scraps of paper that included your hopes, **Dreams**, and desires which have been torn, trodden on, crumpled up, and dispersed among the trash.

164 | **EVICT THE BULLY IN YOUR HEAD**

It is time for you to bring in the cleaning crew! The **Headspace Heroes** are experts in this area and know the negativity must go! They know how to create a fresh space that is encouraging and inviting. They'll get to work immediately, painting the walls, burning the linens, and replacing the putrid scent of **FEAR** and **Doubt** with the refreshing scent of **Peace**.

Thinking has become easier and more focused without the drowning sounds of negativity. The spacious area is now clean and serene. It is bright and cheerful with positive affirmations decorating the walls encouraging growth and leading you to the best version of yourself.

Guarding Your Headspace

The **Headspace Heroes** are fully committed to defending you from the **Bullies,** but part of their ability to protect you is your commitment to protect your **Special Access Gates**. If you don't protect these vulnerable places, the **Bullies** can stroll back in, just as if you sent them an engraved invitation. Today, we are going to talk about your **Ear Gate** and how essential it is that you guard it fiercely.

What is Driving Down Your Mental Highway

Music is one of the great connectors of feelings and emotions and it can imprint on the human brain. Without getting too technical, let's just say the music we listen to affects the way we think, act, and respond. Music travels through our neural network after being allowed access by the **Ear Gate**. If there is no sentry stationed there, the **Bullies** have free and unfettered access to reclaim your brain.

I know you may not want to hear, that the music you are listening to, could be hindering your progress toward becoming the best version of yourself, but the fact is… it might be.

If you want to stay connected with the Headspace Heroes, you need to choose music that has a positive message.

If the music you are listening to is littered with negative topics like **Anger** and violence, it is like leaving an open window for your **Bullies** to crawl back through. Think about how much easier life is when you **Believe** in yourself and recognize the value in your relationships and surroundings. If you are going to deliver toxicity to your subconscious, you will experience the effects of it in your life.

Years ago, when my oldest son Zachariah was in middle school, Al Menconi delivered a presentation to them about negative media and the effect it has on the human brain. He challenged the kids to go on a 30-Day Christian Music Diet. It was a powerful presentation that produced amazing results.

It is fascinating what changes are made in the mind of a teenager when they choose to engage the **Headspace Heroes** instead of the **Bullies** when it comes to entertainment purposes, but it works with adults, too. Let's see who or what, is dominating your **Headspace**.

#GuardYourGate Challenge

The **#GuardYourGate Challenge** is to help you get a better idea of what kind of content you are introducing to your **Headspace** and how heavily it is weighted on one side or the other. It is not a measurement of how good, kind, or respectable someone is. It is simply information to make you more aware.

If you want to get real data from this exercise, don't tell people why you want to know their favorite songs and what's on their playlist. If people think they may be "judged" by their choices, they are more likely to provide a tamer list of music or try to substitute a "clean" version of a song. In my experience, most songs that require a "clean version" are based on topics that are more congruent with the **Bullies** than the **Headspace Heroes**.

If you are doing this challenge with your kids, I recommend you consider not punishing them for inappropriate music. You are trying to prevent the **Bully Brigade** from taking over your child's mind and want to keep them open instead of resentful of the experience.

You can use this process to assess your family, but let's start with analyzing yourself:

1) Select your 5 favorite songs AND the first 5 songs on your playlist. (If they overlap, add some of your other favorites to make a total of 10.)
2) Print out the lyrics to those 10 songs.
3) Give them to your friend, teacher, parent, neighbor, mentor, or coach.
4) Have them read the words out loud, with no music.
5) Have them circle every word that is associated with something negative like death, suicide, murder, violence, racism, **Sex**, **Adultery**, **Drugs**, **Abuse**, **Alcohol**, **Depression**, **Anger**, **Rage**, and **Hate**.

6)   Have them <u>highlight</u> all the positive words or phrases that have to do with **Love**, **Compassion**, **Kindness**, **Joy**, **Forgiveness**, **Empathy**, **Integrity**, and **Honor**.

7)   Add up the total number of words or phrases that are attributed to the **Bullies** and the **Headspace Heroes**.

8)   Compare the number and identify which side is dominating your **Headspace**.

Don't get me wrong. I'm a country music fan and there are plenty of songs about drinking and falling for the wrong person or making decisions that are not the most beneficial in your life. Which side of the scale dominates your feed? Is it even a close call?

If you are filling up your mind with the music that supports the **Bully Brigade**, it will be much harder to break free of their negativity.

If you are serious about wanting to
Evict the Bully in Your Head,
you need to change what is playing in your earbuds.

The words to those songs can and will change what you think about. Let me share about my own experience with you.

Adolescence

Preteen and teen years can be particularly brutal on kids. Their desire to fit in, be liked, and be connected hits an all-time high. Most kids say that junior high and high school are some of their most difficult years. Taking that into consideration, we need to recognize that **Bully Births** often spring up likes Twins, Trips, and Quads during this tumultuous time.

I was no different than many of you. I won't go into all the details here, but I can tell you that during middle school, I found myself listening to a specific type of music to impress a boy. It is a common occurrence among kids to allow something to **Nudge** us off course in an attempt to connect with someone or to be part of the culture. In this particular case, the music I was encouraged to listen to, although some of it was upbeat, had a heavy undertone and a very dark message.

The lyrics spoke of some of the typical adolescent issues of **Rebellion**, **Confusion**, and **FEAR**. **Sex**, **Drugs** and **Alcohol** were the lyricists numbing agents from **Loneliness** and to fill the empty void. Dealing with **FEAR** and **Shame** produced **Anger** and **Rage**. It was an emotional roller coaster and the more I listened, the more resentful I felt about my circumstances. I was in **Pain** from being misunderstood and I was frustrated. I didn't feel loved or appreciated by my family, and when you feel isolated like that, the music can become a "friend" giving unsolicited advice.

Think about that for a moment. Pairing up a hormonal teenager or emotional adult with lyrics that create feelings of **Pain, Anxiety, Resentment, Anger, Loneliness** and **Depression**… throw in a song about suicide being an alternative or a solution to their problems, and you have mixed yourself a cocktail for disaster.

If we are wondering why suicide has become an epidemic, we need to start by recognizing the **Bully Brigade** that we are attracting to ourselves or our children, by not posting a sentry at these **Special Access Gates**.

If you are listening to music that suggests that suicide is the solution to your problems, the **Bully in Your Head** is going to use that as a weapon every time you are struggling. It is like the Pied Piper calling the **Bully Buddies** to come party at your place! **Loneliness, Anger, Frustration, Despair, Resentment, Addiction**, will all be there for a full-on **Bully Bash**!

When this happens at a pivotal time it permeates to our core of who we are. Just like **Shame**, it seeps and oozes into all the little crevices of the subconscious mind. Music matters and we need recognize the harmful effects and take steps to protect ourselves and our children.

If you are a parent, you better **Pull Up Your Bootstraps** because I am about to get real with you. You NEED to know what your kids are listening to and protect them from listening to music that is harmful. That is why I told you to print out the words of those top 10 songs and circle all the negative words that might invite **Bullies** in and highlight the words that support the **Headspace Heroes**.

I was listening to that music out loud on my stereo at home. The beat of the song didn't alarm my parents and they weren't listening to the lyrics. Yet, right under their noses, I was becoming more withdrawn from them because I was commiserating and allowing the **Bullies** free reign in my **Headspace**.

You MUST **Stand Up** for your kids! They will fight you, argue with you, yell at you and maybe even tell you they hate you. But if you continue to allow it, they may eventually **Hate** themselves because they feel **Hopeless**.

I am not suggesting you can control what they consume outside of your environment, but you can stop them from listening to it repeatedly in your own home or when they are with you. I did not become a better, happier, or more connected person by listening to those lyrics. My attitude changed and instead of trying to please my parents, I wanted to embrace **Rebellion** because I thought I would feel better.

Before you start arguing and telling me that you just like the music and aren't really listening to the words, I have news for you… your subconscious is. If you have children who are listening with you in the car or out loud in the house, it is infiltrating them. You are inadvertently inviting **Bullies** into their heads and I can tell you from the voice of experience, that isn't a positive place to be.

The moral of the story is to guard your **Ear Gate #GuardYourGate** and protect yourself and your family from that unguarded entrance for the **Bullies** to sneak back in. (We will discuss other **Special Access Gates** in a future book in the series.)

Now that we understand how to **Clean the Canvas**, we can take what we've learned and share it with others to become **Part of the Solution**.

Chapter 25
Be Part of the Solution

---

*"You can't be against bullying
without actually doing something about it."*
—Randi Weingarten

Being **Part of the Solution** to any problem means we have to be proactive. We want to be the catalyst for creating change not reacting to circumstances. For some of you, this chapter is going to be uncomfortable because up until this part, everything could be done without anyone else knowing. The next part will actually require you to do something more. If you want to change, it's time to take some action.

Difference Maker

Change is always scary, but it is what makes us grow. Just like the caterpillar forms a **Chrysalis** and then struggles to get out and changes into a beautiful butterfly, we need to experience times of difficulty before we can make our biggest transformation.

Becoming a **Difference Maker** can be a bit of a roller coaster. There will be times of **Confidence** and times of **Doubt**. Times of **Courage** and times of **FEAR**. You will feel unstoppable some days. Other days, you will want to hide in the closet and go back to being the person who accepts the

Unacceptable Behavior around you, allowing the **Bullies** to come back to claim your **Headspace**.

As we step into our growth and success, we recognize that helping others is part of the journey. It is imperative that we remember through the ups and downs that we must never, ever, ever, ever, ever give up. When setting the example for others to follow, we strengthen ourselves and lead them to emulate our own growth.

Difference Makers refuse to stay stuck in the **Sea of Status Quo**; they choose action.

Step Up, Stand Up & Speak Up

The **Headspace Heroes** are not part-time participants; they are a full-time, do-the-right-thing kind of crew. They are Heroes.

> **Hero - /ˈhirō/**
> **A person who is admired or idealized for courage, outstanding achievements, or noble qualities.**

It is time for you to find your inner Hero. That doesn't mean you need to go out and buy yourself a cape, but it does mean, you need to **Step Up, Stand Up & Speak Up**.

Heroes…

- **Step Up** to lead with **Integrity** and transparency.
- **Stand Up** for what is right.
- **Speak Up** when someone is being bullied or abused.
- They also…
- Reach out when someone is discouraged or disheartened.
- Recognize the value of people and help others see it, too.
- Appreciate the strength and importance of community.
- Provide insight to others on how to be the best version of themselves.
- Share their struggles to encourage others.

It takes strength and a courageous heart to **Step Up** when you see something wrong. We often want to stick our head in the sand and pretend it isn't happening or convince ourselves it is none of our business. Sometimes, we even tell ourselves that to **Speak Up**, "won't change anything," but it isn't true. Your bold gesture, or strong example, might inspire others now and for generations to come.

A book I read recently spoke of a situation where an elementary class went to see a play about a courageous woman from history. On the bus ride home, an older male student was taunting a developmentally disabled boy by pulling his hair. One of the girls tapped the **bully** on the shoulder and told him he was being mean and to…

"Stop it."

Those two words made all the difference in the world to the boy that was being abused. Those two words spoke volumes. They said:

"I see you."

"I recognize someone is being unkind."

"I am willing to **Stand Up** for you."

"**You Are Not Alone.**" **#YANA**

If those two tiny words, comprised of only six letters, can wield so much power, imagine what can happen when it is amplified. When waves of people are protecting others, recognizing their own value and standing in unity against cruelty or abuse, things will change…

- In our homes
- In our schools
- In our businesses
- In our organizations
- In our relationships
- In our world

That is the power of a movement. It doesn't start as a tsunami. It starts as a ripple. One person, one moment at a time.

In the example above, a young girl was inspired to **Speak Up** for a boy because she had been inspired by a play. When one person is willing to **Stand Up**, just as we talked about the #MeToo movement, others are encouraged to face their **FEAR** and move forward as well.

It's time to
#GetYourHeroOn

Heroes, lead with **Integrity**. Their consistent nature of doing the right thing, even when it is hard, becomes part of who they are. **Integrity, Truth** and **Honor** are always ready to **Stand Up** and defend. So, hold on to that strength for a moment and let's talk about situations in your life that might cause you to pause…

Perhaps a peer is being bullied or harassed at work or on the school campus. You may have secretly shuffled by in the past feeling grateful that it wasn't you being abused. Don't let **Guilt** or **Shame** try to attack you right now.

You weren't equipped to handle it at the time. As you become stronger through these steps, there will be a time when you are ready.

Having the **Courage** just to say, "Stop it." to someone who is being cruel, or "Come on friend." while walking beside them, after someone has been harassing them, can change their lives forever.

When **Loneliness** moves into our **Headspace**, she is like an open invitation for the **Bully Brigade** to dig into the trenches. **Sadness**, **Pity**, **Anger**, **Shame**, **Resentment**, **FEAR** and **Overwhelm** can flood the scene and send the unsuspecting person running straight into **Depression**.

We see an epidemic of tragedies that are reflective of these **Bullies** and the hold they have over the mind. That is why the **Eviction Process** is so critical to healing society because we must see the world through the clear **Filter** of the **Headspace Heroes**. The little things collectively can make a big difference and in order to do that, we must be the catalyst of change.

We have to **Step Up, Stand Up**, and **Speak Up** if we want to make a difference. The next part may get a little bit harder for some of you to handle. **Standing up** for yourself and setting clear boundaries comes first. **Speaking Up** for others is an important second. **Stepping Up** and doing the right thing, even when it is hard, is another critical attribute of a true Hero, so you may want to **Pull Up Your Bootstraps #PUYB,** this could get bumpy.

It's Not My Responsibility

We saw from the previous story that it is important to **Stand Up** to oppressors when we see others being harassed or abused. It may not be a loud and proud cry. It may need to be soft and subtle, like anonymously giving a copy of this book to a coworker. That is a step in the right directions, but what do you do when things require more?

What do you do if you see coworkers stealing from your place of employment?

Some of you consider that a simple question with a simple answer.

- "Of course, I would tell someone!"
- "Heck no, I need my job and will just keep my head down to stay out of the crossfire."

Others of you may feel conflicted by experiencing both of those considerations simultaneously. I am not questioning you or your decision-making process. I am here to expand the way you think and to help you learn to engage the **Headspace Heroes,** so they can keep the **Bullies** from setting up shop in your head again.

Those concerns are based on the **Bullies** convincing you that it is none of your business, not your place, or that you don't want to deal with the consequences or fallout. I'm not judging you or telling you that you are "less than" if you choose to ignore or avoid the situation. What I do want you to understand is when you ignore situations, you are essentially propping a door open for the **Bully Brigade** to come back in whenever they want.

We will explore this topic in more depth in **#*Christianpreneur*** but for now we at least have you thinking in the right direction. The Bullies want to keep you isolated from thinking this way. They want to be your only companionship because they can influence you by making you feel alone. Hold on to this fact:

Loneliness is a Liar.

#YANA – You Are Not Alone

Throughout the first two books of the **#12Books12Months** series, I have used the hashtag **#YANA** to remind you that **You Are Not Alone**. We already know that **Loneliness** can be a very devastating **Bully** to handle. We need a **Tribe** we can count on to keep our eyes on the prize.

I know what it is like to be alone. When my husband left me when I was 21 years old, I didn't want anyone to know. I felt **Shame**, **Humiliation** and **FEAR**. I didn't want to be judged and I didn't know what to do. I was young and on my own. I had options, but **Pride** prevented me from reaching out. I found **Peace** and **Friendship** in **Al-Anon**, the support group for family members of alcoholics.

My friend Denise reached out to make sure I was not alone. She sponsored me, listened to me, comforted me, and lead me back to the path of recognizing who I was. She reminded me that this was a temporary setback and it would not define who I was, or who I would become. I found a **Tribe** there in **Al-Anon**. Most of the other members there weren't like me... some of them were the complete opposite of me, but we had a common thread that bound us together. We had been affected by someone else's **Addiction** to alcohol or drugs. For all the things we didn't have in common, it didn't matter. We were there to support each other in the common interest, or in this case, the **Pain Point** we shared.

I learned so much about myself in that group and I learned to heal in those rooms. I deeply understood the power of a **Tribe**, one that didn't judge or have expectations. I was allowed to cry, or be angry, hurt, sad, or afraid. I was allowed to be me. If I ever wandered off into the **Weeds of Wallowing**, Denise would surely get me back on track. (That girl wielded the power of a the

Fitchslap and she didn't even know it!) I am so grateful for her guiding me to that **Tribe** and for taking my hand and dragging me there (with a bit of **Rebellion** I might add – but you will find out much more about this in *Profit in the Pain*.)

My point in sharing that with you is that **You Are Not Alone**. This journey you are on right now to **Evict the Bully** plaguing your **Headspace**, I've already been there and done that. I found a solution and I am here to share it with you and everyone else that wants relief from **NES**. Don't let **Pride** keep you from finding a group of people that will accept you for who you are and actually engage with you, without expectation. I encourage you to find your **Tribe**, whether it is with us or another group, it doesn't matter to me. I care that you never lose **Hope** and that you always see the value you bring to others.

#JoinTheJourney

If you read *Direct Selling 101*, you know that my clients call me the *#HopeDealer* because I provide a clear vision and the Belief in their Dreams, which gives them Hope, which is what fuel them to keep moving forward. I want to provide that resource to you as well. That is why I took a year of my life to put this content down into bite-sized manageable pieces for you to consume!

This is my "Why" …

- I started this project, so I could provide **Hope** to the world.
- I started the **#YouAreEnough** campaign to provide a global message that no matter your race, color, creed, beliefs, or background that you are enough just the way you are!
- I wrote the **#12Books12Month** series, to encourage, motivate, and inspire you to become the best version of yourself.
- I created the Facebook Group, so you could find a **Tribe** that would accept you unconditionally.
- I interact with the Facebook Group so I can stay connected with you and to share my transparent journey with you and help you find additional resources.
- I use fun analogies is to help you remember the content in a way that is relatable and to remind you not to judge yourself or others.
- I wrote the **Fitchtionary,** so the **Tribe** would have their own fun vocabulary to laugh their way through challenges, and easily identify other **Tribe** members. (You must admit, if you met someone at an event and they said someone deserves a **Fitchslap**… you know you are with your **Tribe**!)

Knowing why someone does what they do allows you to connect with their mission and their message. Knowing how to do it, is what changes your life. It is time to put the **12-Step Bully Eviction Process** into action.

Part II
The Eviction Process

Chapter 26
The 12-Step Bully Eviction Process

"The key to success is action,
and the essential in action is perseverance."
—*Sun Yat-sen*

I n the beginning of the book, I assigned your first lesson of standing up for yourself to include a simple step toward asserting your power. In subsequent chapters, we started to understand a little more about others and a lot more about ourselves. Becoming educated on the **Bullies** and the **Headspace Heroes** provided you new insight on who has had the most influence over you, and how to proactively pursue the changes needed to find the best, strongest, and most confident version of yourself. Now it is time to give you the 12 Steps to freedom. For easy reference, you can download a 1-page infographic at **www.VickiFitch.com/ETB**.

12-Step Bully Eviction Process

1	Believe in Yourself	7	Trust Yourself
2	Stand Up for Yourself	8	Guard Yourself
3	Affirm Yourself	9	Encourage Yourself
4	Support Yourself	10	Love Yourself
5	Know Yourself	11	Strengthen Yourself
6	Stabilize Yourself	12	Focus Outside Yourself

STEP One – Believe in Yourself

Recognizing your own value can be a tricky task. When we are used to the **Bullies** being in charge, it takes a new mindset to actually **Believe** in ourselves. It takes practice and persistence. Now that you know the **Headspace Heroes**, you need to engage them to help you. I recommend you start with **Captain Confidence** and **Corporal Courage**. They are experienced team leaders and are ready, willing, and able to help.

> **Confidence - /ˈkänfədəns/**
> **is the feeling or belief that you can count on someone or something.**

The time has come, for you to **Believe** in YOU.

> **Courage - /ˈkərij/**
> **is the ability to do something when you are frightened, grief-stricken, or in pain.**

I know you might be frightened to take on the task of believing in yourself. It requires being vulnerable and that is a difficult step to take, but **You Are Not Alone #YANA**.

STEP Two – Stand Up for Yourself

It is usually easier to **Stand Up** for someone else than it is to do for yourself. We often have preconceived notions that we are somehow selfish if we take a stand on how we should be treated. By now, you should recognize that a lack of setting boundaries assisted in you in getting into the difficult situations you are in today. Standing up for yourself requires you to act like your own best friend and accept that taking care of yourself is the equivalent of putting your own oxygen mask on first. You must help yourself before you are able to effectively assist others.

- **Engage Step One** – Believe in Yourself
- **Set Boundaries** - You can't expect people to respect boundaries that you haven't set.
- **"Not today, Bully. Not today."** – Your first line of defense to stop the negativity that infiltrates your mind. Keep practicing and it will become easier.
- **#MakeYourMove** – Find your own "Move" (or feel free to use mine with your own flair!) to help keep the **Bullies** at bay. Practice in the mirror! You've got this!

- **Send me your video** – I want to see you! Send it via social channels! Tag me in it and use the **#MadeMyMove** hashtag so we can support you on your journey (I may even feature you in the newsletter!)
- **Don't Accept Unacceptable Behavior** – When people cross the boundaries you've set up, **#DoTheBubbleBump**. Do not allow others to come into your space and treat you poorly. If you don't feel valued, that isn't a healthy relationship.
- **Be Your Own Best Friend** - Act like your own best friend by believing in yourself, trusting yourself, and being willing to take a stand for yourself.

STEP Three – Affirm Yourself

The definition of affirmation should put into perspective what you should expect from yourself:

> **Affirmation - /ˌafərˈmāSH(ə)n/**
> **Emotional support or encouragement.**

If you have been taught that showing emotion is inappropriate (i.e. "Big boys don't cry"), you may have gotten into the habit of stuffing your feelings or considering them irrelevant. Your feelings and emotions make up the person you are. While we should all strive to improve ourselves, we need to accept and affirm ourselves for who we are today.

After implementing the first two steps, we need to immediately start working on affirming ourselves to recognize our intrinsic value. I recommend you start by going to the website and printing up the graphics we created for you so that you can hang them around your house or in your office wherever your **Bully** tends to visit you. **www.VickiFitch.com/ETB.** Here are some samples but coming up with your own that are relevant to you specifically might serve you even better!

I will Evict the Bully in my Head!	I am Confident!
I Choose the Headspace Heroes!	I am Courageous!
I am not afraid of FEAR!	I Trust myself!
I Choose Joy!	I AM Enough!
I Love me...for me!	I am a Rockstar!
I will hold my Boundaries without feeling Guilty!	I Forgive my past mistakes and look forward to my future!

You already know that your **Bully** is mocking you, so let's chat about it for a minute. I want to keep you focused and committed to your goal of removing him forever. You probably know where you tend to hear his voice, but here are some suggestions for where to post some of your signs and how they might support your efforts.

Remember, the one mantra that continues throughout the process and each time you see an affirmation sign, you will start with:

"Not today, Bully. Not today."

The Closet – When you go to choose your clothes for the day, does the **Bully** tell you nothing looks good on you; that you don't have the right body type or wardrobe? Does he try to convince you that others will judge your accessories or that you have no taste or style?

"…I AM Enough!"

Read your sign out loud over and over again until you drown out your **Bully**. **#MakeYourMove** and recognize that **#YouAreEnough**, just the way you are.

The Mirror – Does the **Bully** tell you there is something wrong with the way you look? It's time for you to look at each area you feel is "lacking" and learn to love yourself for who you are today. It is OK for you to set a goal to change because you want to, but you need to accept yourself first.

"…I Love me… for me!"

At first, you may not **Believe** this mantra. It takes time to replace the recording in your head that says you are **Not Enough** with the recognition that **#YouAreEnough** just the way you are. It will serve you well to recognize that each individual part of you is just the way it is supposed to be. Practice makes perfect and finding your value when it is underneath loads of lies can be difficult. I **Believe** in you and I know **You Can Do It! #YCDI**

In Your Car – Driving may be a peaceful or frustrating time for you, but either way it is an easy place for the **Bully** to slide into gear and come at you with attacks like, "You are always late." "You're going to get another ticket!" "You forgot to renew your license and now you will have to pay late fees."

"...I Forgive my past mistakes and look forward to my future!"

We all make mistakes. Obsessing over them only gives the **Bully** more power over you. Forgiving yourself for the past and committing to your future is the best thing you can do.

Your Desk – The office can be a stressful place where your performance is always under review and your coworkers are constantly **Complaining** about your boss, the company, and their lives. It can be difficult to keep the **Bully** away from you when you are feeling the pressures of your coworkers.

"...I Choose Joy!"

This sign is there like a friend in stealth mode advancing on the battleground in front of you. No one knows that the sign is to keep the **Bullies** at bay, and yet it is there, providing an extra layer of protection to help you stay with the **Headspace Heroes**.

Bright Idea: You should probably buy some extra copies of this book and anonymously pass them out to your coworkers. This could be the start of your **Tribe**!

Your front door (inside) – Whether your home feels like a war zone or a safe zone, it is important before you go off into the world every day that you remind yourself that you are going to give your best and you will handle the day with **Dignity** and **Grace**.

"...I am a Rockstar!"

Recognizing your value and giving yourself credit for your talents and skills is important. If you can't wholeheartedly feel this when you say it, keep practicing. Eventually, you will *Believe* it and you will *Receive* it as truth. Practice saying these affirmations every time you see them and eventually, you will start to **Believe** yourself.

Affirmations are another way to keep the **Headspace Heroes** engaged on a daily, hourly, or minute-by-minute basis. Life gets difficult sometimes, but it is consistently easier after you #EvictTheBully.

Print up extra signs and post them wherever you hear the **Bully's** voice. Create habits and affirmations that will support you in your journey. **Believe** in yourself, your abilities, and the constant truth that **#YouAreEnough**. The more you practice, the easier it will become.

STEP Four – Support Yourself

Creating a strong support system is an important part of any change. If we are on a weight loss journey, being around people that won't tempt us with our favorite treats is important to our success. The same applies to supporting yourself against negativity at home, in the workplace, and most importantly, in your own **Headspace**. Knowing there are others who understand your journey, and are eager to support you, provides the extra strength we need.

- **Find your Tribe** – Finding a **Tribe** of positive, energetic, likeminded people is crucial to the **Eviction Process**. It is easier to **Stand Up** to the **Bully Brigade** when you know that **You Are Not Alone #YANA**.
- **Positive Interaction** – Knowing you are going to have a dose of positivity every day can keep you focused on the **Headspace Heroes** and clear some of the dangerous negative debris off your path. I post thought provoking and inspiring quotes and questions on social media every day, so I hope you will take a moment to follow me on your favorite social channel. I also motivate and inspire you on my daily **Livestreams** so feel free to tune in! My handles are in the front of the book, but you can also go to **www.VickiFitch.com/ETB** for a complete list.
- **Connect with Positive People** – You may need to interact more in the group or organizations you are already involved in, or you may need to find a new crowd to spend time with. Take a look at your **Bubbles** and make sure there are some positive people for you to spend time with, otherwise, go on a mission to find some new places to support yourself and enrich your journey.

STEP Five – Know Yourself

In order to know yourself, it is important to know your **Bully** and his **Bully Buddies** to prepare you for their tricks. It is equally important for you to start getting more familiar with the **Headspace Heroes** and how they support you! You can download an easy reference guide at **www.VickiFitch.com/ETB**.

- Read the list of **Bullies** and identify which ones have set up residence in your **Headspace**.
- Fill them in on the **HHJ (Headspace Hero Journal)**

- Read over the **Headspace Heroes**. Really think about who they are and what they mean. Start to embrace them and understand how they will change your life.
- Fill in the chart and match up the **Headspace Heroes** needed to help **#EvictTheBully** you are struggling with. It is OK to recognize that you need more than one **Hero** to support your efforts. They are a team and they work well together.
- In our Facebook Group, share the **Bully** you feel is the most challenging right now. I will try to share lessons during my daily broadcasts or in my blog posts, which will help you with the **Eviction Process**.

STEP Six – Stabilize Yourself

This is your time to stabilize. Just like a boat with a leak, you must seal off the area until the leak has been fixed to prevent it from sinking the entire ship. You must protect the ship by restricting access to that area until the breach has been repaired and the contaminated water has been disposed of. Once the vessel is stable, you can assess if the ship can be salvaged, or if it must be scrapped. The toxic relationships in your life are like those sinking ships. You need to restrict access until you can stabilize yourself, assess the situation, and take the necessary action.

It is time to... **#DoTheBubbleBump**! **BOBO** is here to help you remove the external **bullies** from your life wherever you can. Remember, this is not something you have to announce, it will be reflected in the way you utilized your time and energy. Ongoing maintenance will happen automatically if you are engaging the **Headspace Heroes**.

- Update your **Bubble Balance Chart!** Now that you have come this far, there are probably more relationships you are recognizing are not serving you well. Note in your calendar to do this maintenance every 30 days or so to stay in balance.
- Execute the **Bubble Bumps**. If you make the list, but don't change your behavior, you are setting yourself up for disaster. You must revoke access to the offenders and reduce or eliminate time with toxic or negative people. You can always reengage in the relationship after they read this book and engage the **Headspace Heroes** themselves.
- **NOTE:** When the culprits are teachers, bosses, or authority figures, it is harder to stay away, but careful planning and positive reinforcement from your **Tribe** will keep you moving forward.
- Practice your **"Not today, Bully" Super Stance**. This will strengthen your **Eviction** muscle.

- Prepare your "**Dear John**" letters to all negative influences in your life. (Downloadable one on the Resource page **www.VickiFitch.com/ETB**]

STEP Seven – Trust Yourself

Trusting yourself means to first accept that your initial reaction to someone is a valid starting point. If you know you are being triggered by something, it isn't necessarily the other person's fault. Seek assistance to understand what makes you uncomfortable. Don't allow **FEAR** and **Manipulation** to rule you. While you are working on that, still **Trust** your first instinct. It is better to be safe than sorry.

- **Trust Yourself.** Recognize that you are an amazing person and that your thoughts and feelings are valuable, and they are there for a reason even if you can't identify the reason you are uncomfortable.
- **Remove yourself** from situations that are unhealthy or toxic. You don't need someone else's permission or confirmation to recognize when you are being undervalued.
- **Respect the Intimacy Bubbles** – they will help to protect you. (**BOBO** is your friend!).
- **Excuse yourself** when you are uncomfortable around someone. Stay away from them whenever possible. You do not have to explain it or justify it to anyone.
- **Report abusive people**. I know this one is tricky and can summon a full set of **Bullies** to try to talk you out of it. It might take you some time before you are ready, and it is OK to take this at your own pace. That shouldn't stop you from the rest of the **Eviction Process**. Just move past this if you need to and you can come back here when you are ready. Remember, our **Tribe** is ready to support you in the Facebook Group. Someone else may have already gone through what you are experiencing and might have the advice you need to move forward.

STEP Eight – Guard Yourself

Guarding yourself is an important step in the **Eviction Process** You only have one life. The longer you live with **Bullies**, the less time you will have with the **Heroes** like **Joy**, **Peace**, and **Love**. It is time for you to start guarding yourself from the negative influences of the world.

- **People** – Make sure you are spending time with people who hang out with the **Headspace Heroes**! If they are talking negative about themselves, gossiping, or putting down others, **RUN**!

NOTE: This may be the time to review and do a **Bubble Bump**, if necessary!

- **#GuardYourGate** - Your **Special Access Gates** need to be guarded to prevent the **Bully Brigade** from getting back in. It is important that you insist on positive influences. If want things to change, you must remove any negative influences that you can, from your day to day circumstances. Trying to decide if it is worth it? Remember this:

Definition of Insanity:
"Doing the same thing over and over again
and expecting a different result."

Don't get stuck in the habit loop of choices that aren't serving you. Make definitive changes so the **Headspace Heroes** can **Clean your Canvas**.

- **Take the #GuardYourGate Challenge**
- Print the words to your Top 5 Favorite Songs.
- Print the words to the first five songs on your Playlist.
- Give them to a trusted friend, mentor, coach, advisor or parent.
- Have them read the words out loud, with no music on.
- Have them circle the negative words. (**Bullies**)
- Have them highlight the positive words. (**Headspace Heroes**)
- Add up the number on each side.
- Compare which side has the strongest influence.
- Try the 30-Day Music Detox and evaluate the change in your attitude.
- Share your-results with me on **Social Media**!

STEP Nine – Encourage Yourself

Encouragement is something that needs to be delivered in daily doses. Just like essential vitamins and minerals, we feed on the nutrients it supplies us.

- **Listen** to positive, encouraging, and uplifting people, podcasts, and music.
- **Read** encouraging books, blogs, and literature.
- **Move your Affirmations** around your home so they can provide you that daily dose without becoming stale or blending in with your environment. Move their locations every few weeks so you don't become desensitized to their power, or ask a family member to move them for you, so they will stay fresh!
- **Read a Daily Devotional** of encouraging words and stay in the habit of reading them every day without fail. Remember, like vitamins, we don't often see their effect the same day; it is the cumulative effect that makes the biggest difference.

- **Ask someone** you know and trust for some weekly words of encouragement about what you did right that week.
- **Give Encouragement to others**. It makes you feel good to bless others and it will create a deeper, more meaningful relationship.
- **Share when you are discouraged**. Post in the group and allow others to lift you up. Don't allow **Pride** to interfere with you getting what you need.

STEP Ten – Love Yourself

Loving yourself means accepting yourself for who you are today, right now; not who you want to be or will be, but who you are now. You may have been told by a lot of other people that you are not very valuable, but that was the **Bully**, not the **Headspace Heroes**

Next, we have to complete the actual **Eviction.** The good news is, if you have done the previous steps, it is already in motion. You don't need to do anything else. Most of the **Bullies** ran for the hills as soon as you invited **Captain Confidence** and **Corporal Courage** to the party. The **Headspace Heroes** will escort the **Bullies** out without a lot of fuss. The **Bullies** know the drill. When the **Headspace Heroes** are around, it is time to vacate the premises.

Let's recap:
- Fill out and print out your **Eviction Notices** to each **Bully** by name. (Read them out loud. Let them know you mean business!)
- Have **Captain Confidence** and **Corporal Courage** rally the troops and deliver those **Eviction Notices**.
- Move in your **Headspace Heroes** and make sure they **Clean the Canvas** so that no debris is left behind.
- Keep working with **BOBO** and check your **Bubble Balance** regularly and execute your **Bubble Bumps** whenever needed.
- Review any applicants trying to return from the **Restricted Zone**. Use **BOBO** to decide what, if any access they will be granted.

NOTE: If you are a visual person, keep your all your materials in a binder including your Eviction Notices and pull them out when you need a reminder of how far you've come!

STEP Eleven – Strengthen Yourself

There are many ways to strengthen yourself to prepare for the **Bully Eviction Process** and you should start with the **Headspace Hero Journal** (download from the resources page **www.VickiFitch.com/ETB**) to keep track of which

Bullies you are encountering on a daily basis and which **Heroes** are getting the most action.

Preparing ourselves be strong enough to face those **Bullies** requires we exercise and strengthen ourselves in all three areas, Mental, Physical and Emotional.

- **Mental** – Filling our minds with positive, encouraging words is important. We should also focus on learning new ideas and evaluating other concepts to keep our creative energy flowing. I read and listen to books every day to keep the ideas flourishing. I get inspired by the content and write blog posts, do livestreams, or even add them to chapters of upcoming books. Your mental strength is critical to staying fresh and focused.

- **Physical** - If we physically allow our body to get sedentary, our minds can't utilize all the new information it feeds us. When we find activities, we like such as: walking, swimming, sports, or Zumba, we look forward to the exercise as it benefits our bodies and contributes to our creativity. (I combine Mental & Physical together by listening to books or podcasts while on the treadmill). Check out the **Rock Star Guide to Gettin' It Done**.)

- **Emotional** – Our emotional wellbeing is often one of the most overlooked areas of strength. The world is a busy place and the microwave generation we live in requires us to produce more answers, more solutions, and more content than ever before. If we forget to keep that area of our lives in balance, we can erode our productivity and our ability to problem solve, educate, or lead others. If anyone ever tried to convince you that therapy was a waste of time or money, I challenge you to remember we are in the **Bully Evicting** business and need to kick that thought to the curb. Learning to understand yourself, your **Triggers**, and the things that bring you **Joy** are well worth the time and energy. In my experience, they have helped me to also understand others better, as well, and have given me the unique opportunity to incorporate what I've learned into my writing.

Strengthening yourself can take on different caveats as well such as adding in meditation, hobbies, massage, aromatherapy, bubble baths, retreats, conferences, etc. Remember, there are a plethora of ways to grow stronger. It is up to you how you incorporate them on your journey to becoming the best version of yourself. Be open to the possibilities and focus on your goal.

STEP Twelve – Focus Outside Yourself

As we are girding up our own strength, it is imperative that we take it one step further and be **Part of the Solution** by focusing *outside* of ourselves to help others who may not have the strength or fortitude to **EvictTheBully** on their own.

- **Step Up**, **Stand Up**, and **Speak Up** – We need to **Step Up** to leading ourselves and others with Integrity. **Stand Up** when we see things that are not in alignment with the **Headspace Heroes** and **Speak Up** when necessary and share what we know. All while making sure our motives are strictly about doing what is right.

- **#JoinTheJourney** – Learning these skills is important and will change our lives but we need to be **Difference Makers** and share this message with others, so we can prevent **Bully Births** from happening in the first place.

- **#GetYourHeroOn** – As kids, most of us dreamed of being a superhero at one point or another. This is your big chance. Not only can you start acting like one, but if we come to your company, school, church or organization, I might need you to dress up as one. We will provide the details if we book the engagement.

- **Share the Mission** – If you know someone who is battling the **Bully**, share the content, book, idea, or concept with them. If you know this could benefit your organization, tell them about it. If you **Believe** in your company or organization, you will want them to understand how to **#EvictTheBully**, as well as embrace the **#YouAreEnough** campaign.

- **#JoinTheMovement** – Help me get the word out to the world. The more **Hope** people have and the clearer the direction we give them, will create a safer, more exciting place for all of us.

Those are the steps to do every day to keep the **Bullies** away. Print out your easy reference infographic at **www.VickiFitch.com/ETB.**

Now that you have immersed yourself in the **12-Step Bully Eviction Process**, it is time for you to **#JoinTheMovement**.

Part III
The Mission
#JoinTheMovement

Chapter 27
#JoinTheMovement

> *"Every great dream begins with a dreamer.*
> *Always remember, you have within you*
> *the strength, the patience, and the passion*
> *to reach for the stars to change the world."*
> —*Harriet Tubman*

My Dream

I have a **Dream**... to start a worldwide movement bringing the **#YouAreEnough** campaign into schools, churches, hospitals, prisons, companies and organizations so we can effectively **#EvictTheBully** currently residing in that **Headspace** between our ears.

This mission is focused on helping people recognize their internal value regardless of their circumstances and accept themselves the way they are. It is not a way to provide excuses for people to stunt their own growth with the excuse, "That's just the way I am." It is an opportunity for them to understand that growth should be a personal goal, not a prerequisite for people to accept them.

It also encourages **Compassion**, while setting the immovable boundary of **Don't Accept Unacceptable Behavior** to strengthen the spirit and prevent anyone from becoming a doormat for others to walk on.

In addition, it is an awareness program that reminds us that most people aren't born with a desire to hurt others. They are taught it as part of their environment. Until now, they may not have realized they have a **Bully** instigating some of the things they do by constantly reminding them of the awful lie they've been told that they are **Not Enough**.

Focus for a moment on the change this book would have had on you as a child, or imagine what would be different now if you had grown up believing the best about yourself… Now, make the decision to help spread the word so we can help everyone recognize their value and to reject the idea that they don't measure up.

With the epidemic of suicide rising in the world today, it is evident that there is a lack of **Hope**, while at the same time, an abundance of **FEAR, Discouragement, Depression**, and **Anxiety**. It is time for us to **Evict** those **Bullies**, engage the **Headspace Heroes**, and teach future generations to do the same.

I have a deep desire to connect with children, so we can try to thwart or even eliminate the **Bully Births** from ever happening in the first place. If we can prevent them by inoculating children from **NES** (**Not Enough Syndrome**), we could eradicate the lies the **Bullies** are plaguing them with. This in turn would change the world by raising generations of happier, kinder and more confident people; ones that look at others with **Empathy** instead of **Apathy** and who have a desire to see others for who they really are, instead of through the **Dirty Filter** of **Judgment**.

This book, along with the curriculum and presentations I've created, are designed specifically to reach all audiences from preschoolers to the elderly and are applicable for everyone by reinforcing the message:

#YouAreEnough… Just the way you are!

When people recognize their internal value, they are much less susceptible to the diminishing remarks of others. This book is part of the **#12Books12Months** series, to help you grow, while recognizing and respecting the immeasurable value of others. Whether or not we like them or agree with them makes no difference. When we use the power of the **Headspace Heroes**, we don't need to worry about the unkind things others do or say. We will instinctively look to **Empathy** to find a reason why they are acting the way they are. When we don't *Believe* the insults, we won't *Receive* them and that is a catalyst for change.

> *"If I look at the mass, I will never act.*
> *If I look at the one, I will."*
> —*Mother Teresa*

Mother Teresa made an excellent point in the quote above, that "*If I look at the mass,* (the world or issue as a whole) *I will never act. If I look at the one,* (an individual you know, love and care about) *I will.*" When the concept is generalized, it may sound like a good idea, but it doesn't inspire action. When we think about one specific person in our lives that may be affected by this, we will act.

Can you think of a person in your life who is struggling, angry, frustrated, depressed or just difficult to be around? Do you have a child, friend or co-worker that is struggling to figure out their value? Do you know someone who is depressed, discouraged or disheartened? Have you worried about them but don't know how to get through?

Do any of those things describe you?

Just keep in mind, there is **Hope** and remember **#YANA – You Are Not Alone.**

I'm sure you've seen or felt the effect these **Bullies** can have on you. If you want to see positive change in your home, work environment and life, share this book with your friends, relatives and co-workers. Especially those who are going through a difficult time in their lives. You will experience the satisfaction of knowing your efforts had something to do with their new perspective and the changes you see in them.

If you recognize the challenges with physical and/or virtual bullying in your organization, you know this training needs to happen immediately before it escalates and infects everyone or breaks down someone's emotional boundaries at a dangerous level. It is time for a change and you can make a difference.

Are you a Dream Builder?

In *Direct Selling 101*, I talked about **Dream Builders** as a **Tribe** of strong warriors that are willing to fight for our **Dreams** and for other worthy causes. We recognize the value in healthy relationships and are committed to becoming the best version of ourselves while leading the way for others to follow so our **Dreams** will thrive instead of just survive. I am calling on you **Dream Builders** to help me spread the mission and get the message out there.

The best way to share a movement is exposure, so help me get the word out to anyone you know in the media, or leaders of companies, schools, hospitals and organizations. I know it is a **BHAG (Big Hairy Audacious Goal)** but it is one that is worthy of time and attention and I am asking for your help to make our world a better place to live in.

Let me "Edutain" You

I'd love to come talk to your school or organization, and I believe this movement will be the catalyst for change that the world has been waiting for. Share this book with:

- Corporate Executives and Training Departments
- Business Owners
- School Board Representatives
- Teachers, School Administrators, Professors and Deans
- Training and Development Managers
- Hospital Boards or Training Departments
- Book Club Coordinators
- Bible Study Groups and Group Leaders
- Prisons or Correctional Institutions

Sometimes we don't recognize where we can weave this message into existing training that needs to be done:

- Anti-Bullying & Suicide Prevention
- Diversity & Sensitivity Training
- Peer and Co-Worker Problem Resolution
- Restorative Justice Programs
- Customer Service
- Relationship and Communication Training
- Couples Therapy
- Child Counseling
- Confidence and Team Building
- Attitude or Behavioral Problems

The possibilities are endless and just as you can tell in this book, the way I mix humor with serious struggles, the presentations will be filled with the same.

No one wants another boring speaker to drill principles that have become platitudes. What we need is **A Fresh Perspective** that **Edutains** (**Edu**cates and Enter**tains**) audiences. Someone that can inspire and engage the participants, while helping them retain the content, so it produces a change in their lives.

If you have an event or virtual training that needs that kind of speaker, I'd love to talk with you. You can fill out the form at **www.VickiFitch.com/ETB,** and we will contact you for details We can also provide special bulk pricing for your teams, students, book clubs, employees, members, etc.

We are here to serve you and the community. Now it's up to you to ask.

"I have a Dream…" that we can change the world. I **Believe** we can do it. I need you **Dream Builders** to help me **Achieve** it!

#JoinTheJourney at **www.VickiFitch.com/5K** and let's **#RockThatDream**

Chapter 28
Moving Forward

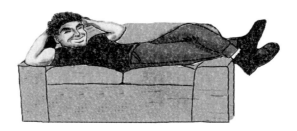

> *"Leadership is the ability to guide others without force*
> *into a direction or decision that leaves them*
> *still feeling empowered and accomplished."*
> —*Lisa Cash Hanson*

I am so excited that you embarked on this journey with me. There are so many more places for us to go and so many more things I want to teach you! Now that you know how to ***Evict the Bully in Your Head***, it is time that you put all your training into action. You have the resources, you have the direction, you have the inspiration to turn the life you are currently living into an even more amazing adventure.

I just want to remind you once again that #**YouAreEnough** just the way you are and when the road gets rocky, the **Tribe** is here to support you. We are all working to become the best version of ourselves which makes the experience richer for all of us.

I have a lot more to tell you about the **Bully in Your Head**, his **Bully Buddies** and the Tools they use. There are many more inspirational stories to share that I have created what I call a **Pseudo-Sequel** coming out later this year as part of the #**12Books12Months** series. It is called ***OWN IT! How to Step Up and Stand Out***: (#**QuirkyIsCool** and Normal is so *Yesterday*.) I am excited to share that with you, but we have some additional layers of support that are needed before we get there!

Speaking of support, I hope you started this series with *Direct Selling 101* because that provided the foundation to support you on the next leg of our journey together. Think of the first book as the rebar you lay before you pour concrete. It doesn't have to be done to pour the slab, but the results will last much longer, and be much stronger, if you do.

Now it's time for us to set sail from **Nough Nation** to learn about leadership, motivation, increasing your potential and boosting your income in Book #3, *Direct Selling 201: Advanced Sales and Leadership Strategies to #RockThatTeam in Direct Sales & Beyond*.

If you aren't in sales or have nothing to do with the Direct Sales Industry, don't worry, this book has a lot of value to offer you! Here is a reminder about what others are saying:

"Don't let the title fool you…

the real power in this book is that it will build your confidence and help you shed the fears and excuses that are holding you back from achieving your Dreams."

*—**Shannon Mattern**; Website Developer and Owner of WP-BFF*

Teaching you to weather the storms of life and business is one of the greatest gifts I can offer, because it will provide **Confidence** for the unknown journeys that still lay ahead of you.

Just like Mr. Miyagi in *The Karate Kid*, the **#12Books12Months** series is teaching you skills, you won't even realize you've learned until the next book, the next conversation or the next situation where your perspective has changed, or you handle things differently.

It is an exciting time to be YOU and living the life of your **Dreams**… is closer than you think. We just need to continue growing, flourishing and leading others to **Step Up**, **Stand Up** and **Speak Up**. Leading others to **Believe** in themselves and recognize their value. And leading others to make a difference.

Understanding how to lead others, especially if you are just learning to be a strong leader or if you are going through challenges yourself, can be tricky. Knowing how to inspire, motivate and encourage others is a skill everyone from children to CEO's need to master.

> *"Everything rises and falls on Leadership,*
> *but knowing how to lead is only half the battle.*
> *Understanding leadership and actually leading*
> *are two different activities."*
> —*John C. Maxwell*

My goal with **Direct Selling 201** is to continue this journey of understanding yourself and others in a way that is unique and extraordinary. So, if you are ready to be the best version of you…batten down the hatches, because there are some turbulent waters like the **Ocean of Overwhelm** and the **Depths of Discouragement** that I want to help you avoid. If you listen to me, I will guide you away from the **Tide of Temptation** and safely deliver you to the **Coast of Consistency** on **Success Island.**

Allow me the honor of being your captain on this voyage. It is time to set sail…

I look forward to seeing you at the dock, and until then, remember to

Dream it

Believe it

Achieve it!

#RockThatDream

Check out all the FREE RESOURCES for the book at

www.VickiFitch.com/ETB

Appendix
Fitchtionary

#12Books12Months	My personal hashtag to brand and identify my **#BHAG** to write 12 Books in 12 Months.
#BHAG	A **B**ig **H**airy **A**udacious **G**oal. A goal that scares you and will make you stretch. *"If you know you can achieve it… it isn't a **#BHAG**."*
#BOBOKnowsBest	A hashtag to remind you that **BOBO** is here to support you and remind you to go through the **Bubbles** One By One!
#Boom	Similar to a **#TruthBomb** A proverbial mic drop that means the content was right on the money and it landed with a loud affirmative thud.
#BrightSide	My hashtag for identifying a situation where the **Bright Side** was recognized or should be recognized. It signifies a choice to find the best in situations. It is also used when people play the **Bright Side** game.
#Christianpreneur	A Christian Entrepreneur and the title of one of the **#12Books12Months** series.
#DoTheBubbleBump	A hashtag to remind yourself and the **Tribe** that you know someone that needs a **Bubble Bump** and you are ready to execute. Or you see someone else who needs to execute one.
#EvictTheBully	My hashtag for acknowledging the active participation needed to *Evict the Bully in Your Head*. It is also a reminder to focus on the power of choosing to **Believe** in yourself and others.
#Fitch5000	The amazing core group of people supporting me on my **#BHAG** of **#12Books12Months**. Thanks to Doug Crowe for giving vision to that!

#FixYourHeart	A reminder from the video clip from Lonnie Chavis that is relevant when dealing with **Trolls**.
#GuardYourGate	A hashtag to remind you that you need to protect the **Special Access Gates** where information and negativity can get in. These locations are also where the **Bullies** can sneak back in undetected!
#GetYourBumpOn	A hashtag to remind someone that they need to execute a **Bubble Bump**.
#GetYourHeroOn	A hashtag to remind you to utilize the **Headspace Heroes** and to stand up to injustice. Be the Hero in someone else's life and your own.
#HopeDealer	A nickname my clients gave me because "working with me is like a drug" and that drug is **Hope**. It is also the name of a book in the **#12Books12Months** series.
#IAmEnough	My hashtag for you to remind yourself that **#YouAreEnough** just the way you are.
#JoinTheJourney	My hashtag to encourage others to join the **#12Books12Months** journey and the **#Fitch5000**. This journey includes becoming the best version of themselves.
#MadeMyMove	A hashtag for you to share your "Move" with me.
#MakeYourMove	A hashtag to identify when you know you need to "Change your State" or change your state of mind.
#ProtectYourBubbles	A hashtag to remind you to use **BOBO** to protect your **V-Zone** and to recognize that the **Bubble Bump** is an important tool in your arsenal.
#QuirkyIsCool	A hashtag I created for my son to remind him that he should embrace who he is, which I've expanded to remind everyone in business and in life to OWN who they are and embrace all that makes you unique.
#PUYB	The hashtag to remind you to **Pull Up Your Bootstraps**. Something challenging is coming or is about to be said.
#QYF	A Twitter sized version of **Quit Your Fitchin'**. Used to remind people to stop complaining.
#RedIsAlwaysRight	A hashtag that was generated from my podcast, *He Said, Red Said*.
#RemoveTheNots	A hashtag to remind you to remove the idea that you are NOT enough, or you can NOT do it.

#RockThatDream	My personal branded hashtag and the methodology I apply toward all I do in business and life. My mission is to help others embrace who they are, so they can truly *#RockThatDream*. Rita Esther is credited with that inspiration! It is also the title of one of the **#12Books12Months** series.
#RockThatDream Ridge	The highest point on **Success Island,** which includes a 360-degree view of all of **Fitchipelago**. It is the home to the coveted **Pinnacle of Peace**, where entrepreneurial **Dreams** live.
#RockThatStream	A crystal-clear stream running between **#RockThatDream Ridge** and the **Pain of Perfectionism Peaks**. It is also the sister hashtag of **#RockThatDream** and my signature step-by-step course to teach you how to *Leverage the Power of Livestreaming: Converting Contacts to Cash*.
#TrollConversion	A hashtag when a **Troll**, changes direction and becomes a fan or follower and engages in positive participation.
#TrollPatrol	A hashtag signifying that I am actively engaging with a **Troll** on a broadcast or in real life.
#TrustBOBO	A hashtag to remind us and others in the community that there is a reason we recommend the **Intimacy Bubbles** be gone through One By One. It is to protect you, so you need to trust the process.
#TruthBomb	My favorite expression when something is right on the money. This term is especially relevant when the information provided is possibly unwanted, but necessary. A **#TruthBomb** at times, can be synonymous with a **#Fitchslap.**
#YANA	A Twitter Sized version of **#YouAreNotAlone**.
#YCDI	A Twitter Sized version of **#YouCanDoIt**.
#YouAreEnough	A reminder that **#YouAreEnough** just the way you are. It is also part of a global campaign that I am launching with the **#12Books12Months** series.
12-Step Bully Eviction Process	My personalized 12-Step process to *Evict the Bully in Your Head*.
A Fresh Perspective	My personal view on things and the name of one of my podcasts: *Vicki Fitch Live: A Fresh Perspective*.

Achieve It Ave	A thoroughfare on **Success Island**.
Active Listening	**Active Listening** requires the listener to fully concentrate on the conversation without being distracted by something else.
All-Access Pass	Allows instant access to your **Vulnerability Zone** and free reign to run around your **Intimacy Bubbles** without **BOBO** escorting them. This is dangerous! You should always use **BOBO**!
Apply for Re-entry	The process of examining someone's motives when they are attempting to come back from the **Restricted Zone**.
Archipelago	A chain or grouping of islands. See **Fitchipelago**.
Asperger's Syndrome	A developmental difference in people who interpret and process information in a different or unique way. Part of the **Autism Spectrum** and usually denotes above average intelligence.
Aspie	A term people with **Asperger's** use to describe themselves or an abbreviated way to say someone has **Asperger's**.
Autism Spectrum	A condition usually characterized by difficulty in communicating and forming relationships as well as working with abstract concepts.
Backpeddling	The act of "moving backwards" or withdrawing a question, suggestion or request, usually due to **FEAR**.
Barter Blvd	A route on **Success Island** that often detours people who are afraid to travel on **Sales Street**.
Behind the Curtain	The context is the *Wizard of Oz* when Toto pulls back the curtain and you see the "real" person "Behind the Curtain". When we look beyond the surface of a situation to the circumstances that might be plaguing others, it gives us the chance to find **Empathy**.
Believe	One of the most powerful words in the world. It is the catalyst to most achievement, and the word I emphasize the strongest in my mantra.
Believe and Receive	Supporting the position that what you *Believe* about yourself, regardless of where the information came from, you will *Receive*, which means to accept it as truth, no matter how false it is.
Believe it Blvd	A thoroughfare on **Success Island**.

Big 3 Bullies	FEAR, Shame & Doubt are the **Big 3** or the **Big 3 Bullies**.
BOBO	BOBO is your personal emotional security guard. He helps you remember to require people go through your **Bubbles, One By One**. He also helps you execute your **Bubble Bumps**! He likes to do that with a little Disco flair!
Bright Side	A game I play with my family, team, and clients to remind everyone that you can find a **Bright Side** in any situation, no matter how frustrating, disappointing or overwhelming it is. **Bright Side** can be ANY idea from the **Obvious to the Outlandish**. The object is to THINK about a positive or funny way to look at the situation. It is a BIG help in keeping a **PMA**.
Brokeville	A town where people that have lost their financial resources tend to hang out.
Bubble	A transparent, but very secure place where we categorize our relationships. See Chapter 7 **Bubble Ology** for more detailed descriptions about your **Bubbles**.
Bubble Balance	When all your **Bubbles** have the right amount of people in them and you are not experiencing any **Bubble Voids**.
Bubble Balance Chart	The place where you record and evaluate the people in your **Bubbles** and identify those who needs a **Bubble Bump**.
Bubble Bliss	A State of **Bubble Balance** that feels like you have everyone in the right location and you are in alignment with your values.
Bubble Boundaries	Your expectations of what you will or will not accept in each of your **Bubbles**. If they are violated, you must do the **Bubble Bump**!
Bubble Breach	An act that violates the integrity of a **Bubble** like betrayal or infidelity.
Bubble Bump	The deliberate decision to move someone to a less vulnerable **Bubble**. This is often executed by singing **#DoTheBubbleBump** with a quick hip check.
Bubble Interloper	Someone who is occupying a **Bubble** promised to someone else.
Bubble Ology	The Study of your **Intimacy Bubbles**.

Bubble Predator	Someone who has less than honorable intentions.
Bubble Talk	Discussions that have to do with your **Bubbles** including **Hopping, Jumping, Bumping & Boundaries** and a whole host of **Bubble Ology**. It is a conversation you can only have with one of our **Tribe**. It's like our own version of Pig Latin (or should I say Igpay Atinlay?)
Bully	**Bully** with a capital "B" represents the **Bully in Your Head**. The one that infects you with **NES**.
bully	"**bully**" with the lowercase "b' represents the **bully** in real life that has a physical presence whether or not you ever meet them in person.
Bully Bay	The **Bay** on the south side of **Eviction Isle** where the **Bullies** are dropped off by the **Eviction Express**.
Bully Baggage	The debris the **Bullies** leave behind in your **Headspace** that carries on into your life and relationships.
Bully Beatdown	The times in your life where you allow the **Bullies** free reign and you accept all their negativity and *Receive* it as if it were truth. This usually leaves you stuck in the **Weeds of Wallowing** because you have convinced yourself this may be what you deserve.
Bully Behavior	When you mentally beat yourself up about mistakes, challenges, or difficult situations.
Bully Birth	The moment that you *Believe* the negative things that are said about you and you *Receive* it as truth. That is when the **Bully** is born.
Bully Brigade	A large group of **Bullies** that attack all at once.
Bully Brothers	Frustration, **Anger**, **Rage** & **Fury** are the **Bully Brothers**. They are like a tag team, if you allow one in the other brothers almost always come along for the ride.
Bully Buddies	The small groups of **Bullies** that like to pal around together and make you miserable playing off each other. Sometimes multiple groups of **Bully Buddies** will come together forming their own **Bully Brigade**.

Bully in Your Head	The voice in your head that infects you with **NES (Not Enough Syndrome)** and tries to convince you that you are **Not Enough.** You must start the **Eviction Process** immediately.
Bully of Bullies	**Shame** receives the title **Bully of Bullies** because she is often the root cause of their existence.
Bully Vacation	When you **Evict** your **Bullies**, but then you let them back in. The goal is a permanent **Bully Eviction**, not a temporary **Bully Vacation**. Do the work and keep them away permanently.
BYT (Bite Your Tongue)	**BYT** stands for **B**ite **Y**our **T**ongue and is used to stop you from **Backpeddling** or filling in the silence that others need to ponder your questions and formulate an answer. It is also used to protect an individual with **TMI Syndrome** from getting a bad reputation by **Gushing** all over other people.
C Sisters	**Comparison, Complaining** and **Criticism** are the infamous **C Sisters**. You should stay away from them whenever possible.
Charisma	A character you will meet in a future book!
Charm	A character you will meet in a future book!
Chrysalis of Change	The place where true transformation takes place.
Clean Your Canvas	Start fresh and remove all the debris so you can get a clear picture of what you need to do moving forward.
Coast of Consistency	A pristine coastline on the northeast shore of **Success Island**.
Comfy Cozy Comfort Zone	The place where you stay wrapped up in what you know instead of braving the trek to where your **Dreams** live.
Confidence Causeway	The connection from **Stability Shore** on to **Success Island**.
Consistency	The person shoveling the coal (**Momentum**) into the fire on the **Habit Train** to keep it moving, and your best friend in business.
Creativity Creek	A place where you can nurture your creativity on **Success Island**.
CTA (Call to Action)	A directive designed to prompt an immediate response from your audience. It is usually done to get them to opt in, make a purchase or engage with you via **Social Media**.

Customer Service Carnival	A Customer Service training ground for entrepreneurs inside the **Entrepreneurial Theme Park** on **Success Island**.
Cyberbully	A person that uses electronic communication to bully another person, group or organization.
Danger Zone	A **Danger Zone** is a place where the we can get ourselves into emotional trouble.
Dear John or **Dear Jane** Letter	A traditional Dear John or Dear Jane letter was a goodbye letter to end a romantic relationship. In **Fitchipelago** it is a letter to remove the toxic people in your life.
Depths of Discouragement	A dangerous place off the coast of **Nough Nation** near the **Ocean of Overwhelm**.
Difference Makers	Someone who practices the **Step Up, Stand Up** and **Speak Up** philosophy.
Dirty Filter	A **Dirty Filter** is one that has been tainted by negative influences and is often a cause of conflict with others.
Dis	A small town in **Not Valley**.
Don't Accept Unacceptable Behavior	An important reminder to cherish yourself enough to set and hold the boundaries that are in alignment with your values.
Double Agent	They start out neutral and can be persuaded by either the **Bullies** or the **Headspace Heroes**.
Dream Builder	A person who is committed to the consistent effort of building their own **Dreams** and helping others to build theirs too.
Dream it Drive	A thoroughfare on **Success Island**.
Dream it, Believe it, Achieve it	My personal mantra and the way I end my **Livestreams**. Emphasis on **Believe it**.
Dream it, Believe it, Achieve it Bridge	The primary path to get off **Fitchslap Island** and onto **Success Island**.
Dream, Dreams	Your **Dream** is something you intensely desire but have often tucked away in a closet to die via **SPD**. Many people have forgotten to **Dream** or have lost their ability to **Believe** in the possibility that they can come true. That is what the **#12Books12Months** series is about. Helping you boldly claim your **Dreams** while developing an execution strategy to reach them.

Dreamicide	**Dreamicide** is the death of your **Dreams** caused by YOU, either by letting them die via **SPD**, allowing others to pick them apart, or allowing the **Bully in Your Head** to influence you to ignore them. **"Leaving the Baby in the closet."** Is committing **Dreamicide**. #NoDreamicide
Dyslexia	A condition that produces difficulty in interpreting words, letters, numbers or shapes that has no relevance to intelligence.
Ear Gate	One of the **Special Access Gates** that needs attention to keep the **Bullies** from using it as a back door to get back to your **Headspace**.
Edutain	The act of **Edu**cating and Enter**tain**ing at the same time, often with laughter.
Entrepreneurial Rock Star	A member of my Facebook Group, the **Entrepreneurial Rock Stars (ERS)**. Or someone who is crushing it in their space.
Entrepreneurial Theme Park	A place on **Success Island** where we learn about being an entrepreneur.
ERS	The abbreviation for my Facebook Group, the **Entrepreneurial Rock Stars**, which is a Group of entrepreneurs who want to *give* at least as much as they *get*.
Evict, Evicted, Eviction	The process of removing any **Bullies** that have inhabited your **Headspace**.
Evict the Bully	A catch phrase that is also used as a hashtag to express a need to remove the negative self-talk going on in your **Headspace**.
Eviction Express	The transportation that brings the **Bullies** that have been **Evicted** to their new home on **Eviction Isle**.
Eviction Isle	The island in **Fitchipelago** that houses the **Bullies** after you have **Evicted** them.
Eviction Notice	The formal notice given to the **Bullies** that they are being **Evicted** and the **Headspace Heroes** are moving in.
Eviction Process	A simplified way of saying the **12-Step Bully Eviction Process** that outlines the steps needed to remove them from your **Headspace**.
Fail	A word the **Bully in Your Head** will try to manipulate you with. **Fail** is a 4-Letter "F" Word and only shows up in this dictionary as a reminder to #EvictTheBully. See **Stepping Stones**.

Fear of Rejection Road	A rarely traveled road on **Success Island** that leads to the fastest route to **#RockThatDream Ridge**.
Filter	**Filters** are created by our life experiences and relationships and they are intensified, both positively and negatively, by our **Self-Esteem**.
Fitch Philosophy	The **Fitch Philosophy** is my perspective on life. It is choosing to look at the **Bright Side**, handling people and problems with **Dignity** and **Grace**, while assuming the best in others. It also focuses on **Empathy** and on actively seeking to understand other people's circumstances. This Philosophy keeps you focused on the positive and helps you to grow as an individual and as an entrepreneur.
Fitchipelago	The chain of islands located in the **M3 (Money, Mindset & Motivation) Triangle**. The Islands include **Success Island**, **Hope Island**, **'Nough Nation**, **Fitchslap Island** and **Eviction Isle**.
Fitchisms	My unique and colorful way of describing things to help you prepare for, understand, and execute things in a fun and progressive way.
Fitchslap	The act of correcting behavior. The **Fitchslap** is a public service. It only comes out when necessary, is always done in **Love**, and is used to redirect the course of someone who has gone astray. It is sometimes necessary to self-inflict a **#Fitchslap** to get you back on course, find the **Bright Side** or help you **Quit Your Fitchin'**.
Fitchslap Island	An island in **Fitchipelago** that you will be visiting during the **#12Books12Months** series.
FitchTap	A **FitchTap** is a gentler reminder of a needed correction in behavior. These are sometimes administered in place of the **Fitchslap** to individuals who are new to the **Fitch Philosophy**, are experiencing some emotional or challenging situation but still need gentle correction or are going in the right direction but need a gentle **Nudge** to get back on track.
Flip-Flopper	Someone that can't make up their mind or randomly changes their mind without notice. It can also apply to people who change their standards whenever it is convenient for them.
Follow Up Ferry	A rarely used mode of transportation throughout **Fitchipelago**.

FOMO	**FOMO** is the **Fear Of Missing Out**. It can often cause us to make decisions that aren't in our best interests.
Group Tasking	Combining activities together that require the same resources, to get them done quicker and more efficiently. See the **Rock Star Guide to Gettin' It Done** for the step-by-step format to achieve success.
Habit Train	The fastest, most efficient way to travel around **Success Island**. Its railcars include: **Planning, Systems, Procedures, Schedules, Routines, Efficiency** and **Productivity**, and the conductor is **Auto Pilot**.
Headspace	The space between your ears that the **Bullies** like to live in.
Headspace Hero	Your volunteer army of positive thoughts and actions. They are the ones that will **Evict the Bullies** and keep your **Headspace** clear of debris. When engaged early, they can inoculate you from **NES** before you are infected.
Headspace Cleaning Crew	All the **Heroes** are great at clean up, but **Forgiveness** and **Peace** are the members assigned to **Clean Your Canvas**. They make sure the trash is disposed of and there are not residual traces of the **Bully Brigade**.
Heebie Jeebies	That uneasy feeling you have when around certain people. You can't always tell why, but you know you are uncomfortable and you don't trust them.
High Ground	The huge mountain range running right through the middle of **Nough Nation**. It is surrounded by two lush valleys and is home to the **Noughs** and the **Nots**.
High Tech	Utilizing technology to allow us to be more efficient with our time and resources. **High Tech** allows us to be **High Touch**.
High Touch	Setting yourself apart from others by using a personal touch to connect with your contacts. **High Tech** is wonderfully effective but should be blended with **High Touch** connection to produces relationships instead of just sales.
Hope Helo	A mode of transportation throughout **Fitchipelago**.
Hope Island	An island in **Fitchipelago** that you will be visiting during the **#12Books12Months** series.

HHH	Vicki's dad's nickname. It stood for Horrible Hollerin' Hank
Hot Spot	They are places that are so sensitive, you have a hard time looking at them or dealing with them. They are also called **Triggers**.
How Can I? (HCI)	The magic question that engages the brain's autonomic response into actively solving the question or problem at hand. It is the replacement phrase for "I can't."
Imposter Syndrome	Feeling like you are a fraud or experiencing the **FEAR** that others will think you are.
Just out of curiosity...	The magical phrase to help you on your entrepreneurial journey.
Keyboard Coward	Another name for a virtual **Troll** that stays behind a keyboard to attack someone.
KLT Factor	Know, Like & Trust Factor. Your goal is to develop the **KLT** with your clients, customers, **Followers**, and **Fans** as quickly as possible. People do business with those they **Know, Like, & Trust**.
Know, Like & Trust (KLT)	The **Know, Like, & Trust** Factor is what people seek before they will do business with you. They need to KNOW who you are, LIKE what you represent, and TRUST that you are honest and full of integrity.
Landmines	A **Landmine** is a **Hot Spot** that is engaged by a word, phrase, or situation that is generally considered neutral or positive to most people; it **Triggers** a negative or hypersensitive response from the other person.
Layering	**Layering** is the process of engaging in multiple activities simultaneously without diluting your **Efficiency** in any of them.
Lens	Your **Lens** is a compilation of your journey through life. In essence, it is your "reality" and how you see the world.
Limbic Lounge	A hangout in your **Headspace** that the **Bullies** like to plan their mischief.
Lisa's Love Story	A very important story to remind us of how subtle a **Nudge** can be and to be vigilant about setting boundaries and recognizing our value.

Livestreaming	**Livestreaming** is the act of streaming live. Therefore, in my opinion it is a VERB, an action word. I have chosen to use it that way throughout most of what I write and until the mainstream catches up, it is a **Fitchism.**
M3	**M3** or M Cubed stands for **Money, Mindset & Motivation** and is the Philosophy that I run my life and my business by.
M3 Philosophy	My Philosophy, that well-rounded growth for an entrepreneur, is created from a healthy balance between the 3 areas of **Money, Mindset & Motivation**.
M3 Triangle	The secret location of **Fitchipelago**. It is similar to the Bermuda Triangle, but this is a place where instead of getting lost, you get found. You find the most authentic, best version of yourself.
Make your Move	This is the physical act of engaging in a specific movement or sequence of movements, which is designed to trigger a change in your current thinking pattern. This is a Tony Robbins suggested activity that is extremely successful in what Tony calls, "Changing your State." (As in changing your state of mind.)
Market Separator	The specialty thing you do, give, or provide that separates you from everyone else who does what you do.
Mobile Classroom	See **University on Wheels**.
Multi-Generational Bully Births	The process of people passing their **Bullies** on to others. It is often a familial transfer, but it doesn't have to be.
Naysayers	**Naysayers** are the people in your life who continue to discourage your ideas, talents and abilities and are often friends or family members that have a lack of vision or lack of **Confidence** in themselves.
NES	The abbreviation for the **Not Enough Syndrome**. The **Bullies** infect you with it and you must engage the **Headspace Heroes** to eradicate it or to inoculate those young ones that haven't been infected yet.
NES Carrier	Someone that spreads **NES** around by discouraging people.

Neutralize	**Truth** is your neutralizer. The **Bully** infects you with **NES** and tries to convince you that you are **Not Enough**. The **Truth** is you are perfect just the way you are. Once you accept that **Truth**, you will **Neutralize** your **Hots Spots**.
Non-Negotiables	Those items in your life that are of the utmost importance; or the items that cannot be changed due to outside circumstances or due to your unwavering commitment to them. The term is used particularly when setting your **Schedule** and is a building block in the **Rock Star Guide to Gettin' It Done**.
Not Valley	A valley on the east side of **High Ground** on the island of **Nough Nation**.
Nough Nation	An island in **Fitchipelago** that is home the beautiful **High Ground** mountain range and is home to the **Noughs** and the **Nots**.
Nough Valley	A valley on the west side of **High Ground** on the island of **Nough Nation**.
Nudge	The tiniest, and sometimes unnoticeable, change in trajectory that keeps you from ending up at your desired destination.
Obvious to Outlandish	My way of giving you freedom to allow your mind the opportunity to explore possibilities. When being a **Problem Solver**, even the Outlandish ideas can lead you to the perfect solution.
Ocean of Overwhelm	A place off the coast of **Fitchslap Island** where people who are overwhelmed get stuck and immobilized.
Overcoming Objections	The process of **Peeling the Onion** to uncover the true **FEAR** or objection that is holding them back, so you can help them resolve it.
Pain of Perfectionism	The agony of always falling short of **Perfectionism** and believing the lie that you are Not Enough the way you are. **#YouAreEnough**
Pain of Perfectionism Peaks	A place on **Success Island** where some entrepreneurs get stranded while pursuing a way to do things "perfectly."

Pain Point	An area of concern or difficulty for a person, family, group, or business. It may be something they are acutely aware of and need to solve, and it may be a problem that hasn't been recognized yet. Solving **Pain Points** is the primary objective in selling your products and services.
Part of the Solution	Your commitment to getting involved and proactively trying to solve the problem or helping to make others aware of its existence.
Peacocking	An expression that means that you are calling attention to yourself. Often because you are **Insecure**. **Cockiness** tends to do this when he is trying to pretend he is **Confidence**.
Peeling the Onion	The act of identifying the real concern that is preventing the client from moving forward. **Peeling the Onion** refers to gently removing each layer until you find that which is truly troubling or causing discomfort.
Perseverating	To get stuck on one thing, even after the original reason or issue has been resolved.
Periscope	Twitter's Livestreaming app.
Pinnacle of Peace	The most coveted place on all of **Success Island**. It is located on the top of **#RockThatDream Ridge**.
Pity Parties	Soirees that **Pity** likes to throw where people can wallow in their problems.
PMA	**PMA** stands for **Positive Mental Attitude**. It is the act of **choosing** to look at the **Bright Side** of things and keeping your attitude and actions in check, while always focusing on the positive possibilities.
Positive Mental Attitude	See **PMA**
Problem Identifier (PI)	Someone who notices everything that is wrong and then dumps it on someone else to resolve.
Problem Solver (PS)	Someone who looks at their problems with optimism and a commitment to finding a solution. **Problem Solvers** always look for at least 3 possible solutions.

Profit in the Pain	A way of looking at your circumstances while recognizing that even in the midst of what is happening, someday you will find Profit (something positive) in the situation. It is also the title of one of the books in the **#12Books12Months** series.
Pseudo-Sequel	My unique way of labeling a book that references the same concept and some of the same characters but is not a true sequel.
Pull Up Your Bootstraps	It means to prepare yourself for a situation or a piece of information you might not like. This statement is often made right before a **#Fitchslap**, a **#TruthBomb** or something that might catch the participant off guard. **#PUYB**
Push-Pull	The dramatic relationship maneuvers of those who desire a strong connection and yet are afraid of getting close. They **Pull** you in and then they **Push** you away.
Quarantine	The separation of people that have either been **Bubble Bumped** to the **Restricted Zone** or where the **Bullies** have been **Evicted**.
Queen of Consistency	A title given to me by my team, due to the **Consistency** in my **Schedule** and activities.
Quit Your Fitchin' (#QYF)	A term that means to stop complaining and to get your attitude right. After being told to **Quit Your Fitchin'**, one should immediately look for the **Bright Side** and start moving themselves toward a **PMA**.
Quit Your Fitchin' Cave	A place on **Fitchslap Island** where many of the **Problem Identifiers** hang out together.
Reassurance Reef	A gorgeous reef off the west side of **Success Island** that has the warm water from the **Sea of Tranquility** lapping against it.
Recruiting Road	The fastest and easiest way to get to **#RockThatDream Ridge**.
Reframe, Reframed, Reframing	To look at something with a different perspective or by applying a different **Filter**. It often requires the concentrated effort of **Empathy** regarding another person or situation.
Rejection Ridge	A place that is feared because of its name. The ridge looks scary from one side, but there is a soft slope that leads right to **Recruiting Road**.

Remove the NOTs	The act of taking the word NOT out of your life when it is in reference to what you can Do, Be or Achieve.
Restricted Zone	The place where you **Bubble Bump** those that have broken your **Trust** or have violated your **Bubble Boundaries**.
Rock Star or **Rockstar**	Someone who doesn't follow the rules, they make their own. They go out of their way to be extraordinary, different from everyone else.
Rock Star Guide to Gettin' It Done	The Step-by-Step Organization & Execution System designed to help you get MORE done in LESS time. *"It will change your life… if you let it."*
Rooter of the Underdog	My quirky way of saying I am a hopeless romantic and I always root for the underdog.
RSG2GID	The abbreviation for the **Rock Star Guide to Gettin' It Done**.
Sales Street	A thoroughfare on **Success Island**.
Salesy Shore	A place people get washed up on **Fitchslap Island** when they use **Sales, Sleazy or Cheesy** tactics.
Scope	An abbreviation for a live broadcast on **Periscope**.
Sea of Mediocrity	One of the **Sister Seas**, The **Sea of Mediocrity** is a place where people who lack vision and ideas float along aimlessly, without commitment or dedication. They get by with the minimum effort required.
Sea of Sameness	Another of the **Sister Seas,** the **Sea of Sameness** is a place people go when they refuse to *Step Up & Stand Out*. Their entire purpose is to seamlessly blend in and never be singled out, lest someone actually have an expectation that they can be more than they are. This is where the average person gets stuck as the **Tide of Temptation** drags them away from reaching their **Dreams**. Everyone and everything here looks and acts exactly the same. #NoCreativityAllowed

Sea of Status Quo	Nestled between the **Sea of Mediocrity** and 'he **Sea of Sameness**, you'll find the Middle Sister, the **Sea of Status Quo**. She desperately wants to keep everything the same. Control is her vice. Everyone travels in the same direction and making waves is forbidden. Any attempt to Rock the Boat and you will be abandoned, destined to be tossed against the rocky reef or to wash up on the shore of **Not Valley**. **#DontRockTheBoat**
Sea of Tranquility	A place off the southwest side of **Success Island** that is nestled up against **Reassurance Reef**. These calm waters allow for easy navigation.
Serial Entrepreneur	An entrepreneur that establishes a business or enterprise, gets it running smoothly, and then sells it or delegates the responsibilities to a qualified person, so they can repeat the process over again.
Shaming Slam	A private party hosted by **Shame** where she invites all the **Bullies** over to rehash your most humiliating moments.
Shiny Object Syndrome	The tendency to leave projects uncompleted because you see something else and run after it because it is new and shiny.
Sister Seas	The **Sea of Sameness**, **Sea of Status Quo** and **Sea of Mediocrity** create the triad, called the **Sister Seas**.
Slow Painful Death (SPD)	**Slow Painful Death** references the dying of anything that you are not actively investing your energy in. Particularly used to refer to your **Dreams** and the act of committing **Dreamicide**.
SM	Short for **Social Media**.
Social Media	Any new or existing platform that primarily uses social interaction and user generated content on the internet as a way to communicate and connect people together.
Special Access Gates	The **Ear Gate**, **Eye Gate** and **Mouth Gate** are three of the specialty access points that allow the **Bullies** free access to enter or to sneak back in after they have been **Evicted**.
SPD	See **Slow Painful Death.**
Stability Shore	The northeastern shore of **Success Island**.

Step Up, Stand Up, and **Speak Up**	We must **Step Up** and take on challenges to make a difference. We must **Stand Up** to oppressors and **Bullies** and for what we believe is right. We must **Speak Up** for those who cannot or will not do so for themselves. These are the actions of a **Difference Maker.**
Stepping Stones	When the results of something are less than you anticipated, the **Bully in Your Head** will call it a **Failure,** but that is a lie. It is a **Stepping Stone** that leads you to growth and strength. **#ProfitInThePain**
Success Island	The center of **Fitchipelago** and home to **#RockThatDream Ridge** and the coveted **Pinnacle of Peace.**
Super Stance	The position you take to stand up to the **Bully in Your Head.** Your positioning grows stronger the more you practice, and it often includes your special "move" to add extra senses in to the process.
Tide of Temptation	The **Tide of Temptation** sweeps many people away from reaching **Success Island** and often leaves them floating aimlessly in the **Ocean of Overwhelm.**
Time Saving Twins	**Group Tasking** and **Layering** are also known as the **Time Saving Twins.**
TMI Syndrome	Too Much Information **Syndrome (TMI Syndrome)** is a disease that needs to be eradicated quickly to prevent it from causing permanent damage to your reputation. A **#Fitchslap** is often needed for proper inoculation.
Tribe	A **Tribe** is a group of people with similar interests, goals or passions. Your **Tribe** is a group of people who enjoy your content and have connected with you to support your efforts.
Triggers	A term that identifies things that induce intense emotions. They are your **Hot Spots.**
Troll	A **Troll** is someone who intentionally tries to emotionally harm or distract you in the online world. Specifically, those who come into your **Livestream** simply to disrupt it, or to get attention.
Unacceptable Behavior	Behavior that is unbecoming of someone of exceptional character and behavior you refuse to accept from anyone, including yourself.

Uncle Ichabod	Is representative a person that is close or is working at getting closer to you or your family with the purpose of exploitation. He represents a **Predator** and/or a pedophile.
University on Wheels	Learning "on the go." Listening to books, podcasts, or other content while traveling or engaging in another activity that doesn't require the active part of your brain.
Vibe with my Tribe	An expression used to suggest that the people who **Follow** you or connect with your mission or message will likely get along with (**Vibe**) with your other supporters (**Tribe**).
Vultures	People in the online space that are out for your money. They may or may not provide great value, but when you are out of money, they are out of time for you, and will kick you to the curb.
Vulnerability Zone	The section of **Intimacy Bubbles** where you are the most vulnerable.
V-Zone	An abbreviation for **Vulnerability Zone**.
Weeds of Wallowing	A place on **Fitchslap Island** where many people get stuck wallowing in their problems.
WIIFM	What's **In It For Me**? The question we must always answer if we want to keep people engaged.
Woulda Coulda Shoulda	Many of the **Bullies** use this, but it is **Regrets** tool of choice. Berating you with what you "Could have" done, "Should have" done or she "Would have" done. You can't win because there is always an alternative to what you did that she will try to convince you was better.

#Fitch5000

NOTE: If you don't see your name here and you are part of the **#Fitch5000**, or if you want to be part of the **Tribe** so your name will show up in future books, go to **www.VickiFitch.com/5K** and let us know. Remember that the content is submitted long before the book is officially published, so you may be showing up in a later book, but feel free to let us know!

Charter Members

Carmela Mae Acot
Mikayla Rose Alley
Sarah Belle Alley
Iris Aroa
Mary Aurellano
John John Andrews
Karen Barrows
Kim Bates
Kelli Beirow
Lisa Benson
April Bowen
Callum Bowen
Dan Bowen
Eliza Bowen
Judah Bowen
Olive Bowen
Dorothy Boyd
Stacy Braiuca
Lise Brake
Ross Brand
Erin Burch
Dean Burt
Suzanne Burt
Nyra Carranza
Rebecca Caroe
Erin Cell
Yanna Cerez

Mia Linda Chapa
Joel Comm
Melissa Compani
Anthony Conklin
Doug Crowe
Diego Dalessandro
Jeremy Dalton
Kira Dawson
Shanon Dean
Stacey DePolo
Wagner dos Santos
Spike Edwards
Jill Elliott
Lisa Elliott
Rosalie Elliott
Irv Federman
Amellali Figueroa
Andrew Fitch
Becky Fitch
Doris Fitch*
Elijah Fitch
Eric Fitch
Erika Fitch
Garrett Fitch
Hudson Fitch
Jack Fitch
Jason Fitch

Jeff Fitch
Justin Fitch
Layton Fitch
Liam Fitch
Lucas Fitch
Michelle Fitch
Olivia Fitch
Palma Fitch
Suzie Fitch
Ted Fitch
Terry Fitch
Zach Fitch
Trisha Fitzgerald
Wanita Fourie
Hanz Freller
Brittney Frewing
Dave Frewing
Jacob Frewing
Janet Frewing
Justin Frewing
Jay Garrett
Marsha Garrett
Bryan Germain
Carolyn Gialamas
Joe Girard
Laurie Goldman
David Gonzales

Joy Gouge
Lyne Goulet
Mike Grear
Henry (Hank) Hainault*
Joan Hainault*
Steve Hainault
David Hancock
Grover Harp
Randall Harp
Stacy Harp
Tug Harp
Dawn Harper
Johnny Harrell
Malia Hassenbien
Mara Hassenbien
TJ Hassenbien
Tom Hassenbien
Tyler Hassenbien
Bryce Heggen
Brynn Heggen
Kamryn Heggen
Kennedy Heggen
Kim Heggen
Rob Heggen
Karla Henry
Cindy Hettinga
Harvey Hettinga
Helene Hettinga
John Hettinga
Pete Hettinga
Debra Hiller
Marsha Hirschhorn
MoniQue Hoffman
Debbie Hogshead
Kathi Hollingsworth
Jim Bob Howard
Tom Iwema
Jenny Jones
Raul Jusino
Adam Kirk
Addie Kirk
Jennifer Kirk
Kendyl Kirk
Megan Kirk
Kara Lambert
D Jay Lareno
Amy Lazare

Jeannie Lokey
Jim Lokey
Brandon Love
Debbie Lovett
Jennifer Lucas
Moonshadow Machado
Gideon Madsen
Josie Madsen
Julien Madsen
Kevin Madsen
Trisha Madsen
Laura Mandzok
Shannon Mattern
Calvin Mattoon
Madison Mattoon
Martin Mattoon
David McCormack
Tom McDowell
Sean McKenna
Jay McKey
Christine Mercado
Maureen Messersmith
Susan Metzger
Adam Migacz
Jennifer Montague
Avery Jean Morales
Adam Nally
Eric Neitzel
Craig Nelson
Peter Nez
Jeannie Nie
Michelle Oxley
Lisa O'Loughlin
David Parsons
Jimmy (James Jr.)
Parsons
Pa (James Sr.) Parsons
Shanna Sheerie Parsons
Judy Peacock
Ernie Perry
Victor Pierantoni
Jennifer Quinn
Érick Ramirez
Leisa Reid
Russ Repass
Melissa Rost
Aaron Roth

Anna Rounseville
Ted Rubin
Elis San Jose
Madison Sanders
Wendy Sanders
Claudia Santiago
Drew Sasser
Érick Saúl
Kiki Schirr
Stasia Schmidt
Kelly Schuh
Jackie Schulte
Kevin Schulte
Lexi Schulte
Roy Schulte
Chloe Shannon
Hunter Shannon
Rik Shannon
Riky Shannon
Susan Shannon
Walter Shannon
Karen Shillieto
Frances Shurley
Reddy Kumara Simha
Lucy Simpson
Nicole Soh
Patricia Sommer
Tiffany Souhrada
Amber St. John
Barry St. John
Brandon St. John
Jan St. John
Jeffrey Stipe
Andrea Stonerook-Nunn
Lisa Sulsenti
Jody Summers
Linda Thierry
Maria Thompson
Eric Thorsell
Kathy Thorsell
Amar Trivedi
Dee Trivedi
Jan Turley
Teresa Velardi
Stevie Lynn Vine
Mia Voss
Ben Warren

Jack Warren	Abby Wiegers	Trevor Williams
Mitchel Warren	Claire Williams	Melanie Wiser
Taylor Warren	Darryl Williams	Rafferty Yao
Tera Warren	Harrison Williams	Jason Zara
Teri Werner	Lydia Williams	

*Honoring those who had an impact on this journey
but are not longer with us.

Join the Tribe and get your name in the next books!

www.VickiFitch.com/5K

What's Next...

Order your copy of Book #3 in the Series NOW!

www.VickiFitch.com/201

About the Author

Vicki started her first business at 12, bought her first house at the age of 19 and started her first company when she was 20. She calls herself a "Serial Entrepreneur" because building and selling businesses became a way of life. She entered the Direct Sales industry over 20 years ago and spent a decade celebrating Top 10 in Sales and Recruiting worldwide, while raising a family, including a child with special needs.

She specializes in helping people of all ages to become the best version of themselves and is passionate about her **#YouAreEnough** campaign to help everyone recognize their value just the way they are. She believes if we start helping children **#EvictTheBully** in their heads, we will build a stronger, more confident generation of leaders that will benefit the future.

Her world recognized speaking and coaching programs have expanded her consulting business to 6 countries across the globe. As a well-rounded entrepreneur that understands all aspects of business, she helps companies to see a greater vision, as well as streamline and automate some of their efforts. She is highly trained in sales funnel automation and explains how to use *"High Tech" so you can be "High Touch"* to create authentic, long lasting relationships.

Her Weekly Podcasts including *He Said, Red Said* and *Vicki Fitch Live: A Fresh Perspective* were the first to go on Facebook Live and she delivers value daily on Instagram, Periscope, Facebook Live and YouTube, training on *"Sales to Social Media & Everything in Between."*

Social Media is one of her strengths and **Livestreaming** is one of her passions. Vicki generated a six figure income in less than 1 year from her live video platforms and created a Free Course called **#RockThatStream** to help others develop their talents in this rapidly emerging area.

Vicki shares a **"Never Give Up!"** philosophy and is empathetic to those who have gone through difficulties since she experienced a multitude of trials herself. Those include losing a baby, losing both of her parents and spending 3 ½ years in a wheelchair. She had to learn to refine her skills and reinvent herself in an online world since she had to spend a significant time in bed. She is often referred to as the **#HopeDealer** because her clients say, *"Working with Vicki is like a drug."* and she reminds her clients that feeling is called **Hope**.

Her love of helping others and contributing to a positive community led her to connect quality entrepreneurs in her Facebook Group, The **Entrepreneurial Rock Stars** and as a Christian Entrepreneur she and her husband contributed by running a Non-Profit Organization (CYAA-Christian Youth Athletics Association) for over ten years.

Vicki lives in Southern California with her husband Terry of 20+ years and their two boys. She is blessed to also have two amazing step-children who have enriched her life personally and by the five grandchildren they have brought into the world that fill her heart with joy. Her business is her ministry and she believes that it is her opportunity to inspire others through her writing and speaking. God has blessed her greatly and as paraphrased from Luke 12:48… *"To whom much is given… much will be required."* It is her honor to share the message of **Hope** to the world… one book, one **Livestream**, or one event at a time.